# Banking On
# AMERICA

# Banking On
# AMERICA

## HOW TD BANK ROSE TO THE TOP AND TOOK ON THE U.S.A.

## HOWARD GREEN

HARPERCOLLINS PUBLISHERS LTD

Published by HarperCollins Publishers Ltd

First edition

HarperCollins books may be purchased for educational, business, or sales promotional
use through our Special Markets Department.

HarperCollins Publishers Ltd
2 Bloor Street East, 20th Floor
Toronto, Ontario, Canada
M4W 1A8

*www.harpercollins.ca*

Library and Archives Canada Cataloguing in Publication
information is available upon request

ISBN 978-1-44340-776-2

Printed and bound in the United States
RRD 9 8 7 6 5 4 3 2

To Lynne

# Contents

# INTRODUCTION

In the fall of 1980 I was twenty-one years old and in my last year at Carleton University in Ottawa. I was a journalism student, but I had also taken a ragtag collection of half a dozen economics courses, many of which I have to confess I slept through. Somehow, after a summer of reporting for the local television news in my hometown of Halifax, I had finagled my way into a part-time reporting gig from Parliament Hill, no less, filling in for a guy who ran a brisk business supplying dispatches from Ottawa to various regional stations across the country.

I shudder to think about that wet-behind-the-ears, freckled, baby-faced reporter proclaiming from the mount. But there I was and it was around that time that the name Ed Clark entered my consciousness. It's only a dim memory, but one day a document called the National Energy Program (NEP) landed on us scribes in the press gallery, bound like a big workbook. It was part of the fall 1980 federal budget, but was deemed to be so important that it was a stand-alone document. The energy minister at the time, Marc Lalonde, was a close confidant of Liberal Prime Minister Pierre Trudeau, who had risen from the political ashes one more time for what would be his last four years in office. I did not know what Ed Clark looked like or whether he was in the room when Lalonde announced the NEP and faced the press, but it was as though a bomb had dropped.

Leafing through the pages of the National Energy Program, I struggled to understand it. I have no idea how I managed to cobble together a report for the evening news. But it didn't really matter. Those who needed to know about it let the rest of the country know what it meant. The oil- and gas-producing province of Alberta was in a rage. Here was Ottawa trying to run its business. The oil barons pointed their fingers in one direction, at a young civil servant named Ed Clark, the assistant deputy minister of energy who had written the National Energy Program. To them, he was a socialist.

Clark, however, managed to keep his job in Ottawa. Even better, he was soon named Civil Servant of the Year and got to take a paid sabbatical in Paris. But when the Progressive Conservative Party of Brian Mulroney came to power in 1984, the new government pushed the eject button and Clark was gone.

A period passed when I lost track of this shooting and falling star. In the 1990s, though, I noticed the name Ed Clark on brochures when I'd wander into Canada Trust, an upstart financial institution that was stealing market share from the big banks with crazy giveaways and promotions. (My first credit card was a Canada Trust MasterCard with a $500 limit, bestowed on me during my last year at Carleton.) Could this be the same Ed Clark?

Clark shot to national prominence again in 1999–2000 when TD Bank bought Canada Trust. Here was this guy who at one point was viewed as a pinko now in line to run one of the country's big banks. An intellectual, cool-headed, self-proclaimed people person with a gift for communication, Clark was suddenly centre stage and would soon embark on one of the most ambitious forays by any Canadian company into the shark-infested U.S. market.

The first time I met Ed Clark was in late 2003. He had been CEO of TD for about a year and I had arranged to meet him for a coffee. We met in Clark's fourth-floor office and sat at his conference table, both of us having removed our jackets. His first line to me was "You're a Maritimer!" and he went on to talk about how great East Coasters were, how they didn't take themselves too seriously. My initial internal reaction was *What a suck-up this guy is.*

But he cursed like an ordinary guy, which made him seem unaffected and likeable. We went on to talk about books and then politics and finally got around to banking. In particular, we talked about the juicy topic of whether bank mergers were possible or necessary in Canada. At one point, I brought up the argument made by Clark's predecessor, Charles Baillie, that in Canadian banking you needed more scale to compete internationally. In other words, it would be to the banks' advantage to spread their considerable costs over a bigger array of branches and services. At the time, Clark said that therein lay the difference between him and Baillie. That view would obviously change, because Clark would make more major acquisitions than any Canadian bank CEO of his era—or of any era. Knowing the politics of Ottawa cold, he clearly concluded that in-country mergers would never happen in Canada and set his course directly for the United States, the Bermuda Triangle for several Canadian CEOs who'd gone before him.

Later, I read Gerald Pencer's book *The Ride of My Life*. Pencer was a controversial, hyper-aggressive entrepreneur. Clark was hired to clean up Pencer's mess at Financial Trustco. Of Clark he wrote, "He proved to be an excellent negotiator. He's Mr. Smooth. He should go down as one of the best bullshitters of all time."[1] Pencer meant the latter description as a compliment. This guy Clark was someone who could talk and persuade. You'd leave a session with Ed convinced he was the most clear-headed, down-to-earth guy ever and that everyone else was full of it.

Before Ed Clark's time at TD, though, there was a senior executive named Keith Gray. I first met Gray in late 1996. I had phoned Toronto-Dominion Bank, trying to drum up something to shoot for *Venture*, a popular CBC-TV magazine program that chronicled the exploits of business people. Charles Baillie had recently taken the reins as TD CEO, and I thought it would be fun, and saleable, to shoot a feature on the new man at the top. I was curious about banking. Canadian banks had a mystique. They were big and made a lot of money. Their leaders were the top drawer of the country's elite. I was nosy and I wanted to take viewers inside the hallowed halls along with me.

I got a phone call back from a woman in the communications department of the bank, Heather Conway. She sounded almost bored, as though this call wasn't much of a priority. Conway said the new boss, Baillie, would be happy to participate in a *Venture* feature, but he would prefer if it were about the bank's burgeoning discount brokerage division rather than about him. At the time, it didn't matter much to me. I was selling my wares story by story to

*Venture.* If I could tell the show's executive producer that I was in the door at the bank, that was good enough to bag another job. I arranged a meeting with Keith Gray and his colleague Duncan Gibson.

Keith Gray was Mr. Discount Brokerage. At the time, he was CEO of TD Green Line, the discount brokerage business within the bank. Gibson, a tall, polite man with a thin face, was ostensibly Gray's boss. He was executive vice-president of wealth management, running one of the bank's key business lines into which Gray's Green Line reported. But when we sat down, it was clear that Gibson was Gray's boss in name only. Gray dominated the meeting. He had once been Gibson's boss and he still acted as though he were.

We discussed what would be required if we were to do a mini-documentary on the discount division. They wanted to know if they could see the program before it aired. I said no. I also told them that while we would not try to trip them up, if we witnessed conflict while we were filming, we would reserve the right to show any bun fights on the air. Warts and all was the agreement. The discussion then turned to the subject of whom we would follow. Gray was the more intriguing character. He had spunk. He was the entrepreneur. *Venture* thrived on following people like him, and the whole notion of an entrepreneur within a fusty old bank had the makings of a story.

Because I would be hearing sensitive information that could move the stock, the bank presented me with a form. By signing it, I would become a temporary "insider" of the bank, privy to information with all the attendant responsibilities, principally abiding by the law that I not trade on that information or tip off anyone else about it. Today, given everything that's happened in public markets since the late 1990s—the financial crisis, the Enron and WorldCom cases, Martha Stewart, and so on—it's hard to imagine a publicly traded company signing in a journalist as an insider. But this was a more innocent time. Joy Crysdale, my boss at *Venture,* would not let me sign the document. She said the president of the CBC, Perrin Beatty, was the only one who could take that responsibility or, at the very least, a CBC lawyer. It seemed pretty unlikely I could make that happen quickly enough, but somehow, we worked it out and started shooting.

On our first day of shooting, Gray was clearly nervous. We started rolling during a meeting he was chairing. He kept looking over at us. I thought, *Jeez, this guy is going to be a stiff. How long will it take him to loosen up?* Normally, the first day of these productions is a bit perfunctory. The subjects are excited the cameras are there and they're acutely aware of your presence. The second day, the novelty has mostly worn off. By the third day, they're wondering why they let you in the door, you've become such a pain. By the fourth day, they've forgotten about you. But Gray was more nervous than most. He was sixty-two, he'd been successful and didn't want to blow it on national TV.

Gray was co-operative, and ultimately very natural. He was also honest. He'd bark in your face if he wanted to call you on something. He'd also take responsibility.

One morning we were shooting on the trading floor where the call centre was located. All of a sudden, there was pandemonium. It was the time of the infamous Bre-X fraud. The gold stock that had the whole country talking and speculating turned out to be a bust. There was no gold in the much vaunted Indonesian mine, people lost millions, and a geologist died having "fallen" from a helicopter. Up until now, a decade and a half later, in a scathing indictment of lax regulatory enforcement, no one has gone to jail for perpetrating the fraud.

The day of our shoot was the day the Bre-X reality hit. People were dumping their shares. TD operators were making margin calls. The supervisor of the floor, his hands on a couple of phones at once, was trying to keep it all together, veins bulging in his neck. We were shooting it all. Then, a PR person put her hand in front of the lens. The bank was throwing us out. We included that ridiculous communications department clampdown in the segment that went to air.

Later that morning, I complained to Gray about the Soviet-style treatment. He waved me off. "I did that. I told them to throw you out. You've got to give them [the operators] a chance." On another occasion, he shot back at me, showing his fangs, when I suggested a certain seating plan for a meeting. "I thought you didn't want to set anything up," he snarled. This guy had a bit of a short fuse. He was bossy, but up-front. I liked him.

After the story aired, I didn't hear from Gray. A year or two later, though, I called him about another story I was working on, this time about the day trading craze. We talked, and ultimately arranged lunch. As the years went by, the lunches and emails became more frequent. Bit by bit, he started telling me his story. It's a good one, just as good as Ed Clark's, and just as relevant to the TD odyssey.

Gray and Clark embody the evolution and growth of Toronto-Dominion. Gray was a crucial player in the generation—which included the formidable CEOs he worked for—that took risks to set the stage. Clark is the inheritor who has written a plotline for the bank that few in Gray's troupe could have foretold. In less than ten years, Clark has dotted the American landscape with more TD branches than the bank had built in Canada over its previous 150 years. While all the major Canadian banks are strong and applauded globally, TD is arguably the most respected bank in Canada, one of the most admired in the United States and perhaps on the planet.

Although I did not begin working on it until early 2010, over time I've come to realize that this book has been percolating inside me, subconsciously and then consciously, since the late 1990s. It tells the story of the people who transformed an institution, from the Keith Grays to the Ed Clarks and many others. They took TD from the sleepy, stuffy and small-minded Canada of the 1950s, when the modern bank was formed by the union of The Bank of Toronto and The Dominion Bank, to the second decade of the twenty-first century. This is a time of aggressively daring to outdo Americans, generating fat profits while preaching social awareness—not to mention trying to control angst inside the bank—as TD prepares itself for life after Ed Clark.

# ED'S ON THE TUBE AGAIN

*Selling TD in the U.S.*

Not only is he on American TV again, for an hour after the closing bell of equity trading in New York, Ed Clark is co-hosting—yes, co-hosting—on the business channel CNBC with none other than the "Money Honey," Maria Bartiromo. With her cat's eyes and full lips, Bartiromo conjures up a fortyish Sophia Loren. Clark, who at the time is sixty-three, lanky and with a face that's both boyish and pleasantly nerdy, looks slightly uncomfortable, unusual for a person so bursting with confidence. He later described the experience of being Bartiromo's co-pilot as "terrifying" but fun.[2] This CEO is apparently willing to endure a bit of terror. He is regularly found flogging his bank's story in the United States (often repeating the same lines), where TD now has more branches than in Canada.

Going on Bartiromo's show is a way of getting in the face of Americans. It's also a way to win the hearts and minds of Clark's approximately 27,000 employees in the United States, close to a third of the bank's total. As Clark puts it, his American staffers can look up at the TV and proudly say, "There's my guy." It's a way of giving market and street cred to a bank that's trying to beat the Yanks at their own game.

Clark has his rap down cold for his U.S. audience. "You put us on a corner, where there are three other banks, and when people find out we're open longer, have better service, roll their pennies for free, and have treats for their dogs, they'll come to TD and we'll take market share."[3]

He repeats his *shtick* over and over again, wherever and whenever he can. For someone who says he sometimes has trouble with words, Clark is second to none as a communicator. This is a deep-thinking, strategically precise intellectual who would seem equally at home telling people why they should buy a Veg-O-Matic on the boardwalk at Coney Island. Described as someone who plays chess in 3-D, Clark may be a Harvard PhD, but he is also a salesman, and he is pitching to America like you wouldn't believe. So much so that TD now has just over 1,300 branches in the United States versus 1,150 in Canada—and it only started buying retail banks in the U.S. in 2005, investing some $19 billion USD to gain the critical mass it believes is necessary to be a player on American soil.

In just a handful of years during Clark's tenure, TD has barged across the border and planted itself toe-to-toe with enormous and legendary American banks like JPMorgan Chase, Bank of America and Wells Fargo. Clark started in sleepy New England and then crept into the outskirts of Manhattan. Through some lucky timing, in late 2007, just as the financial world was going on red alert, Clark pounced on a bank with a cult-like focus on customers called Commerce Bank. TD suddenly had branches in New York City and its metropolitan area, a market that has roughly the deposit base of all of Canada. In a brazen move, to show New Yorkers it wasn't just some hick bank, TD did what's known in advertising as a "takeover." It bought every inch of ad space in the iconic Grand Central Station, including the umbrellas on the hot dog stands outside, blanketing the joint in TD's colour, which is green for money.* Its goal is to move from being the number five bank in Manhattan to number three by 2015. It's a slight exaggeration, but one top financial sector observer has said that there are now as many TD branches in New York as there are Starbucks.

Clark's opportunistic purchase of Commerce also gave TD a hub in New Jersey, Philadelphia and Washington, and a toehold in Florida. The 2008–09 financial crisis would challenge bankers like Ed Clark as they'd never been challenged before, but the turmoil would also present him with other pigeons he could pick off to build his flock of banks in the U.S. Looking at a map

---

* The Grand Central Station takeover, or "station domination," cost $300,000. For that price, TD was also able to blanket 30th Street Station in Philadelphia and Boston's North Station.

might make you think TD is the "I-95 Bank," its branches roughly tracking the famed interstate that runs down the eastern seaboard.

It didn't hurt that Canadian banks did not implode during the financial crisis like their brethren in the U.S. or the U.K. Believe it or not, staid Canadian bankers are now the rock stars of the global banking club. Their banks did not engage in the loose lending and hanky-panky that destroyed banks in the U.S. and forced its government to bail out the economy and financial system. Canada's banks, long considered big and boring, have proved that boring is what you want in a bank. They make gobs of money and in September of 2012 were named the soundest on earth by the World Economic Forum for the fifth year in a row. Since the crisis, these dullards of finance have had the world's attention.

During the crisis, although its stock was halved and it sold new shares to the public to shore up its bunker of protective capital, TD still earned $3.8 billion during the worst year of the meltdown. This strength allowed it to take advantage of opportunities that arose because others found themselves in precarious states.

TD, it should be said, sits in an exclusive club. There are really only six Canadian banks of note:[†] Royal Bank of Canada (RBC), Toronto-Dominion (TD), Bank of Nova Scotia (Scotiabank), Bank of Montreal (BMO), Canadian Imperial Bank of Commerce (CIBC) and National Bank. They are known as the Big Six and each has hundreds of billions in assets, although National is concentrated in Quebec and is considerably smaller than the other five. Critics will jump at the chance to say that Canada's banks enjoy an oligopoly, which is true, but they omit that the same is true in countries like Australia and France. In contrast, the U.S. has 7,300 banks, from community banks with just a few branches and mere millions in assets, to JPMorgan Chase with more than $2 trillion.[‡]

---

[†] The major domestic banks are known as Schedule 1 institutions. According to the Canadian Bankers Association, based on information from the Office of the Superintendent of Financial Institutions Canada, there are 23 of them. Aside from the Big Six, they include Laurentian Bank, Canadian Western Bank, President's Choice Bank and Canadian Tire Bank. The Schedule 2 category is made up of subsidiaries of foreign banks such as HSBC Bank Canada. They can take deposits like Schedule 1 banks and are eligible for deposit insurance under CDIC. There are 25 of them. Schedule 3 banks are branches of foreign banks. There are 29 of those.

[‡] Although the U.S. has about 7,300 banks, it should be noted that half a dozen large institutions dominate and conduct at least half of the country's banking business.

Canada's banks, with a limited market of 34 million people, have looked longingly at the gigantic yet fragmented market south of the border. Restricted from merging in Canada, they need to find other places to do deals and grow earnings to satisfy the one-half of Canadians who, directly or indirectly, through mutual funds or pension funds, own their shares and rely on their quarterly dividends. The most obvious target of the bankers' lust has been the United States. While far from a fatal attraction, this obsession with expanding into the U.S. has not been without its difficulties.

From Maine to Florida, TD is suddenly everywhere, with a forceful presence in moneyed counties and major cities like Boston, New York, Philadelphia and Washington, and throughout Florida.

Americans could be forgiven for wondering just who these TD people are. On June 13, 2011, it was game six of the Stanley Cup final between the Vancouver Canucks and the Boston Bruins. Vancouver was ahead in the series three games to two. This could have been the Canucks' night. But they were playing on the Bruins' home ice, which was no longer called Boston Garden, but rather TD Garden. Every time the director cut to a shot of the Canucks' bench, viewers got a look at repeating TD logos. When the players fought for the puck along the boards, there was the TD logo. It also stared back from under the ice. Ultimately, the Canucks lost and Boston went on to win the Stanley Cup. Although no Canadian team has won the NHL championship in nearly two decades, the winning team was playing in an arena named for a Canadian bank. Clark enjoyed imagining that other Canadian bank CEOs were watching the game, grinding their teeth every time the TD shield appeared.

\* \* \* \*

In a story that's now legendary among the brass of the bank and a favourite of Ed Clark's, a few years ago TD held its annual general meeting in Saint John, New Brunswick. One of the top executives was out on the street when a group of American tourists from a visiting cruise ship walked past and one noticed a TD branch on Canadian soil. "Hey, guys," the tourist said, "they've got TD up here too!"

It wasn't always thus. After a merger of The Bank of Toronto and The Dominion Bank in 1955, Toronto-Dominion, or TD, as it was now called, was for decades stuck as Canada's fifth-largest bank. It was known to be well run, with specialties in certain areas, such as its discount brokerage, and was the number one lender in the world to the cable television industry, funding entrepreneurs like Ted Rogers. But TD wasn't climbing in the rankings versus its four main competitors in Canada.

TD had tried foreign adventures a few times. In the early 1960s, the bank opened talks with David Rockefeller, grandson of the legendary John D. Rockefeller. David was CEO of Chase Manhattan Bank and had engaged in conversations with TD's boss at the time, Allen Lambert, about some sort of stake in each other's enterprise. According to Lambert's assistant, future CEO Dick Thomson, Rockefeller secretly wanted to buy TD but was thwarted by the government of Prime Minister Lester Pearson. In the early 1970s, TD bought a few bank branches in ritzy neighbourhoods in California, but the experiment didn't work. The operation was too small to make inroads and TD finally sold the unit in California to the Japanese in 1983. Bizarrely, TD even once had branches in Lebanon. In the mid-70s, someone (the bank suspects it was an employee) fired a bazooka into the vault of one of the branches in Beirut, destroying it. Two other branches in Lebanon were also obliterated, ending that chapter in the bank's history.

As the century ended and a new one started, the transformation began. TD bought Canada Trust, a company that set the standard for customer service, showing up the stodgy and crusty banks with its underdog gimmicks. Along with that purchase, TD got Ed Clark, an unbanker-like CEO if there ever was one. After establishing himself as boss and refocusing the bank on retail, rather than fancy financial products and corporate lending, Clark embarked on a fearless U.S. buying spree.

When Clark took over from Charlie Baillie at the end of 2002, TD's assets stood at $278 billion. By the end of the third quarter of 2012, they were $806 billion, second only to Canada's largest bank and company, Royal Bank, and placing TD as the sixth-largest bank in North America (by assets, deposits and market value) and the only bank traded on the New York Stock Exchange with a triple-A credit rating from Moody's. Although Royal Bank has a higher market value, TD continues to gather assets at a faster clip. As of the end of the third quarter of 2012, RBC had just $18 billion more assets than TD ($824 billion versus TD's $806 billion). As for profitability, TD earned upwards of a billion dollars more than Royal in 2011 and now has more branches than RBC.

Ed Clark is an outlier because he wasn't always a banker. There was a time when those who ended up at the top of financial institutions like TD were lifers who'd started as tellers. Some still are, but Clark didn't take that route. He was a scholar who ended up with a notorious and controversial history in government before being tossed aside and landing in the financial industry.

In the 1970s, Ed Clark graduated from Harvard with a PhD in economics and eschewed the family tradition of heading into academia. Even though he was offered professorships at both Harvard and Stanford upon graduation, he blew them off, likely to the chagrin of his father, who was a leading academic, having founded the sociology department at the University of Toronto. Instead, William Edmund Clark went to work as a civil servant in Ottawa, the furthest thing from being a banker.

Arriving in 1947, Clark was born into the second year of the baby boomer era. He was sixteen when the Beatles appeared on *Ed Sullivan*—a child of the change-the-world-for-the-better-generation. Like many brainy kids at that time, he wanted to work for the government of Pierre Trudeau, which had an activist bent. Clark is one of the rare few to have been honoured as both Civil Servant of the Year and CEO of the Year. During his time in the Department of Energy, Clark wrote what came to be called the National Energy Program (NEP).

In the aftermath of the global oil shocks of the 1970s, the thrust of the NEP was threefold: to tax the sector more heavily so Ottawa could get what it considered a fair share of revenues, to achieve a greater degree of Canadian ownership of the industry and to protect the consumer from the impact of high oil prices. Westerners were appalled because they considered oil and gas their resource, not Ottawa's. Clark was dubbed "Red Ed" by the oil patch. It didn't help that he had written his doctoral thesis about the socialist regime in Tanzania.[4]

So how did this guy become CEO of the best-run bank in Canada, the country with the best-run banks in the world, and also one of the most powerful bankers in the United States of America? Ed Clark recounts a scene from an annual banking event in 2010, a CEO-fest he attended with the likes of Jamie Dimon of JPMorgan and John Stumpf of Wells Fargo. Amidst the wreckage of U.S. banking, these two were relative standouts. Clark burbles with delight as he describes running into Dimon and Stumpf: "They bow down and say, 'The triple-A bank is here.' Four years ago, it would have been 'What do you do? Who are you?'"

Clark says that most Canadian businesses have two approaches to breaking into the U.S. market: either they don't have the guts to do it or they go down there and blow their brains out trying. TD, so far, doesn't fall into either camp. It's made the leap and isn't losing money having done so.

Given the shipwrecks of Canadian businesses that have tried to sail into the American market, how did a Canadian bank manage to pull it off? In June 2011, Royal Bank was the most recent casualty in the long list of Canadian companies that have tried their luck in the U.S. After spending billions over a ten-year period, RBC finally cried uncle and sold its retail banking business in the U.S. to PNC Financial Services Group Inc. of Pittsburgh for $3.62 billion USD. It was a loss for Royal, but at least the division wouldn't be a ball and chain anymore and it wouldn't have to answer recurring and irritating questions from analysts, investors and the media. What is it about the United States? Even a company like Tim Hortons that has made its fortune on donuts and coffee can't seem to make its simple formula work down south.

A cartoon that appeared in the *New Yorker* a few years back sums up the subtle differences between Canadians and Americans. It shows a man and woman out at dinner, leaning in over their meals. One says to the other, "You seem familiar, yet somehow strange—are you by any chance Canadian?"[5] While we share great similarities, there are also significant differences, and TD must cater to each one depending in which country it's operating.

It has been one of the great misapprehensions—that Canadians are just like Americans and vice versa. While we are allies and exuberant trading partners and friends, we are not the same. We may look alike, share tastes in movies, music and sports, drive similar cars and spend our winter holidays in the

13

same places. Arguably Americans are more enthusiastic, more entrepreneurial, more gregarious and more socially conservative than Canadians, who are perceived as more standoffish, less flashy, more cautious and deferential to authority. You won't find a drive-thru daiquiri bar in Ontario as you will in Louisiana. Some might say that Canadians are changing to become more like Americans as the country has become more confident, more patriotic, more willing to compete on the world stage economically and culturally.

Still, there are many cleavages in our national personalities. As a result, a Canadian firm looking to attract U.S. consumers requires an in-depth understanding of the psychology of Americans. Slapping your shingle on a few locations and thinking that the market, which is ten times larger than Canada's, will suddenly flock to your door is delusional. Canadian Tire (twice), Mark's Work Wearhouse, Danier Leather, Future Shop, Jean Coutu, Shoppers Drug Mart, Tim Hortons and RBC have all learned this lesson the hard way.

What did these companies miss? Larry Stevenson, who was CEO of the Canadian bookstore chain Chapters and then held the same position at the U.S automotive repair chain Pep Boys, says that it's very different for U.S. companies coming to compete in Canada than the other way around. For U.S. companies, adding Canada is like adding California. While a big addition, it's not akin to betting the company. As well, when a major U.S. chain moves into Canada, Canadians are already aware of the brand. Every Canadian knew Walmart before it arrived. Everyone knew Home Depot. The next big incursion will be by clothing retailer Target, familiar to many cross-border shoppers. Canadian customers and retailers here have been anticipating the chain's arrival for five years.[6] In contrast, when a Canadian retailer or a Canadian bank heads south, there is no instant brand awareness. As well, U.S. retailers are huge and used to lots of competition. Canadian companies are not used to as much pushback, and many have tried to enter the American market with just a few stores—not enough to fend off rivals.

Keith Howlett, a highly regarded retail and consumer products analyst who works with Desjardins Securities, says it's hard to find a profitable franchise chain in the United States with fewer than 500 stores. Howlett gets wound up about cross-border retail. He says that the home improvement chain Lowe's, which entered the Canadian market in 2007, had racked up cumulative losses of $300 million by mid-2011, yet during the company's quarterly conference calls none of the analysts who covered the stock even asked about it. "They can absorb this. They can sustain that type of loss over four years without every-one shouting and screaming, 'You have to stop this!' Lowe's is [losing] $300 million and no one asks them anything. Whereas Mark's [Work Wearhouse] with two or three [U.S.] stores is getting pummelled."

On the issue of competition, Howlett says U.S. retailers are used to doing molecular research when they enter a new market like Canada, whereas Canadian retailers traditionally have not done the same level of analysis when entering the U.S. At the same time, he is critical of Canadian investors who ham-mer the nation's companies for their overseas ventures. "Canadian investors are really nervous Nellies" on foreign investments, he says. "It's just reflexive; if they hear about a company going to the U.S., they remember all the errors."

Lululemon Athletica has been a recent success story. The yoga-wear retailer caught the wave of popularity around yoga, taking something that had all the sizzle of a self-righteous health food store and turning it into a fashion state-ment. "They really understand their business and they have a really distinctive consumer proposition. Lululemon, it's such a beautifully branded message," says Howlett.

The fact remains that there have been a lot of U.S. misadventures. Experienced observers put Canadians' success ratio at about one in ten. In the case of Jean Coutu Group, which bought Eckerd Corporation, Howlett says that "their mistake was not retaining American management" of the drug chain, whereas Alimentation Couche-Tard, which retained local management in its U.S. operations (which include On the Run and Circle K convenience stores), has been successful. The worst screwups, he says, have been Canadian companies carrying a pocketful of capital across the border, thinking they can just throw money at a retail mess in the U.S. "Those are usually the ones that are the complete blowups. You think you're going to fix it. The Royal Bank is good, but do they know anything about banking in Georgia? You can be a long way removed from how to sell mortgages in Biloxi, Mississippi."

While his specialty is retail and consumer products, Howlett also brushed up against banking when he covered Imasco, the parent company of Ed Clark's old haunt, Canada Trust. Imasco, at the time run by Purdy Crawford and Brian Levitt, owned not only Canada Trust, but also Shoppers Drug Mart, which made a couple of abortive U.S. forays of its own.

Brian Levitt, current chairman of TD, talks about how the United States is actually several countries. There's the south, there's the northeast, there's Texas, the Midwest and California. The latter alone has a population and GDP the size of Canada's. Competition is off the charts in the U.S. and Americans are so obsessed with the pursuit of economic success that they are willing to work very hard. Their annual vacations are shorter than those of Canadians. It is also a winner-take-all culture. Coming in second or being a good sport is not celebrated.

The United States is also a breakaway country. It fought a war for its independence. It also had a protracted civil war. Aside from the two world wars in which it was successful, it has been embroiled in many conflicts abroad with mixed results. The scar tissue from more than a decade in Vietnam is still sensitive and informs policy. In the new millennium, the U.S. has also been a country under attack. The horrific destruction of September 11, 2001, shattered the American nervous system. The U.S. was no longer invincible, and ever since Americans have heard footsteps and looked over their shoulders, on guard for another attack. Later in the decade, they would discover that their banks were also not invincible. Beginning in late 2007 and culminating in 2008 and 2009, the United States experienced a devastating shock to the financial system courtesy of a banking crisis that had its roots in the American Dream of a house for every family. The economic foundation of the country was shaken to the core, the worst pocketbook scare since the Great Depression of the 1930s.

While Ed Clark gets all the glowing press, he is sitting on top of an institution that has a history of building brick by brick. While savvy, strategic and smarter than most, Clark has the benefit of following three other successful CEOs and many other sharp TD executives, both current and past. In fact, the beginnings of TD's U.S. invasion can be traced back to the moxie of someone who began as a lowly clerk in 1954, the year before the historic merger that created Toronto-Dominion.

16

Although he never reached the heights of president or CEO like Ed Clark, Keith Gray became one of the most effective executives in the bank's modern history. Not only did he not get degrees from Harvard like Ed Clark, or Clark's two predecessors, Dick Thomson and Charlie Baillie (the first two MBA grads to be bosses at TD), Gray didn't even graduate from high school. Keith Gray shares Clark's difficulty with words, going so far as to say he is dyslexic. Gray fared poorly in school and professes to be a slow reader even today. He clawed his way up from junior clerk to the higher reaches of the bank, and his working-class roots made him the chalk to the upper-class cheese of other senior managers. Although he is now a wealthy man, with homes in Toronto, Muskoka and Sarasota and a membership to the exclusive Rosedale Golf Club, he still feels he is not "one of them."

But Gray's outsider status also made him an entrepreneur, and he became the bank's rebel inside the castle. Without his enterprising ways, which often made his bosses nervous, the bank might never have grown the financial spine to build the business to where it is today.

Few remember it now, but TD was the one major bank to spurn the idea of buying an investment bank when the opportunity arose in the 1980s. Instead, from scratch, Gray was busy building the bank's discount brokerage business, Green Line, into the dominant player in Canada, ultimately gaining 72 percent market share.

He started out filling inkwells at a rural branch in southwestern Ontario in the 1950s. Those were the days when banks still kept revolvers onsite, just in case. There were no computers. Banks were open only from 10 a.m. until 3 p.m. and they closed Wednesday afternoons. The ballpoint pen wasn't even in the picture. Gray says that when he joined the bank, employees were prohibited from owning motorcycles, and if a male staffer wanted to get married, head office had to be notified.* By 2011, TD was displaying brochures targeting gay

---

* TD archivist Anne Spruin says in the late 1800s and early 1900s all Canadian banks had a rule requiring employees to seek permission to marry if their salary was below a certain level. There was worry that an employee trying to support a family with an entry-level wage would be more likely to go into debt or commit fraud. It was also easier to transfer an unmarried employee. Spruin says it's unclear when the rule was repealed, but prior to the 1955 merger, employees had to advise head office that they were getting married.

and lesbian customers and sponsoring the Pride Parade in several Canadian and American cities. In just over half a century, the spectrum of social change is on full view at the bank. The evolution of financial services in North America can also be charted along the same timeline.

In the 1970s, the financial world began to do away with many regulations, arguably going too far and setting the world up for the financial crisis that would hit like a vicious cyclone in 2008. But an early change to the rules that helped TD was the elimination of fixed brokerage commissions. That opened the door for discount brokers to enter the market, companies like Charles Schwab in the United States, which allowed the average guy to trade in and out of stocks cheaply. TD decided to build a discount brokerage too. It would be a business inside the bank. Gray was the architect and engineer, and by the late 1980s he was buying other companies with the bank's chequebook.

Those smaller deals set the stage for Gray's landmark purchase of U.S. discounter Waterhouse Securities in 1996, TD's biggest acquisition ever to that point. Not only did it put the TD shield in front of Americans, it turned out to have been one of the best financial services transactions anyone in the business can recall. Gray and the bank put together a deal for Waterhouse that made it essentially free to TD. That, and a lucrative related transaction, paved the way for Toronto-Dominion to buy Canada Trust, a transformative deal. In Canada Trust, TD nabbed the country's premier retail financial institution, positioning TD to become a banking colossus. It also got Ed Clark, enabling him to make the bank's next big move, the U.S. expansion.

Now, as it settles into the second decade of the new millennium, the United States faces enormous debts at all levels of government, a stubbornly high unemployment rate and a national aversion to taxes that dates to the War of Independence. Ed Clark knows more about the U.S. than the average Canadian. In his early teens, he spent time in California, where his father taught at the University of California, Berkeley. In his twenties, Clark was at Harvard doing his master's and a doctorate. As CEO of Canada Trust in the 1990s, he sold off a U.S. division. While his PhD may be in economics, you could say his post-doc work has focused on U.S. banking.

At the bank's annual meeting in March 2012, Clark said that he is in his final years as CEO. His legacy depends on how well his bet on the United States turns out. It might be many years before investors know for certain whether TD can avoid the fate of RBC when it attempted to be a retail banker in the United States.

Canadian bankers proved their worth during the financial crisis. Could it be their time to shine outside of Canada? Ed Clark likes to say it's better to be lucky than smart. He certainly has the brain wattage, but he may also have lucked into the right time to lead a Canadian bank's invasion of the United States—or not, depending on how you view the future of that country.

## 2

# POOR BOY DROPOUT

*From the Foundry to Bank Clerk*

Keith Gray grew up "very poor" in rural southwestern Ontario. His parents, Jim and Lyla Gray, had already lost the family farm in Lambton County's Moore Township when Keith was born in 1935. They'd abandoned it and rented another farm in the same county, but thirty-five kilometres away. With no choice about how to move there, they walked to their new tract of land in Plympton Township, along with their (then) five sons, fifteen head of cattle, and a few horses.

Growing up in this part of the country was tough, but it also imbued the young Gray with characteristics that served him well decades later in business. His second wife, Wendy Leaney, who worked for Gray when he ran the main branch of the bank and later became an investment banker at TD, calls such quiet determination the "southwestern Ontario way."

"We keep things close to the vest, don't show our hands," says Gray. "That's the way I was and that's the way my dad was. It worked well. I had to use it 'cause I didn't have the education. Sit back, watch, bide my time and make a move. I don't confide. I wasn't as smart as the other guys, so I'd better use the cards-against-the-vest theory. Even during the Green Line days, I didn't confide."

Although he had little in the way of formal education, Gray's favourite word was *why*. "Why, why, why? I always had to know why. People would tell me, stop asking so many damn questions."

21

When the Second World War began, four of his brothers (Goldwin, Kenneth, Alex and Eugene) enlisted in the military. Goldwin and Alex had been "riding the rails" because of a lack of work. Two brothers were wounded, one was declared missing in action, and the youngest to serve, Eugene, a tail gunner in the Royal Canadian Air Force, was killed at nineteen when his plane crashed returning from Germany. Eugene is buried in Scotland, with the rest of his crew.

"It's touching. Hard to keep the tears from flowing," says Gray, describing visits to the cemetery. He and his brother Bill, too young to serve, were at home during the war, along with their sister, Lois.

"I remember this period as a very sad and traumatic time for my mother and father. It was not a very happy time in our lives," Gray recalls. Sitting at the dining room table in his Sarasota condo, Gray speaks quietly, his eyes moist. He describes the United Church minister coming down the lane, informing families in the area that a son had been killed or wounded.

"I remember my dad sitting looking at my brother Eugene in a picture, and wishing it had been him. That was really a tough time for a family."

As if the sacrifices of their sons were not enough, in the spring of 1940 the farmhouse the Grays had bought in the late 1930s (after renting it) burned to the ground.

"We moved to a farmhouse across the road that was sitting empty and for sale. It had no electricity, plumbing or indoor bathroom, but it was someplace to live." The owners allowed the family to move in after the fire at their previous home, and the Grays soon bought the property.

Surrounded by such life-and-death problems, the young Gray had little encouragement to do well at his studies. Classes were held in a one-room schoolhouse a couple of kilometres from home, where eight grades were taught. Gray got the strap numerous times for transgressions such as "looking up girl's dresses." Once he got whacked because he couldn't spell, something that, being dyslexic, he still can't do well. "I did not like school and wished out of there," he says.

During high school in Petrolia, about ten kilometres from the farm, Gray developed a bad case of the skin disease psoriasis on his face and body. As a result, the school would not allow him to take physical education. He dropped out after grade eleven and went to work in a foundry in Sarnia for six months at $50 a week. His father, who was in poor health and barely able to withstand the physical demands of farming, had worked in the same foundry during the war at sixty cents an hour.

Notwithstanding the litany of hardships in his early life, Gray was born in what was arguably one of the luckiest years in the twentieth century. In his book *Outliers,* Malcolm Gladwell describes how being born in the mid-1930s put you in a select group.[7] If you had been born ten years earlier you'd be serving in World War Two, and perhaps not coming back, like Eugene Gray. It was also the Depression and there were fewer babies, which would make for less competition in the job market during the 1950s. Gray agrees, saying that ten years later, "I'd never have got in the bank. Timing and luck is everything."

Keith's luck arrived one day in late 1954. Gray's dad was in the Bank of Toronto in Wyoming, Ontario when the manager, a fellow named Bob Richardson, asked him if Keith would consider joining the bank.[*]

At the time, banks did not hire university graduates. Men—they were almost all men—were hired straight out of high school and trained in a way similar to the Scottish system of apprenticeship. Gray took the job at the Bank of Toronto (established 1855), which merged a year later with the Dominion Bank (established 1871), one of the last noteworthy bank mergers in Canada, to form what is now known as Toronto-Dominion. Gray contends that from 1954 until about 1980, there was an "us and them" feeling inside the merged bank, describing the Bank of Toronto as "tightass" and the Dominion Bank as "gamblers." In any event, the bank job paid a paltry $1,200 a year, a huge cut from the $3,000 he was making at the foundry. "It was warm," is the reason Gray gives for making the switch. "It wasn't dirty."

The branch had six employees and his first job was as a junior clerk at $23.08 a week. That meant he sat at the back, on a stool, where he had the grand duty of looking after the mailbox. At night, he would write in the general ledger, marking down deposits and withdrawals, "like Scrooge." There

---

[*] Gray's sister, Lois, thinks her father, not the bank manager, may actually have been the one who asked on behalf of Keith.

was an adding machine, but it wouldn't subtract. "If you were caught using it, you were considered a weakling," Gray recalls.

The bank was open from 10 a.m. until 3 p.m., as was the custom for many years. While the restricted hours seem archaic and sleepy now, they were a practical necessity in the days before personal computers, when tellers needed the extra time to balance their tills accurately. Gray's job wasn't quite as lofty as a teller's. He was to turn the light out in the vault. Each Tuesday, he had to replace the pen nibs and fill up the inkwells. He had to mix the ink, which came in powder form.

There were also rules for people who worked at banks in the 1950s. Aside from not being allowed to own a motorcycle and having to notify the company if you planned to get married, it was generally accepted that you wore a hat, and you most certainly had to wear a jacket and tie to work, which Gray did for forty-three years.

Today, there is still a TD in Wyoming, but it is now staffed and managed by women. These rural branches were once described by long-serving TD Chairman and President Allen Lambert as the backbone of the bank. They are often also full of unclaimed deposits that just sit there—chockablock with what Gray calls "cold money." "You talk about hot money. The money in those little communities is as cold as it gets. It's stable, stable money."

Promoted to teller, Gray worked in a cage and always had a revolver on the desk. He would place the gun on the counter so it would be in plain view of any would-be robbers. Every six months, he was required to check that the gun worked, so he would take it down to the basement and fire a few rounds into the coal bin.

As a teller, he had to make up any unaccounted shortfalls out of his own pocket. Unfortunately, he once lost track of $50, which he had to pay back at $2.50 a month over the course of twenty months.

After about a year, he was moved to Kerwood (near Strathroy) for two years, where he admits he did virtually nothing at the bank. There were just three employees in the branch. The manager sat around reading the sports section all day. Some days, only two or three customers would come in. The bank would be shut from noon till 1 p.m. Once they locked the door over the lunch hour and forgot to unlock it. It didn't matter. There were no customers the rest of the afternoon so no one even noticed the bank was locked.

"I was in Kerwood for two very boring years," Gray says. "Nonetheless, the experience maintaining and balancing the books, by hand, was very valuable training."

In 1956, he was transferred to Meaford, Ontario, on the shores of Georgian Bay, where the Protestant farm boy roomed with a Jewish family. His job was assistant accountant and he was there a little over a year. "The work was not difficult and I enjoyed the girls."

The Meaford branch manager, Norm Hazel, gave his young employee some advice: Don't trust even your own grandmother. This counsel would prove valuable when Gray became a lending officer, with progressively higher limits, and later when he oversaw commercial and industrial banking for all of Canada.

What followed Meaford was a seemingly endless series of moves to Hamilton, Bronte (near Oakville), back to Hamilton, and Winnipeg. Hamilton was Gray's first full-time experience in a city, and an intimidating one. He'd never before ridden on a public bus. He lived in a boarding house with three other men. Unfortunately, the psoriasis became quite severe on his face, and the bank thought it best to hide him in a small town. Just four months after arriving in Hamilton, the bank shipped Gray to Bronte, where he became the branch's accountant. While in Bronte he was, for the only time in his career, lured away from the bank. He had been making $3,500 a year, but in late 1959 or early 1960, an offer of double the money from the parents of Olympic skater Otto Jelinek proved irresistible. The Jelineks ran an import sporting goods business and were customers of the bank. Since he was planning to get married that year, Gray found the offer to be one he couldn't refuse. But it didn't work out.

"I had grown up in the TD and found I was lost outside," Gray admits. He eventually went back to the bank at the same salary he had when he left. "After being out of the bank, I realized it was a good place to make a living and it was all I knew. So I re-entered with a determination to work hard, and if I was lucky, become a branch manager."

Now in his late twenties, Gray began to apply himself. He studied all the bank's regulation manuals, took internal courses and knew he had to score top of the class whenever there was a bank inspection. There were three rating categories—above average, average, and below standard, which was cause for dismissal. His branch was called "outstanding," a highly unusual rating, and he was immediately notified he would be promoted.

Head office told Gray his choices were to move to a larger branch, become an inspector at headquarters or be trained to become an operations and efficiency expert. He picked the third option. It turned out to be a prescient move. Based in Toronto between 1962 and 1965, Gray started learning about computer programming (the language was COBOL) and how to measure efficiency. Learning computers from the early days would prove invaluable later when he built the discount brokerage business just as the Internet was blossoming.\*

Cost cutting was just as popular in the 60s as it is today. Gray would visit small-town branches to see where they could improve. He hit a high note on a trip to review the bank's Winnipeg operations, somehow managing to winnow down the number of employees from one hundred to seventy.

Having worked there earlier in his career, Gray hated Winnipeg. Head office, however, wasn't interested in people's likes or dislikes. Six months later, Gray's Toronto bosses asked him to move back to Winnipeg to become supervisor of operations/administration for the bank in western Canada. No way, he said. Told in no uncertain terms that if he wanted to keep his career with the bank he'd better go, he moved with his wife, Diane, whom he had married in 1961, and their small daughter, Christine.†

Gray's Western Division territory was a vast geographical area stretching from Marathon, Ontario, 300 kilometres east of Thunder Bay, to the Alberta border. Gray immediately began telling his general manager, Tom Easton, how things were done in the East. Anyone familiar with the sensitivities of

---

\* In the late 1960s, Gray took delivery of the first computer for TD Bank in western Canada, the second in the bank's system. It was an IBM that required a 280-square-metre (3,000 sq. ft.) room with a raised floor that he rented in Winnipeg's Grain Exchange Building.

† All three of Gray's daughters—Christine, Kelly and Kerry—would work for the bank. Christine and Kelly still do.

regional Canadian politics knows that attitude can make you enemies quickly. "We know where head office is, but we don't pay any attention to anything they say," Easton responded. "You have a lot to learn. Be at my home at 8 a.m. on Monday morning and I will show you this division. Tell your wife you'll be back late on Friday afternoon."

On Monday morning, Gray began touring the division in Easton's chauffeur-driven Cadillac. The area was so huge, it took seven hours to reach the first branch. Before he'd left, he'd asked the supervisor of human resources, Bob Good, if there was anything he needed to know for the tour. Good told him to take $500 and two bottles of Dewar's Scotch for Easton.

Sure enough, once inside the Caddy, Easton asked Gray if he'd brought any money and how much.

"$500."

"Did you bring any Scotch?"

"Two bottles."

"What kind?"

"Dewar's."

That was the extent of the conversation for the next seven hours as they drove across the Prairies. Gray, who didn't drink Scotch then, says he didn't see any of it, and figures Easton drank it when he was on his own at night.

Eventually, Gray developed a working relationship with Easton and he was given the job of preparing basic layout drawings for new or renovated bank branches. One day, Easton asked him to prepare two, one for Rocanville, Saskatchewan, the other for Gravelbourg, Saskatchewan. He told Gray there was no rush, that two or three weeks would be fine. About four days later, on a Friday, Easton wanted to see the plans. Gray said they weren't ready because he was under the impression they were due in a few weeks.

"I don't care what you think, have them on my desk Monday morning," Easton said.

Gray worked all weekend on the plans. Each branch was supposed to have a different look or design. The rush job resulted in the two plans being almost exactly the same, except that Gravelbourg's was three metres longer than Rocanville's. Gray had taken a risk and was relieved when Easton didn't notice the similarity.

He soon took another risk and turned down a transfer to Montreal, which could have been a fatal career move. Easton defended him, saying he was too important to let go. Gray stayed for a total of five years in Winnipeg and his middle daughter, Kelly, was born there in St. Boniface Hospital.

He was learning the banking business in the trenches, branch by branch, sometimes in quarters too close for comfort. He describes a trip to a small town in Saskatchewan with another employee of the bank. The two men had to stay in a seedy motel that had only one vacancy—and had to share the one and only bed in the shabby room with a bare bulb hanging from the ceiling. "I had to sleep with the guy!" Gray says, laughing.

By 1970, the bank had seen enough of a spark in the farm boy to send him to Harvard for a three-month advanced management program. This was a *huge* break. Harvard was a major spawning ground for future bank executives. Dick Thomson, the longtime TD CEO, was a Harvard MBA, as was his right-hand man, TD President Robin Korthals. Thomson's successor, Charlie Baillie, was as well. (And Ed Clark has both a master's and a PhD in economics from the prestigious university.) It was no longer enough to work your way up from being a teller. It was becoming de rigueur to sport a degree from an Ivy League school. This was where valuable contacts were made and where the financial establishment perpetuated itself. Studying hard and doing well there could help propel you to the top.

Gray's few months in Harvard Yard changed him, giving him more confidence. He goes so far as to say they changed his life, describing the experience as extremely intimidating. "Talk about being shell shocked," he says.

Until 1956, the bank did not hire university graduates. Dick Thomson was the person who changed that. "Probably the best thing I did for the bank," Thomson says of convincing the head of human resources to start hiring MBAs (four were hired in 1963 and all became vice-chairs of the bank). Thomson's own stint at Harvard almost worked against him when he joined the bank in 1957. The future CEO also had an undergraduate degree in engi-

---

* One of those future vice-chairs would be Sydney "Bud" McMorran. He says there were just 100 MBA graduates in all of Canada in 1963 and each got five job offers upon graduation. As for Charlie Baillie, Dick Thomson hired him out of Harvard Business School.

neering. The recruiter at the bank, a hard-boiled character named Harold Burns, told Thomson, "We don't hire people like you."

"Pretend I'm a clerk, will you hire me?" Thomson shot back. Burns did, for $275 a month. Thomson's Harvard education would ultimately help pave his way to the corner office. He was eventually made assistant to the chairman and president, Allen Lambert, a position from which he launched his own stellar career.

"Dick decided we've got to get some men some education," Gray recalls. Starting in the mid-1960s, the bank would send a couple of people a year to Harvard, even those with no university education.

Gray recalls there were 106 men and three women from twenty-five or thirty countries in the program—PhDs, doctors, scientists, government bureaucrats, economists, military personnel and others. In a strange coincidence, Ed Clark was at Harvard at the same time. "All had university degrees except a chap from England and me—and I was the only high school dropout."

Gray's dorm was Hamilton Hall—four rooms, each one housing two students, and one bathroom for eight guys, known in campus lingo as a "can group." The workload was crushing, classes six days a week, and more homework than Gray could possibly get through. Each night, he had to study three or four of the famous Harvard business cases. "I was and am a very slow reader and so I was advised by members of my can group to pick one or two cases and work on those and just hope you did not get asked a question in class."

At first, because he was self-conscious, Gray was very quiet in class. Soon enough, though, he came to the realization that many classmates were naïve in the ways of business. After all, he was now thirty-five and had been in banking for sixteen years, learning from the bottom up. "I am sure they were very knowledgeable [about their] chosen discipline; however, they knew very little about managing businesses or people. Their opinions were off the wall. I slowly built confidence and participated openly in class."

With Harvard behind him, Gray would soon see his career become airborne. Again, good luck would intervene.

3

# THE BOMB THREAT

*What a Way to Get Promoted*

On his return to Toronto in 1971, Keith Gray was sent to the branch at Spadina and Adelaide, the centre of the city's *schmatta* business, or needle trade. "An excellent place to learn when—and when not—to make a loan," Gray says of his eighteen months there.

He outlines the three most important conditions a lender has to assess before making a loan. The first is character. Do you trust the borrower? The second is capacity. Can the person or business pay back the loan? The third is collateral. Gray calls this third condition the "sleeping pill," meaning that there is something to back up the loan if it goes sour. The rule of thumb back then was that you could finance up to 75 percent of sixty days' worth of receivables. In other words, the money these businesses were expecting to receive from buyers for sixty days would allow for a loan at three-quarters of that value. Borrowers were also eligible for financing of up to 50 percent of their inventory. Due diligence, however, meant the banker went out to the warehouse to check the shelves—a far cry from the NINA (No Income, No Assets) mortgages that were one of the causes of the U.S. subprime mortgage crisis.

"We're going out kicking boxes," Gray would say of his inventory-checking visits. He told one smart-aleck *schmatta* merchant that he needed to see proof of receivables in order to lend him money.

"You want receivables, I'll give you receivables," the customer said. In other words, if you want me to lie to you, I'll lie to you.

If the boys in the needle trade liked you, they'd invite you to their synagogue or their home. Lamenting the decline of person-to-person banking, where character was king, Gray says it's now all about computerized credit scoring, with applications sent to head office. Instead of kicking the boxes, it's about checking the boxes, an objective assessment instead of what used to be a much more subjective, judgment-based decision. The managers of branches were out in the community, "helping build churches, helping build curling rinks."

"On Spadina, we'd call on customers once a month. And they loved it. We were in a partnership. We were excited when the customer did well."

Still, the advice of his manager in Meaford, Norm Hazel, kept coming back to Gray. Don't trust even your own grandmother. "You never know what a man will do when his back is to the wall and his family is starving. He'll lie. And he'll cheat," says Gray.

The garment district taught him not only more about lending, it brought Gray closer to head office, just blocks away, yet another world. But his next move landed him at the main branch at the corner of King and Bay streets, the heart of Toronto's financial district, in the famed TD Tower, the architectural masterpiece finished in 1967. Within a year, Gray was deputy manager of the biggest branch in the system and responsible for 350 to 400 employees. "If I failed, I would be written off as to future potential in the TD," he recounts. As usual, not only did he not fail, he also got lucky.

One day in the early 1970s, Gray was sitting at his desk when a security officer handed him an envelope addressed simply to "TD Bank." He opened it to find a bomb threat. The would-be bomber was demanding $1 million CDN and $250,000 USD from TD and the same amount from CIBC across the street. The drops were to be made by a top-management person of each bank who were instructed to deliver the funds "alone" (underlined) to the northwest corner of Bay and Adelaide streets. "No two serial numbers will be in consecutive order. No unused bills. No silver," the note instructed.

Upon hearing of the threat, Gray's boss said, "I gotta visit some customers—you handle it." Gray was suddenly on his own. He called bank security, who immediately called Toronto Police.

Aside from the conditions laid out by the bomber, the other three pages of the letter went into detail about the nature of the incendiary device and the damage it could do:

> *Located in one of the rooms (office, service, storage, etc.), is a collection of equipment. In that room are two aquariums of large proportions. They are full of kerosene. Each aquarium is covered and sealed to prevent fumes escaping. The aquariums hold one hundred and eighty gallons each. Suspended in each are several glass containers containing nitric acid (HN03). Taped to the glass containers are several standard blasting caps. They, and the wires attached to them, are sealed in plastic. Also suspended in the aquariums are six two-pound packets of powdered chemicals. When the blasting caps explode, they shatter the glass containers. Nitric acid will act as an oxidant and the kerosene as a combustible. Combustion is spontaneous and ignition is not required. This combination is a common liquid rocket fuel. The resulting explosion and flash fire is quite spectacular. The selection of the site of the device was carefully considered to render the most damage. The architectural plans of the tower were carefully studied. Total damage from fire and explosion alone might make the tower structurally unsafe . . .*
>
> *But there is more. Remember the packets of chemicals? Under combustion conditions, this powder burns with an unusual effect. Toxic fumes are produced. These gases are extremely corrosive to anything with a plastic or rubber base, and are quite deadly to human metabolism when absorbed in lung tissue. Even in minute quantities, they usually prove lethal . . . if the device were to be set off NOW for example, I would expect that over twenty thousand persons would die or be injured before lunchtime today.*

The letter went on to describe how the bomb's timer was controlled via a telephone hookup:

*"If no telephone call is received, the device blows on schedule via the timer. Thanks to Bell, the touchtone generator takes care of additional instructions. A very ordinary telephone answering machine is wired to a live telephone that was installed some months ago. A touchtone switching system, stolen from Bell, is hooked in sequence to that. Got it so far?"*

And there was more:

*This may come as a surprise to you, but this is a duplicate of a letter sent to your neighbour across the street. That's right, the other bank. The device is located in one of the two towers (TD or Commerce). I suggest you read the conditions, then contact that other bank. The conditions must be followed exactly and no extension or deviation will be considered. If you consider this a bluff, that is also fine. A copy of this letter will be given to the media immediately after the explosion and fire. After the public furor dies down, we set up exactly the same situation somewhere else (World Trade Ctr.?) and we are sure there would be no problems then.*

Gray contacted the executive offices and asked for Robin Korthals, then VP of Administration, who was in a meeting. Gray told him about the bomb threat, adding that a senior executive of the bank was required to make the drop.

"Well, you're now a senior executive of the bank," Korthals drily informed him. With that, Gray was dispatched with a satchel to the corner of Bay and Adelaide, where he waited with an undercover cop. "We had missed the first drop," Gray says. The bomber had then called the bank to say that they had just a half-hour to get there with the money.

Accompanied by a police officer posing as the CIBC executive, Gray was carrying a gunnysack full of blank cheques. They stood there for forty-five minutes to an hour. Meanwhile, a plane was standing by at the airport, as per the bomber's instructions.

Since it was the lunch hour, it wasn't long before the crowd from Winston's, the restaurant of choice for the financial elite at the time, started to stumble out after their three-martini lunches. "Gray, what the hell are you doing here?

Gray, what are you standing there for?" a few started yelling. He tried to shoo them along.

"The cop was standing next to me, shaking like you wouldn't believe," Gray says. Suddenly, a cab pulled up and the driver asked if they had a delivery. They said yes and the cabbie instructed them to put it in the trunk. Gray's orders were to go back to the office to report on what happened. But in an instant, the cop jumped in the back seat and pulled his gun, at which point the cabbie jumped out of the car.

"You get back into the car and drive where you're supposed to go with this," the cop ordered.

The cabbie drove them to the underground parking lot at City Hall, just a few blocks away, where the bomber was waiting in a pickup truck. The police closed off all the exits and captured the criminal, who happened to be a customer of the TD Bank with an outstanding loan of $1,500. (Gray says they always joked at the bank that the bomber borrowed the money to buy the gun and the typewriter.) The cop, meanwhile, was named Toronto Policeman of the Year. Keith Gray got a $300 bonus cheque, but his name did not appear in the papers. (As for the bomb, it was a hoax.)

The bank, though, was true to its word. The episode did lead to the farm boy dropout becoming a senior executive. In 1980, Gray became the vice-president and manager at the main branch at King and Bay. He could now lend up to $250,000 without approval (at Spadina and Adelaide his limit had been $15,000). But as a harsh recession kicked into gear, he'd spend much of his time supervising the collection of delinquent loans—the black-hatted banker from the old movies. "I was told I was the right man for the times," Gray laughs.

Gray's outsider status also gave him a competitive advantage. In the starchy world of Canadian banking, he thought like an entrepreneur. In a few years, president Robin Korthals and CEO Dick Thomson would see a perfect fit for Keith Gray and the bank—one that would lay the foundation for the bank's expansion in Canada and what it has gone on to build in the United States.

4

# BUILDING A BUSINESS INSIDE
# (OR OUTSIDE) THE BANK

*The Rise of Green Line*

Dick Thomson and Robin Korthals are eight weeks apart in age, Korthals being the older of the two. For years, they were a winning tag team atop TD Bank. Korthals came from an investment bank and joined TD on Canada's 100th birthday, July 1, 1967. From then on, he worked only on the executive floor and was president of TD from 1981 until 1995. Thomson, after apprenticing with Allen Lambert, became chief general manager in 1967, before he turned thirty-five, moved up to president in 1972 and CEO in 1977, adding the chairman's title in 1978, which he held until 1998, a year after he relinquished the CEO job to Charlie Baillie.

"Dick was an extraordinary banker. The combination of Dick and Robin was unbeatable. I'm talking in a North American context. They didn't follow the crowd," says one former executive, adding, "I think Robin was the insurance policy in case Dick was run over by a truck." Korthals could have run any bank, he adds, an opinion shared by Thomson.

"We called him Special K," jokes Keith Gray.

Bob Kelly, the former chairman and CEO of Bank of New York Mellon, who was once chief financial officer of TD (and heir apparent to Charlie Baillie before Ed Clark came along), says of Korthals, "He was the smartest guy I ever worked for."

Korthals pioneered what they called "lending on cash flow." At the time, few banks would finance cable television companies. In those early days, the only asset cable companies had was their "pole rental agreements" with telephone and power companies. Most banks worried about getting their money back if a cable business soured. Many in the investment community worried about the amount of debt required by cable companies, viewing them as bad bets. Korthals, however, saw the business differently. He came to the view that "you'll give up your refrigerator before your cable television." He pushed the bank into lending to the likes of Ted Rogers, who founded the empire that became Rogers Communications. (The bank would later extend this philosophy to financing the wireless telecom industry.)

"We enriched quite a few Canadians," Korthals says, adding that if you had a cable licence, you got a loan. Besides Rogers, TD also loaned to JR Shaw of Shaw Communications, as well as to the Audets of Cogeco and Chagnons of Vidéotron. Ted Rogers, though, proved to be a wild one. Korthals says Rogers flipped out when he informed him there would be covenants, or specific conditions that had to be met, in order for Rogers to keep a loan. "I don't want anything like that. I've never done that before," Rogers protested loudly.

Korthals told him he wasn't sure he could approve the loan without providing protection for the bank. With that, the volatile Rogers took a set of keys and hurled them onto Korthals' desk, yelling, "Here. You can have the whole goddamn business if this is what I have to do!" The keys were to Rogers' office and his blue Dodge convertible.

This was the world of Robin Korthals and Dick Thomson—corporate banking—a world Ed Clark would reduce TD's exposure to years later. It's believed by some who worked under the duo that for a time they didn't talk because of issues surrounding succession. If that was the case, there's no sign of animosity now and each speaks highly of the other.*

Both Thomson and Korthals trained as engineers, both had Harvard MBAs, both had fathers who were executives and both enjoyed investing in stocks, buying and selling shares as a hobby. "We didn't use investment

---

* Twice a year, Thomson and Korthals, along with some twenty executives they worked with, gather for a lunch, something Korthals describes as "highly unusual" in the corporate world.

managers ourselves. We thought we could pick our own stocks. We loved it," Thomson says during an interview in the spacious office (with assistant) he still has at the bank.

As Thomson puts it, it didn't take a genius to figure out which were the top ten companies in Canada. That's true, but it's also easy for Dick Thomson to say. His father had been chief general manager of the Imperial Bank (which later merged with Commerce to become CIBC), and Thomson himself had a spectacular run as boss of TD for decades. He knew everyone who mattered in Canadian business. He and Robin Korthals lent to many of them. If anyone in Canada knew the country's best companies, it was these two fellows.

Korthals, who had grown up on the Caribbean island of Curaçao, where his father ran the Shell refinery, had watched his dad buy stocks during the Great Depression when no one bought stocks. In the 1950s, the stock market recovered from a twenty-five-year funk and his father was left sitting on a big pot of money. Korthals took notice and got interested in the market, buying his first stock in 1953, a Saskatchewan gold company. The two top bankers at TD couldn't help wondering why they were paying their stockbrokers so much money to buy and sell stocks when anyone who put a little time into researching could have a shot at making as good a call as the garden-variety investment advisor.

"I thought like an investor and I had the frustrations of an investor. I thought, Why did I have to pay 5 percent to execute my intellectual property? So it [the discount brokerage business] was a good fit with my history," Korthals recalls.

Korthals and Thomson's thinking coincided with an era that saw the regulatory shackles come off the investment industry. It happened in the United States in the 1970s and soon followed in Canada. In the U.S., though, entrepreneurs seemed to have a heightened sense of smell compared with Canadians, and they jumped on the new opportunity. TD's multiyear stealth raid on the brokerage and banking sector in the United States can be traced back to 1971, with the establishment of a new type of financial company. That firm was Charles Schwab, the company founded by the entrepreneur of the same name, which would revolutionize the brokerage business around the world.

In 1974, the Securities and Exchange Commission (SEC) allowed Schwab a trial period when it could offer discounts on commissions for very large or very small securities transactions. Then on May 1, 1975, things changed for good. The SEC put an end to fixed commissions in the brokerage industry, clearing the way for discounters like Schwab to ramp up for real. It was deregulation. Of course, the traditional brokerage types loathed this new entrant. They could loathe all they wanted, but Schwab wasn't going away.

At the same time, computing power was beginning to develop critical mass, just what a discounter like Schwab needed to process trades. Discount brokerage was a telephone order business that required volume to be profitable, and volume processing to be efficient. Efficiency meant the Schwabs of the world could charge 75 percent less for a stock transaction than the traditional broker charged, and make money.

Schwab's growth did not go unnoticed in other quarters, particularly at TD Bank, where Robin Korthals observed this new industry from afar. Still, it would be more than a decade before TD's answer to the trend, known as Green Line, was established in Canada. But TD can thank Schwab for breaking new ground.

Chuck Schwab, as he's known, was an entrepreneur from the get-go. Born in Sacramento, California, in 1937, his first job as a boy was picking walnuts, sacking them and selling them at $5 for each 100-pound sack. By the time he was twelve, he had graduated to the chicken business, selling eggs door to door. At thirteen, Schwab owned a few chickens himself. After a series of jobs such as driving a tractor, harvesting sugar beets, working in the oil fields, and being a railroad switch man, an insurance salesman and a bank teller, he ended up at Stanford University, then at Stanford Graduate School of Business. By twenty-three he was working in the investment business.[8]

It would be almost fifteen years of hanging on until Charles Schwab & Co. took off in 1975. With capital from his uncle Bill, Chuck Schwab's company was turning a profit a year later and getting loans from banks that were eager to lend. Of course, Chuck had to secure the loans with his home, a gutsy move typical of entrepreneurs.[9]

Among the banks that turned him down more than once was Bank of America. But in 1984 that bank bought Schwab for $53 million, making

Chuck Schwab the largest shareholder of B of A. It was a very unhappy marriage, and would later fall apart. By that time, just when TD Green Line was opening its doors, Schwab had 1.2 million customers dealing with his salary-only brokers.[10]

In his book *How to Be Your Own Stockbroker*, Schwab says the company had four "secrets" to its success: direct response marketing that included photographs of Schwab himself to humanize the company, "cutting edge" computer technology that made possible the twenty-second transaction, "risk innovation" such as introducing 24/7 order entry and, finally, never acknowledging defeat, even under the toughest circumstances.[11]

Schwab also paints himself as market seer. In what now appears to be quaint and naïve advice, given the scorching of investors during the recent financial crisis, the king of discount brokers makes some outlandish statements. For instance, Schwab writes of the gains to be made on equities, "26 percent yearly is obtainable, if you know what you are doing."[12] That may be possible if you are a leading hedge fund operator, but even those high rollers have many, many negative years owing to huge bets that go wrong.

When Schwab wrote the book in 1984, no doubt he was inhaling the fumes of what would be a two-decade bull market in equities. But he also dumps on bonds, basically saying they're not worth the time of day. What Schwab missed predicting was that bonds were in the early stages of a three-decade rally. At one point, he also says a "12 percent return isn't that much."[13] These days, 12 percent with minimal inflation would be spectacular. But in the early 1980s, interest rates were very high. It didn't take much effort to get 12 percent on your money when you could stuff your cash into a guaranteed investment certificate in Canada or certificate of deposit in the U.S. that gave you double-digit returns. But with inflation in the double digits, real returns were much lower.

Schwab's investing advice aside, Korthals and Thomson were ready to take a stab at discount brokerage. In 1983, TD was the fifth largest Canadian bank—just a bit more than half the size of Royal—and it was looking for novel ways to grow.[14] One day, the two TD bankers wandered over to the offices of Loewen, Ondaatje, McCutcheon to have lunch with the investment banking partners. Chuck Loewen, who was a friend of Korthals, had been following the monthly revenue stats of the brokerage industry. "You've got to look at these people offering [discount] brokerage and look at this growth, and we should really do something," he told Korthals.

According to Korthals, in Ondaatje's office there was, of all things, a sandbox with black leather sides in the middle of a conference table that this group of blue chippers sat around. Presumably, the idea was to foster playful thought and creativity. As Thomson and Korthals sat there, the investment bankers across from them began to draw a picture in the sand of a simple organizational structure for a discount brokerage partnership with TD Bank.[15]

After the meeting, the two men were walking back along King Street when Thomson asked Korthals what he thought. Korthals said TD should go into partnership with Loewen, Ondaatje, which would handle the so-called back office of the business. This was the conception of Green Line that Keith Gray would build up to control more than 70 percent of the market in Canada before heading to the United States, a huge step in the evolution of TD.

One day in 1983, Gray was sitting in Korthals' office when the president reached for a file on his desk and asked him a question. "What do you know about brokerage? We're thinking of setting up a discount brokerage operation similar to Schwab." Gray admitted he had heard of discount brokerages but was not sure what they were doing.

Korthals transferred the assignment to Gray, who happened to like stockbrokers. He had, as he put it, "banked them" when he ran the branch at King and Bay. Gray started studying Schwab, even paying Chuck a visit in California.

Korthals and Thomson chose Gray because he knew technology from his experience with TD's earliest computer systems, he had an entrepreneurial spark and he was a hardboiled character who had done a lot of the bank's dirty work during the brutal recession of the early 1980s. By then, he was handling big loans, with authorization to lend up to $50 million. Lending also meant putting the screws to people, some of them very powerful. Thomson once sent Gray on a mission to put pressure on none other than a friend of Thomson's who was also a director of the bank. The man, a well-known member of the Canadian business establishment, was behind on his loan to TD.

Gray recalls Thomson's instructions, "Keith, you gotta get tougher with his account."

"Dick, he's a director of the bank," Gray pleaded.

"Leave that up to me. You be tough on the account." So there Gray was, going over to the man's office.

"If you don't bring this loan down, we're going to close you up," Gray told him.

"Does Dick know about this?"

"As a matter of fact, Dick asked me to look after it."

"Jesus, you're going to give me a heart attack."

"Well, it's not too good for my constitution either," Gray countered, squeezing the man where it hurt. As one of the *schmatta* merchants on Spadina had told him, "Gray, you'll go a long way. You've got shit in your blood," (meaning that he was tough).

As for discount brokerage and TD's new business, Green Line, Korthals laughingly recalls thinking that "one day it will take up a whole floor of the TD Tower." He could not have imagined that, through various acquisitions and metamorphoses, the discount brokerage would one day process more trades per day than any other comparable company on the planet, be a major plank in TD's growth as a retail bank and lay the foundation for Ed Clark's aggressive expansion into the United States two decades later.

The bank, however, was in for a fight. The investment dealer establishment declared war. The status quo was terrified its business would be destroyed by a discount brokerage, much like small merchants lash out when Walmart comes to town. Schwab had experienced the same reaction in the U.S. As Keith Gray puts it in the colourful idiom of the farm boy, Charles Schwab was "like a skunk at a garden party."

TD's case for a licence went before the regulator, the Ontario Securities Commission (OSC), in 1983. Carrying the spear for the brokerage industry was the hulking Austin Taylor, six and a half feet tall and not much less in girth. The head of investment dealer McLeod Young & Weir (later bought by Bank of Nova Scotia), Taylor was the brother-in-law of conservative commentator William F. Buckley. Taylor was renowned for speaking in hushed, whisper-like tones, which some say was a manipulative way to get people's attention by drawing them closer.

The OSC hearing went on for some time. Gray testified for two full days. The lead lawyer for the securities industry was none other than the legendary Purdy Crawford.* He would also be central to the evolution of future TD CEO Ed Clark. Crawford later became chairman and CEO of Imasco, the parent company of Canada Trust that Clark would run prior to joining TD. Crawford, it also turns out, had been instrumental in helping Clark get a job on Bay Street after the federal government sacked him. When Keith Gray testified, Crawford had had another lawyer on his team question him. "I have always believed this was because I had been his banker when I was manager at the King and Yonge branch," says Gray.

Austin Taylor didn't hold back. He went on at length about how bankers didn't have the right mentality for the securities industry, referring to Gray and his band of discounters as "leeches."

Gray testified that TD only wanted to do what Canadian banks had been doing for many years, telling the commission that in the early twentieth century, banks had been given permission for branches across the country to take orders from customers for the purchase and sale of securities. The orders, he said, were then forwarded to a bank's regional or head office, where they were passed on to a stockbroker for execution, with the proceeds or the purchased securities passed back to the customer. This process was common in small towns and villages across Canada, where there were no brokerage offices.

In the end TD won and was allowed to launch the discount brokerage. Korthals estimates the OSC battle cost the bank $500,000, a lot at the time but a small price to pay given the eventual rewards.

A year later, Green Line was launched with eight people and just two or three telephone lines. The OSC hearing turned out to be fantastic publicity

---

* In his late seventies, Crawford came to the rescue and helped mop up the $32 billion Asset Backed Commercial Paper (ABCP) scandal, in which investors saw what they thought were risk-free investments freeze up during the financial crisis of 2007–09. Again, one can't help but note the concentration of the Canadian business elite. As one former TD executive put it, 300 people run the country and the bank CEOs know all of them.

for TD and Green Line. People knew all about the service before it started operating.

"An hour after approval, he (Austin Taylor) was on the phone wanting to do our back office!" Gray chuckled.

Gray's business plan for Green Line was a model of simplicity. "We're order takers. That's all we are," he'd say, as if any other interpretation of the discount brokerage business were ridiculous. This view would resonate with Ed Clark in later years, in his belief that customer service is everything. Gray had a basic model and he would stick to it, resisting pressure from above. For starters, Gray was dead set against the discounter giving advice to customers, particularly on the phone.

The key was to execute as many trades as possible by automating "to the fullest." Ultimately, the target was to get each phone call down to 117 seconds. Gray chose 117 seconds rather than two minutes "for effect." The idea was that if you lowered the amount of time required to take an order over the phone, the fewer people you would need manning the phones, thereby squeezing out more profit. Gray knew that if he could bring down the transaction time by just three seconds, he could increase the bottom line.

Every business has a unit of operation, says Gray. In the nursing home business, it's beds. In discount brokerage, it's the trade. If it took more than 120 seconds to do a trade, Green Line was losing money. TD was charging $29.95 per trade, but the processing cost was $54, recalls Robin Korthals, and "You could never predict the volume."

But the attraction of the discount business was simple: big balances sitting in accounts. "I didn't give a damn if we made money on a security transaction as long as they left a balance. This is a balance-attracting business. The balances were terrific," says Korthals. Customers who'd sold stock or deposited money in a brokerage account would "just leave it lying around"—sometimes millions for a day or two. The bank would pay little (if any) interest on these balances and lend the money out at much higher rates.

"If we could break even on the trading, the balances were gravy," Gray says, adding that the bank could make good money on margin loans (lending to investors to make stock purchases). A no-nonsense banker, he dismisses all the hedge fund–like trading banks do today, politely known as proprietary trading, as "all that other bullshit."

Gray's other hard rule was to keep the business separate from the bank, as Ted Rogers had advised him to do in order to maintain an entrepreneurial culture. Rogers was a kindred spirit, a 24/7 entrepreneur who plotted his own course, a billionaire who would call customers directly to hear their complaints.

Gray liked to refer to Green Line as the "skunk works," perhaps a subconscious holdover from his foundry days in Sarnia. Green Line started operations in 1984. With approximately 1,000 TD branches across the country boasting millions of customers, there was a lot of interest generated by the OSC hearing and considerable pent-up demand from investors who wanted to open accounts in this new service that promised to save them money.

"We were like the dog that chases the bus. What do you do with it when you catch it? We were expected to open within thirty days and we had two people to answer the phones and one person to work on processing orders."

One of the first people Gray worked with at Green Line was a TD systems man, John Davies. "How do we clear trades?" Gray asked him.

"Don't ask me. I don't have any idea," he answered.

Davies describes Gray boldly picking up the phone and calling Schwab and asking, "Do you mind if we come to visit?" So Gray and Davies flew down to San Francisco, presenting themselves as "just a bunch of hicks from Canada."

"We were absolutely no threat," Gray laughs.

Schwab echoed Ted Rogers' advice, telling him to keep the business outside of the bank. He told them they had to have branches, saying his firm almost went under without them. Gray started advocating for branches and Korthals went along, sharing the belief that customers don't trust you if you don't have an office. "We learned it was important to have physical premises in different communities. If you didn't answer the phone, they wanted to kick in your door," says Korthals.

"The day we opened, Korthals, with all the press watching, did the first trade," Gray recalls. "It turns out it was illegal! TD was in a trading blackout period [typical in the few weeks preceding a quarterly earnings release to prevent illegal insider trading based on non-public knowledge] and Korthals, being a director, was not allowed to trade. It was simply an error. The quarter had ended, Korthals says, but he hadn't seen the results. The technically off-side trade for 100 shares of TD Bank was cancelled.

After such a dubious beginning, Gray and his little troupe found themselves swamped. There were now five people handling five ordinary phone lines and three more people processing new account applications and stock trades, which had to be passed on to Loewen, Ondaatje. For the first few years, Gray found himself working eighteen hours a day. "With much debate, fighting, arguing, threatening, et cetera for more resources, we were able to get more people and space. By the way, this internal fighting went on for the next six years."

"It was hell when he was building Green Line," says his wife, Wendy, who also rose in the ranks at TD and knew and worked with many of the top people there. "There was a lot of jealousy. Keith was really breaking new ground. There were a lot of knives out for him."

Gray says Thomson and Korthals understood answering phones and the link Green Line needed to the stock exchange, but appeared to have no understanding of what was required in the back office. The executives, for their part, believe they gave Gray the full weight of their support.

Gray begs to differ. "Why do you have 300 people there pushing paper?" they'd ask him. "'Cause you won't give me the money to automate it!" was his frustrated response.

After a few months of chaos Loewen, Ondaatje called to say it wanted out of the partnership, that it was unable to handle the heavy volume. Korthals remembers events differently. He says that Chuck Loewen called discount brokerage a *schlock* business. "It's not for us," Korthals recalls Loewen saying.

The result was that TD took in the back-office part of the business—a mixed blessing for TD. Loewen, Ondaatje hadn't been doing a great job of executing the trades. On the other hand, it was a full-flight brokerage and the bank needed one to handle the part of the business it could not.

"Korthals agreed to give them $100,000 and we would take over their work and their share of the business," Gray recounts. "I then had to run around Bay Street like an idiot to get another 'introducing broker.' Many doors were slammed in my face. We had just gone through an OSC hearing with these same firms strenuously objecting to our getting into the business."

Gray convinced none other than McLeod Young Weir, the firm run by Austin Taylor, along with a company called Watt Carmichael, to share the business with TD. "Needless to say, they increased the processing fee considerably, which made my job of turning a profit and getting resources much more difficult."

Green Line's first full year of operation was 1985. The fledgling business opened 10,000 accounts, did 50,000 trades—and lost $3.6 million. In 1986, new account growth was 156 percent, trading increased by 160 percent and losses increased as well, to $4 million. The red ink grew to $4.8 million in 1987, but trading more than doubled and Green Line doubled the number of accounts. The brass didn't seem to care about doubling this or doubling that, focusing instead on the losses, which at the time were considered huge. "We came under heavy pressure to stop the bleeding or close the business," Gray recalls.

The company struggled to keep up. The computer system wasn't up to snuff. IBM had the brokerage business locked up in Canada with a system known as Bitsy, "a terrible system," Gray says, because IBM had stopped investing in it.

In brokerage, unlike banking, which is essentially debt and credit, there are dozens of potential paths for a transaction—dividends, stock splits, buy, sell, margin—and if you can't reconcile properly, it can "bring you down," says Gray.

In the small fish tank that is the Canadian business establishment, the man running IBM at the time was Bill Etherington. Later, he would go on to become chairman of CIBC during the bank's trying times with Enron-related legal issues and exposure to the toxic subprime mortgage market in the United States. Still later, another head of IBM Canada, John Thompson, would become chairman of TD Bank during Ed Clark's tenure as CEO (he'd been brought in as a board member in the late 1980s when Thomson was still CEO).

Gray was dissatisfied with the computer systems right up until his retirement. "I was under extreme pressure for the first five years," he says. "I was losing money and they were trying to shut me down." The bank's finance gnomes would go to Dick Thomson and "badmouth us." According to an internal memo to TD executives, the precise amount of money Green Line had lost from inception in 1985 until 1990 was $33 million. Those losses would put Robin Korthals under the gun and then he would dump on Gray.

"I couldn't get a telephone switch [call-routing system]. We were using ordinary phones and we needed a switch. I had talked to Schwab and they told me what they were using. In my entrepreneurial way, I just ordered the goddamn thing from Texas."

The "goddamn thing" was something called an Advanced Call Distribution system and in the late 1980s it sold for about $300,000. It could keep track of all the calls, and most important, it would time them. "It came to the border at Fort Erie and Finance wouldn't pay for it so it sat at the border for a month," Gray says.

This was without a doubt one of the most excruciating times for Gray in his forty-three years at the bank. Lying awake in the middle of the night, he said to his wife, Wendy, "They can fire me, they can take away my pension, but the one thing they can't do is kill me."

Just before Christmas, he went to Korthals to beg for another management person. "He said, 'Do it yourself.'"

"I don't have any goddamned time!" he replied.

"Well, tell me to fuck off," Gray recalls Korthals saying.

"Robin, I respect you and the position too much to tell you to fuck off."

Korthals doesn't recall the exchange but does not refute it. Gray didn't get the additional manager.

The bank couldn't have had a better guy than Gray, says Korthals. "For a while, it was not very rewarding for him personally, but he never lost faith and gradually costs came down and down and down."

"He was loved by his people. He was very down to earth. He knew banking from the guts up," says John Davies.

For an entrepreneur to survive in a large corporation is next to impossible, but by now, Gray was in deep. Korthals had offered him a position back home, so to speak, as senior vice-president in southwestern Ontario. It was a get-out-of-jail-free pass for Gray if he wanted out of running discount brokerage.

"You're betting your career on this," Korthals cautioned him. "Let's face it, you're losing a lot of money for the bank."

"I said, 'No, I'm going to stay here,'"—even though finally going back home would have been, according to Gray, something of a dream come true. Wendy says, "Robin would have been devastated if Keith had taken that," adding that her husband is a "pretty pigheaded guy who excels under pressure."

\* \* \* \*

Ted Rogers gave Keith Gray and the TD board of directors a grim warning. With more than 70 percent market share, you have nowhere to go but down. While Green Line may have been profit-challenged for several years, it had become the dominant name in discount brokerage in Canada. What to do? Acquisitions are always a tricky business. Many purchases end up on the slag heap because companies pay too much or don't understand what they're buying. They then try to crowbar the company they've bought into their existing business, often bending the asset into something unrecognizable, destroying what they sought. Bank of America's purchase of Charles Schwab was a case in point, a dismal failure. A big, bureaucratic bank trying to absorb an entrepreneurial culture like Schwab's was like trying to mix oil and water.[16]

A bonus for Keith Gray was that a button-down TD banker named Charlie Baillie loved discount brokerage and would become an ally when Gray made his biggest move, the purchase of Waterhouse in the U.S. Baillie argued that as a discounter, you want record-keeping expertise, stability and execution, all things the bank had. It also turned out, he said, that discount brokerage customers are "wonderful" retail bank customers. Retail business in the bank started growing faster because people who'd opened accounts with Green Line said they might as well bank with TD too.

Unlike Schwab at Bank of America, Green Line was already "of" the bank, although operating on the periphery, so that Gray could keep the bureaucracy from suffocating his fledgling business. The question became: What could he buy to keep the business on top?

Dick Thomson says, "Keith Gray's job [was] to figure out what to do to get bigger." The get-big-fast theory would come into play in a much more significant way in the Ed Clark era when TD began buying American banks.

It would still be a few years before the bank felt buff and bold enough to take on the United States. There were some competitors in Canada that TD took over first, not only to acquire customers, but also to learn how to integrate its acquisitions. The Gardiner Group was one of them. In the fall of 1987, Gray heard rumblings that CIBC was looking to buy the company, the discount brokerage operations of Toronto establishment man George Gardiner, the former chairman of the Toronto Stock Exchange and an entrepreneur in his own right.* He had built the first discount brokerage in Canada, and it was now the third largest. With just 12 percent market share it was much smaller than Green Line, but it had something TD didn't have—a back office for processing trades and keeping records. (At the time, TD was dependent on other brokerage firms. Gray says he was afraid if he did business with just one, that company might cut Green Line off since it was still viewed as the black sheep on the street. "If you only have one, they'll up the price on you like crazy. They're a bunch of whores.")

Gray knew Gardiner and called him on October 13, 1987, but didn't hear back. The next day, Gray called him again and got him to agree to a meeting. Gray and Charlie Baillie went over to see him on the following Friday afternoon.

"What do you want?" Gardiner asked. Gray and Baillie told him they wanted to buy his firm, knowing Gardiner already had a bid from CIBC.

"By the time the meeting ended, we'd done a deal with him," Baillie says. Gardiner wryly told the two bankers that he wanted to bring his wife to the press conference to introduce her to his new boss, TD's CEO Dick Thomson, because Gardiner had never had a boss during his entire career. TD paid $14.8 million, a price per customer of $750.

Looking back, Dick Thomson laughs and says, "We basically paid what everybody asked." It was more important to be on strategy, get big and get the right asset than to pay less for Gardiner. The move would establish something

---

* The Gardiner Museum of Ceramic Art in Toronto is the result of a $15 million donation in 1984 by George and Helen Gardiner and houses their personal collection.

of a pattern for TD in future acquisitions, with the market often viewing the bank as having overpaid for purchases, at least initially. CIBC had lost out. In the ensuing years, CIBC would slip to fifth place in size and arguably be the most accident prone of the Big Five, its mishaps costing the bank billions due to a 2005 legal settlement in connection with Enron, and later, write-offs associated with the subprime mortgage market in the United States. Things did not markedly improve until 2010.*

The Saturday after the Gardiner acquisition, Keith Gray and Robin Korthals had their picture on the front page of the *Globe and Mail*'s "Report on Business." Gray planned to leave town the next day to visit the ten Gardiner branches in western Canada. Dick Thomson asked him if he wanted to take the company jet. Gray said no. "I was in the discount business. It would not look right to be travelling by private jet."

The $14.8 million Gardiner purchase brought lots of equity market expertise to Green Line, as well as an electronic order entry system that put an end to having to phone the floor to do a trade. For TD, it was the beginning of modern brokerage. The purchase also added eleven offices across Canada. But, as in most acquisitions, it didn't go down easily. No two companies are alike and when executives stir them together in a deal, there is often much tension and unhappiness as employees try to figure out the new ground rules. Different procedures, different styles, different histories can create a volcanic cocktail. About a quarter of the Gardiner people quit.

"For many of the staff of the Gardiner Group, the amalgamation was a shock," according to a case study written for the Richard Ivey School of Business at the University of Western Ontario. "The Gardiner people were used to a paternalistic, small-business environment run by Mr. George Gardiner. The company had been run informally. The atmosphere changed as they moved to the more bureaucratic, large-company environment at The Toronto-Dominion Bank."[17]

---

\* In May of 2012, *Bloomberg Markets* ranked CIBC the third "strongest" bank in the world. TD was ranked fourth. Strength was judged by capitalization, quality of the loan portfolio, reserves and other measures— not strategy, management or profitability.

Gray puts it more plainly: "The brokerage side was much more aggressive and in-your-face types. Bank culture is laid-back—do as you are told. Over time, we lost most of the Gardiner people."

For George Gardiner, his timing was pitch perfect. Mere days after he agreed to sell, calamity struck North American stock markets. October 19, 1987, has gone down in market history as "Black Monday." On that day alone, the Dow Jones Industrial Average dropped 22 percent and the Toronto Stock Exchange fell 11 percent. Gray and another TD executive were in Victoria at the Gardiner office when the crash hit. "I had never seen anything like it. Our customers were panicking and our staff bewildered. We also visited the Green Line office and found they also were in turmoil."

Gray and his colleague flew home on the red-eye to Toronto. The market panic was too much for investors, who went into hibernation for the next nine months. Trading dropped by a third. Because Green Line was a high-fixed-cost business, a falloff in trades had a serious impact on earnings. According to the Ivey case study, this was an epiphany for Gray. He realized he had to learn how to systematically manage the business by understanding what costs to watch. "If you can't measure it, you can't manage it," he is quoted as saying.[18]

By 1990, the market cloud had lifted and people were back investing. By then, Green Line had become a 24/7 business, open all the time, in stark contrast to the full-service, nine-to-five brokerages offered by the other big banks. Still, Gray struggled to get respect from the upper reaches of TD.

According to Gray, "During this period, Korthals did not like to tell the street or the press how well we were doing so we could keep our growth going. I recall he was once asked if he felt Green Line was good business for the TD to be in and he said, 'No it is not.' When I complained to him that this had upset our staff, he said he made the comment in hopes of keeping the other banks out or at least reducing their investment in the business." Bob Kelly backs up Korthals' approach, saying he "never disclosed results, never said how well [the discount brokerage business was doing]. Kelly adds that Korthals "kept it very quiet very intentionally" to throw the other banks off the scent. Whatever Korthals thought, the comments bothered Gray; it was as if he had carted the *schmatta* business from Spadina Avenue to the august corridors of Bay Street, embarrassing the pinstriped crowd at the bank.

The Gardiner acquisition was, however, a huge learning experience for Gray. In deference to George Gardiner's reputation, Dick Thomson decided to make him the chairman of Green Line. Past retirement age for directors, Gardiner was too old to be on the board of the bank, but there was nothing stopping Thomson from installing him on the board of the internal company. Charlie Baillie, the future CEO of TD, was also selected to be on the Green Line board, setting him up to be a major ally of Keith Gray in the years ahead.

"George Gardiner really helped me a lot," Gray says. Gardiner taught him how to run a board meeting: "Take charge, always control the agenda. If you let the agenda stray, you'll lose control." Gardiner was also known for barking out tough questions, a characteristic Gray also exhibits. Gardiner could be intimidating and not above humiliating directors who had not read the minutes before coming to the meeting.

"Has everyone read the minutes?" he'd ask. If someone said no, Gardiner would instruct that person to read them aloud to everyone in the boardroom, like a headmaster cracking the whip in class. If two guys were whispering back and forth to each other, Gardiner would get them to say aloud whatever it was they were saying to each other.

He also counselled Gray on the need for a "road map." To make the point, he asked the young executive of the freshly minted discounter how much he would like to make in profit.

"A million a month," Gray responded.

"Okay. Let's make a million a month," Gardiner said, as if he could wave a magic wand and make profits materialize. But they did. Gray's "skunk works" turned its first profit in 1991, seven years after it was launched. It made all of $28,000 that year, but by 1993 Green Line was making $2 million a month, the beginning of a stream of profits that today add up to billions. Gray contends that no analyst or MBA could have told the bank the need for discount brokerage even existed. Steve Jobs would later say the same thing about Apple products: Customers didn't know what they wanted until you showed it to them.[19] "It's a great example of a need building up in society that we didn't know about. It took off. I think it took off faster and hotter in Canada than it did in the U.S.," says Gray.

Because Green Line was an upstart operation, Gray tried to foster innovation. He encouraged his employees to "think wild," to try things. Sure, many of the ideas failed, but some worked. The attitude emboldened staff because their ideas weren't always being shot down. As for marketing, corny was the flavour.

"Corn sells," he says. This resonates today for TD in the U.S., where corny advertising and the coin-rolling machines known as "Penny Arcade" have been a smash success with customers.

Around this time, in a little-known story, TD Bank also contributed to saving its ancestor in discount brokerage, Charles Schwab. Schwab, it turns out, had allowed a single customer to expose it to potentially company-wrecking losses related to the 1987 stock market crash.

When Gray arrived home from Vancouver on the red-eye flight after Black Monday, Wendy gave him a message from a Schwab executive by the name of Tom Seip, asking that he call immediately because the U.S.-based discounter needed help with a "big problem" in Hong Kong. Gray called Seip at his San Francisco home. The executive told him that a customer by the name of Teh-Huei (Teddy) Wang, after borrowing from Schwab, had been heavily exposed to the equity market through options.* Wang's wrong-way bet was now underwater somewhere in the vicinity of $100 million.

These days, a $100 million loss for a big firm is serious, but not necessarily life threatening. Back then, for Schwab, it was huge money. Not long before, the discount brokerage had issued about $60 million in equity (sold stock in the company) to buy itself back from Bank of America after the disastrous merger. Having borrowed from Schwab to make his ill-fated market wager, Wang now owed the company more than it was worth. When stocks plummeted in the crash, the brokerage called Wang and told him he had to cover what he owed. According to John Kador's book about Schwab, Wang had "accumulated liabilities representing more than a third of the company's total revenues for

---

* Options give the investor the right, but not an obligation to buy or sell a stock, currency, commodity, or other instrument at a set price for a set amount of time.

the year."[20] The fact that Schwab had allowed one customer to expose it to so much risk is astonishing, but it happened. Kador contends Wang actually owed Schwab $124 million. Although Kador does not mention TD in describing the episode, internal bank documents corroborate the scope of the problem. In a memo to TD's general counsel from the bank's general manager in Asia at the time, "The amount involved can run into the hundreds of millions."

Meanwhile, Seip informed Keith Gray that Wang had "significant deposits" at the TD branch in Hong Kong and other banks totalling about $35 million. If that was the case, Schwab wanted the money frozen so it could begin to recoup Wang's losses. Out of the cash Wang and his wife had spread around various banks, $9,080,329.32 was on deposit at TD.[21] Schwab's people also believed that Wang was moving the money out of Hong Kong. Gray, through TD's international office, was able to confirm that Wang was in fact trying to get his money out, possibly to Taiwan. He informed Seip.

As a result of the information Gray provided to Schwab, the stricken company was able to get a court injunction to freeze the funds. Within two weeks, TD and Gray were served with a $250 million lawsuit from Mr. Wang saying the bank and the banker had violated his confidentiality rights by divulging information related to his account to an unauthorized party without his consent. Gray had been either fearless or reckless in giving out the customer information. Once again, he was the maverick going offline to do things his way. "I may have been wrong to tell Schwab what I did; however, they had been and continued to be a great help in the building of our business. I had no regrets."

Ultimately, Wang's wife negotiated with Schwab and the couple paid the company eighty cents on the dollar.[22] After Schwab settled with Wang, the latter agreed to drop the lawsuit against Gray and TD.*

Gray and Green Line took their next big gulp in 1993, acquiring what had been the number-two discounter in size, Lawrence Bloomberg's Marathon Brokerage. The sticker price was a lot higher than what TD paid for Gardiner Group, and the bank could have paid a lot less had flat-footed negotiating not taken place.

---

* Chuck Schwab did not respond to a request to be interviewed for this book.

In mid-1992, Gray heard that Bloomberg wanted to sell. Marathon had about a quarter the number of accounts as Green Line and eleven offices, but Bloomberg felt he had reached an inflection point. Among other things, the banks were getting tougher to compete with and he would have to make hefty investments in technology and management to sustain profitability.[23]

Lawrence Bloomberg, according to Gray, was cocky, nervy and a tough customer. Some might say the same about Keith Gray. Nevertheless, he aggressively tried to convince the bank to buy Bloomberg's operation. It had a good base of accounts, and TD's purchase would stand in the way of another bank getting a leg up in discount brokerage. At the time, Green Line was finally making money after eight years of racking up $40 million in losses and Keith Gray comes up with a plan to spend another $35 million! The brass at TD finally agreed it was a good idea, but Gray was told he couldn't spend more than $33 million.

"Bloomberg was very upset with me because he thought I was jerking him around and said $35 million or nothing. We had to walk away." Gray believes Korthals was willing to pay more, but Dick Thomson was unwilling to go higher.

"You never knew if Dick and Robin were talking," he says. However, both Thomson and Korthals say they had a great working relationship, a "partnership," as Thomson describes it. Korthals says he and Thomson are very similar, citing similar parents and values, adding that they "saw eye to eye on a high percentage of things." A complicating factor is that they are just two months apart in age, making it difficult for Korthals to have succeeded Thomson as CEO. Ultimately, the top job would go to Baillie, who is younger. Korthals would go on to become chairman of the Ontario Teachers' Pension Plan and the real estate firm Cadillac Fairview. "We wouldn't still be good buddies if he [Korthals] felt he got a raw deal," Thomson says.

A year later, in the spring of 1993, Gray was in Zurich visiting the Swiss bank UBS on behalf of TD. While in a meeting, he was passed a note saying that Dick Thomson wanted him to call as soon as possible.

"This was unheard of. Dick very seldom called me when I was in Toronto, let alone when I was out of the country. Not knowing what he wanted, and concerned, I left the meeting and went back to the privacy of my hotel room and called Dick. He came on the phone and said that he had had a visit from Bloomberg and he still wanted to sell his discount broker to us but now wanted $60 million." Furthermore, Thomson told him, "Bob wants to do it." Bob was Bob Kelly, a Haligonian who had just been made chief financial officer of TD and would later go on to be, for a time, one of the top bankers in the United States.

In his dark-panelled, elegant office at National Bank Financial in Toronto, Lawrence Bloomberg recalled Green Line's prowess during an interview. "They were good. TD was good. It had a good CEO, I think a guy by the name of Gray. He was very good and I was impressed with what they were doing."

Although Bloomberg's company had been a first mover in Canada with discount brokerage, Bloomberg wasn't sure if he could compete with the banks longer term because they had an edge in technology. He says he engaged in discussions with Charles Schwab, but negotiations proved too difficult. Still, a dance with Schwab gave the shrewd Lawrence Bloomberg leverage with TD.

"I picked up the phone one day and I called Dick Thomson and I said: 'Dick, there's an American in my office and he's looking to buy our discount business. Do you think we should chat?' He said, 'Come on over.' So I went over."

Describing the negotiation, Bloomberg says that, after the pleasantries, Thomson asked him how much he wanted for his discount business. He recalls TD's boss making a counter offer of $57 million. Thomson has a slightly different recollection, laughing about the encounter and Bloomberg's stubbornness about his asking price. "I can remember vividly saying to him, 'Did you ever pay the offering price? Or did you negotiate when you were trying to buy something?'"

Bloomberg said, "Yeah, I negotiate."

"Well, then, why don't you let me negotiate here?"

"What do you mean?"

"Let me get $1 million off that."

Bloomberg smiled and shot back, "That's your negotiation?" and then he agreed. Once again, TD basically paid asking price.

In the end, Marathon cost TD $59 million for 92,000 accounts, of which just over 47,000 were active, establishing a new price per account of more than $1,200.[24] Gray, knowing that TD could have had Bloomberg for just over half this price a year before, was opposed to the deal. Again, Dick Thomson saw the big picture, but to Gray the new sticker price of almost $60 million was the kind of money his operation, Green Line, had been losing—and he'd gotten hell for it. But his view did not prevail. "Dick called me back and said we're going to do it." Many in the investment community applauded Bloomberg for offloading a lowly discounter onto what appeared to be a naïve bank.

TD, however, was now making money from Green Line and senior management could see the potential of the discount brokerage business. Top executives, contrary to the popular view that they are savvy enough to buy low and sell high, often buy high, just like retail investors. In spite of the higher price, TD was getting staff and accounts and eleven offices as it embarked on bulking up Green Line. Marathon also had more active customers than Green Line, and they were more likely to trade in a wider array of products, such as options. Gray's staff, however, was less than thrilled at the prospect of integrating another company.

"I said to my staff, 'We've just done another acquisition.' They said, 'Oh, God!' One woman cried." Gray likened the situation to stacking wood. A truck comes along every morning and deposits a load of wood out front, and you start stacking it, but you don't get it all done before another truck comes the next day and drops more. "It piles up over and over again."

Meanwhile, business was exploding. Canadians, led by the baby boomers, were beginning to invest for their retirements and were glomming onto the idea that mutual funds would be their salvation. They made this connection for good reason. They were sold aggressively through intense marketing campaigns by mutual fund companies, as well as by the banks, which were becoming huge players in the mutual fund game. At the time, mutual funds were seen almost as a no-lose proposition. By investing in a fund, you were mitigating the risks associated with holding one or two stocks that could go down the drain. A mutual fund might hold thirty or forty stocks, with the portfolios managed by professionals (although over the years, investors would discover some are more professional than others). Aside from warnings like "Past performance is no indication of future performance," these funds looked like a hassle-free, relatively risk-free way to invest in the stock market. After all, no one wanted to go to a cocktail party to hear some loudmouth talk about how well he was doing in the market, and then drive home feeling like a chump because he wasn't in the game. As a result, mutual funds multiplied like rabbits, to the point where there were more funds for sale than there were stocks on what was then known as the TSE. You could buy a Canadian equity fund, a U.S. equity fund, a bond fund, an emerging market fund, a gold fund. If it moved, fund companies found a way to call it something and sell it, usually just as a particular fad was waning and the real pros were getting out of a sector. In any event, there was more and more product available, and the order takers like TD Green Line were standing by to sell it all. As with any retail business, there are good and bad products on the shelves.

This was the era of what's been called the "democratization" of stock markets. Everyone could get involved and trade and try to build a retirement nest egg. In spite of the equity market being one of the few arenas on earth—casinos being another—where amateurs compete with the pros, people jumped in holus-bolus.

"In good times, you'd say it was excellent. In bad times, you'd say they shouldn't be making their own decisions," Gray says when asked if on balance, self-directed investing has been good for people. In fact, many of the pros can easily blow it. Often they have no better information than amateurs and can be led astray just as easily, or fenced in by the challenges of moving large blocks of stock, a problem that comes with managing a lot of money.

Full-service brokers often have stock in inventory that they have to get rid of, the "overhang" the firm is left with from an underwriting. To whom could they sell it? John and Martha in Moose Jaw, that's who. "Put some lipstick on this pig" is the line brokers use, or "Stuff this stock," meaning push it out to retail clients to get it off the firm's books. Gray knew this to be true because he had "banked" many brokers when he ran the main branch of TD, and they'd come running to him for thirty-day loans to cover those overhangs. "We'd bank it for them until they could stuff it into clients' accounts."

In the early 90s, the challenges of growth were beginning to become apparent. During a six-month period ending in May 1994, volumes mushroomed as though Green Line had added two-and-a-half more Marathons. The staff couldn't handle it all and customers got annoyed. Satisfaction levels plummeted from 93 percent down to just 62 percent. There were also thousands of what they called "breaks," trades that came down the pike but wouldn't reconcile, for one reason or another. Customers were on their backs, and so was the regulator. The OSC warned Green Line to correct the problems or they'd stop the company from opening new accounts, threatening to make the information public.

Since the inception of Green Line, however, it had been, for the most part, a very good time to be an investor. Even with the crash of 1987, from 1982 until 2000, the stock market had been a profitable place to park your money. Its direction was pretty much one-way—up. The rah-rah glow of Reagan-era deregulation, the investment dollars of the boomers, the liberalization of trade, and the broadening of stock ownership among the masses pushed more and more money into the market. It wasn't just stocks. If you were a bond-holder during this period, you probably made money too. From 1982 until 2000, interest rates steadily fell. Someone holding a bond with a high rate of interest in the 1980s watched the face value of that bond rise through the 1990s as interest rates fell, making older bonds more valuable than newly issued ones (bond prices and yields move in opposite directions). All of this played into the growing stature and profitability of Green Line. By 1996, profits at the business Gray built hit almost $74 million. He and TD were now ready for the biggest bite ever, a slice of American pie.

# 5

# HUNTING LARRY WATERHOUSE

*TD Buys in America*

Waterhouse Investor Services was a firm built by Lawrence M. Waterhouse Jr., a hard-bitten and shrewd ex-Marine and former employee of Chemical Bank. He started his discount brokerage in 1979, a two-man shop. According to those who knew him well, he didn't mind people thinking he was part of the global accounting and consulting firm Price Waterhouse, even though there was no connection. His office at 100 Wall Street in Lower Manhattan was adorned with statues of a bull, a bear and a pig. "Bulls make money, bears make money, pigs get slaughtered," he sermonized as I looked over the sculptures in early 1997.

Waterhouse inspired respect, if not a touch of fear. With a deep voice and a large head, he was a presence. When I met him for the first time, he gave me the once-over, taking a friendly pot shot at the suit I was wearing. In a staff meeting that I attended, the grunts followed his lead. When Waterhouse took off his suit jacket, they took off theirs. Getting impatient, hurrying along the meeting, he toyed with them. "C'mon, let's get this over with. I've gotta get back to Flahrida," he said, jokingly adopting the tone of a fat cat—which he was, having personally just coined $121 million for selling his baby to Keith Gray and TD Bank. Since 1997, the TD stock he received has been divided among more than two dozen family members and Waterhouse says not one share has been sold.*

---

* As of April 2012, 16 years after the bank bought Waterhouse, the market value of TD was $76.37 billion, eight times what it was at the end of 1996 ($9.5 billion). The increase in market value does not include the dividends Waterhouse and his family would have received during all the years since. On market value

The holding makes him and his family among the largest non-institutional shareholders of TD Bank. "Every once in a while [we] think of diversifying but don't do it," he laughs.

In the mid-90s, by his own admission, Waterhouse was spending more and more time in Florida playing golf. He was tired and ready to cash out. Gray had been eyeing him for a couple of years, getting to know him, waiting in the weeds, claiming he already had an understanding with Waterhouse to "sell to us" for $15 a share, but he kept that to himself. The bank, as usual, would end up paying much more a couple of years later.

Gray's Green Line was finally making money, and good money. Banks like to measure their success by a yardstick called return on equity (ROE), the number you get when you divide net income by the shareholders' equity in the company. It yields a number that reflects information from two key financial documents, the income statement and the balance sheet. The banks target the high teens for a respectable return on equity (perhaps unrealistic in the wake of the financial crisis, given new rules being crafted by regulators that require banks to hold more capital as a buffer against tough economic times or financial shocks). Green Line's ROE was now better than that of the bank as a whole and the brokerage was becoming a noteworthy contributor to TD's earnings. It was clear, however, that with a 70 percent market share in Canada, Green Line could only get so big. As a result, Gray had his eye on the United States and the notion of buying into the U.S. discount brokerage market.

Schwab was the biggest company and too big a bite for TD. Fidelity Investments was number two, but also an unlikely candidate because it didn't want to sell. Fidelity viewed its discount division as being a bit like having an outlet mall for Fidelity mutual funds, the company's main product. The other two discounters of note were Quick & Reilly and Waterhouse. Dick Thomson knew Leslie (Les) Quick Jr. from their Florida neighbourhood. Like Gray, Thomson was big on personal relationships, one of the characteristics that

---

alone, his stake would be $972 million. At a dividend yield of 3.42 percent, he would receive more than $33 million in dividends annually. Between 1996 and 2012, the bank's dividend has increased by 478 percent. With dividends and dividend increases, Waterhouse made well over $1 billion selling to TD.

made him a successful corporate lender. Thomson also had shares in Quick & Reilly. But the firm was eliminated for two reasons. According to then-CFO Bob Kelly, Quick had several children who were involved in the company and it would have been "messy" to attempt a buyout. Quick was also not interested in selling and not co-operative, despite being a neighbour of Thomson.

Although Larry Waterhouse had initially said he wasn't interested in selling either, he was more open to the idea. He didn't see a Canadian bank as a threat, so he happily spoke with Gray, to whom buying Waterhouse was looking like an attractive way to enter the U.S. market in a meaningful way, and in a way that distinguished TD from the other big Canadian banks. In 1995 alone, Waterhouse Investor Services had opened 80,000 new accounts. It had seventy offices, and had the advantage of a wholly owned subsidiary, Waterhouse National Bank. TD could buy a discount brokerage and bag a banking licence on the same drive-by. Two issues had to be considered: would someone else get to Waterhouse first, and would TD have to pay a rich price, with the market having shot up so much? Gray started to get to know his quarry. It would be almost three years of bird-dogging.

"I was always interested in what was going on in the States. I would go down to visit." On these visits, Gray knocked on doors of several acquisition targets (he didn't use investment bankers to find prospective purchases), saying he was there to learn from their successes, and tried to get to know their owners as people because he thought that was the best route with entrepreneurs. "They're very proud and you have to be careful not to insult them. I would cultivate my relationship with Schwab, cultivate my relationship with Larry Waterhouse." It's Gray's contention that entrepreneurs are dying to tell you their stories, where they came from, how they once had ten cents in their pockets—a lot like Gray himself.

"I was a much better negotiator with people like myself, entrepreneurs. I knew how proud they were. I'd be positive. 'You've done a wonderful job. You must be very proud.' That's how I got Larry Waterhouse. That was my negotiating style. I'm just a farm boy from Canada and want to buy your firm. I'd never brag. Entrepreneurs don't want to hear what you've done, they want to tell you what *they've* done."

Although Waterhouse's stock traded on the exchange, it was volatile—down in the single digits, then in the low teens, then back down. "It was up and down like a toilet seat," Gray recalls.

Meanwhile, Gray had convinced TD in 1995 that Green Line should open an office in New York. He wanted an outpost from which to track his prey, setting up with four people on the eighth floor of a building on Park Avenue near the Waldorf-Astoria. "I wanted to get a feel, understand the regulation." He tried to buy Muriel Siebert & Co., Inc. (its founder was the first woman to have a seat on the New York Stock Exchange). Siebert was helpful, but she wouldn't sell. Hers was just one of many small discount brokers in New York.

It soon dawned on Gray, though, that Larry Waterhouse had reasons to sell. Not unlike the situation that faced Lawrence Bloomberg, because of the competitive nature of the business, Waterhouse would have to grow very fast, and to do so he needed to invest big dollars in technology. The American held the right to vote 5 million of the 11.5 million outstanding shares of the company (he owned 3.2 million shares, with the right to vote another 1.8 million), but the brokerage couldn't generate enough cash to support the investment needed in systems. Waterhouse had built a great business, but had taken it about as far as he could. A big player with deep pockets was now required. Enter Gray with the TD chequebook. By then, Gray knew Larry Waterhouse was being tracked and hunted by others in the U.S., in particular a large American bank. Richard Neiman, the former top bank regulator in New York, who worked for Waterhouse at the time, believes it was NationsBank (which later became Bank of America).

Being acquired by a bank had its pros and cons. Charles Schwab had already been through the process, having been purchased by Bank of America in the late 1980s. It was a disaster, once again proving the risks of trying to run an entrepreneurial operation inside a large bureaucracy. Schwab and his senior team ended up buying back the firm from B of A, building it to be the discount house to beat, with 3.2 million accounts.

Waterhouse's business had grown exponentially. After incorporating in 1979, in its first full year of operations the company made $1.36 million

USD in commissions out of two offices, New York and San Francisco. In the space of seventeen years, Waterhouse went from thirteen staff to 1,000. Business slowed down in only one year. That was 1987, the year the Dow crashed 25 percent and Waterhouse lost money. That was also the year the company went public at $7 USD a share, raising $5.7 million from selling 40 percent of the firm. By 1989, Waterhouse was paying a dividend to share-holders, and by 1991 it was a parabolic stock, straight up, six times what it was in 1990.

Waterhouse generated revenue of $131 million USD in 1995, up from $102 million the year before. Over the period from 1991 to 1995, its compounded annual revenue growth rate was 45 percent.[25] It was, like Green Line, catching a wave. Its accounts had grown to 450,000 by the end of its 1995 fiscal year, roughly on par with Green Line's, a leap of 100,000 from the year before. By April of 1996, when it announced it was selling to TD, it had 500,000 accounts, revenue of almost $172 million and net income of $22.3 million.

Well behind Schwab and Fidelity, Waterhouse had just 6 percent of the discount brokerage market share in the United States. An active customer would make about eight trades a year, with the average commission per trade around $50. But its ROE, that magic number in the banking industry, was a whopping 33 percent. Its market value or capitalization (share price multi-plied by number of shares outstanding) was $262 million USD. TD would obviously have to pay a premium, but even so it was well within the bank's range. However, Larry Waterhouse had built and run his own show and the ex-Marine wasn't about to give it away.

"Why would I ever sell to a Canadian bank? What the hell are you?" is what Waterhouse said to Gray. "If I wanted to sell, I would sell to a Citibank or another bank; that way I'd have a U.S. account base. You don't have any. Why would I sell to you?"

"'Cause I'm a nice guy" was Gray's response.

It turns out that Larry Waterhouse's grandmother was Canadian. That alone did not influence his final decision, but it was one of the many little things dur-ing the courtship that made him curious to hear what this bank from Canada had to say. With the stock at $13.50, Gray thought he had Waterhouse ready to sell. For his part, Waterhouse was ready to head to the chapel. According to Robin Korthals, Waterhouse had told TD, "If you want to buy the firm, I'm not going to shop it around." In other words, it was TD's for the right price.

Gray went back to Robin Korthals and told him he thought TD could get Waterhouse for $20 a share, a significant premium over the $13.50 market price, but given the bank's habit of paying top dollar, not out of the realm.

"Keith, I think we should go ahead and buy in the U.S. If we do buy, you'll have to move to the U.S. We'll find Wendy a job there as well," Gray recalls Korthals telling him. He wrote a letter giving his subordinate the authority to start negotiating more convincingly. Korthals always signed his notes in green ink, just with the letter "K." Gray was recommending TD offer $18 per share, hoping to get it for $20, but Dick Thomson wasn't ready. Gray claims that in front of a group of top executives including Korthals, Baillie, Kelly and others, Thomson threw him out of his office.

"You've got enough troubles in Canada. We're not buying retail operations in the United States," Gray claims Thomson said. Others, including Thomson, do not corroborate the story. For his part, Thomson simply says it didn't happen. Baillie doesn't recall the specific meeting, but says he was probably there. "It may have been something Keith took more personally than anybody else, because I don't remember Dick saying no. Dick could intimidate people without intending to, but I never heard him disparage Keith," Baillie says.

Thomson's version is that Waterhouse wasn't ready to sell, and if he wasn't ready to sell, there was no point making an offer because they'd waste their time and might end up paying too much. After whatever happened in Thomson's office, Gray confronted Korthals, who he said had told him to make the proposal. "You prick, you didn't even support me!" is how Gray phrases his response years later, although he concedes it's unlikely he used such a noun to describe his boss at the time.

Gray felt that Korthals had left him in the lurch after giving him a clear signal to negotiate. It seemed to Gray as though Korthals had "lost the desire." For his part, Korthals does not dispute that he wrote Gray the letter. But things had changed. Korthals explains, "I supported him [Thomson] because our balance sheet had deteriorated. It was a slippery situation and it had changed.

I think Dick was very concerned about a deteriorating situation and he was battening down the hatches. It's worrisome when your assets start to slide on you. If they had continued to slide and we made the acquisition, you'd lose your job. I couldn't fight Dick on that. We had a lot of respect for Keith and his entrepreneurial drive. But you have to look after the whole bank. I don't fault Dick. I don't fault Keith. I felt badly. But he got his way in the end. And thank God he did" (since the Waterhouse acquisition turned out to be such a spectacularly successful purchase).

Korthals says that the first time the Waterhouse idea surfaced the bank was in no position to consider it. It was the early 1990s, and after a collapse of the commercial real estate market, major banks were crippled by bad loans. Although TD had avoided the troubled loans other Canadian banks faced, which were associated with the failure of the Reichmann family's storied Olympia & York, along with its Canary Wharf project in London, the bank had its own real estate mess on its books.

Thomson says he had other reasons for not jumping at Waterhouse. Unbeknownst to Gray, the CEO wanted to buy a Bay Street investment dealer, something the bank had declined to do when the other Canadian banks were doing so (it may not have been allowed, given Green Line's market share). "I had a deal, basically a deal, that we were going to buy Richardson Securities at the time," says Thomson. Richardson was part of the empire of the wealthy Richardson clan of Manitoba. Thomson called them up and asked them to wait five months for him to buy. Richardson wouldn't wait and sold to Royal Bank. (Another former executive says TD was also looking at buying the mutual fund firm Altamira, which was highly regarded at the time.)

Gray, ever the rebel, continued to maintain contact with Waterhouse over the next several months. The American was an entrepreneurial kindred spirit. He'd built the company from nothing. He'd even written all the ads himself, placing them only in the *Wall Street Journal*. ("I wrote every frickin' ad from top to bottom," Waterhouse said.) They all had the word free in them "about ten times," leading to an avalanche of business.

When Waterhouse took the company public in 1987, every employee, even those working in the mailroom, got stock. They would come to love TD

Bank after the Canadian company bought out Waterhouse. The shares they'd purchased for $5 apiece would one day be worth almost eight times that. Waterhouse would also come to respect Gray and his approach. "It was very soft. It was getting acquainted, so it did take a period of time. Keith and Bob Kelly were the masterminds of that at the time. It wasn't like 'we wanna buy you, here's the price, c'mon.'" They got to know each other, with no investment bankers involved as matchmakers. "Keith is a very personable, great salesman. Great guy and smart. But Keith—Christ, I could have told him 500 times to go away and he wouldn't have gone away," says Waterhouse.

Things accelerated when Green Line found itself on the other side of an American court ruling that said it couldn't have U.S.-based clients with Canadian accounts. From the point of view of American law, these account holders were trying to avoid taxes in the U.S., and the state of Massachusetts had fined the Canadian brokerage firm Midland Walwyn, later acquired by Merrill Lynch.

Dick Thomson was furious, according to Gray, afraid TD would be sued, or worse—that someone from the bank might go to jail in the U.S. Thomson called a meeting and tore into Gray again.

"I believe he fired me," Gray says, although if it was a dismissal, it apparently didn't stick.

Gray's handwritten notes from January 16, 1995, indicate the level of his angst. They are talking points he assembled to prepare for a follow-up meeting with Dick Thomson. *Not certain where I stand—fired at worst, reputation at low ebb at best. Very disappointed in colleagues—I was left out to dry. Ask that you allow me to clarify some very important aspects leading up to last Friday.*

Gray says he tried to set up a follow-up meeting but was unsuccessful. Thomson says, "He [Gray] was never at risk of being fired. This was one of those things that comes along when you start a new business." Thomson says he was worried the bank had done something it shouldn't have. "I suggested that he should get out of that problem as fast as he could," he adds. Both Charlie Baillie and another top executive, former vice-chairman Bud McMorran, back up Thomson, saying they doubt Gray was ever in danger of being fired. Bob Kelly, the former vice-chair and CFO, says Gray was "being a little hard on himself" and that Thomson "had enormous respect for Keith," which is why he was tapped by Korthals to build the discount brokerage.

Gray, of course, hadn't been getting to know Larry Waterhouse just to kill time. Now he called up Waterhouse and asked him for a favour: "Will you take our U.S. dollar accounts?" There weren't very many, but Waterhouse agreed, solving TD's regulatory problem without asking for anything in return.

To thank him, a few months later Gray invited Waterhouse to Toronto to play golf at Glen Abbey. The course is the Jack Nicklaus–designed, frequent home of the Canadian Open PGA tournament. TD had at one time been a lender to Nicklaus' business, again through Thomson's personal contacts. After the game, the plan was to have dinner with a handful of TD executives, including future CEO Charlie Baillie and CFO Bob Kelly.

The group was to dine on the fifty-fourth floor of the TD Tower. Thomson had overseen the development of the modernist masterpiece at the behest of Allen Lambert, who thought the building would raise the bank's profile. The tower put TD on the map in the Toronto financial community.* Larry Waterhouse, however, wasn't interested in architecture. He wanted to measure manhood. He wanted to see the size of Keith Gray's office, to see if he was dealing with a real executive.

Soon the phone rang in Gray's office. It was Dick Thomson.

"What's Larry Waterhouse doing here?" came the now-familiar growl.

"I'm taking him for a game of golf and we're having a dinner for him."

"Why?"

"He took those accounts off our hands,"

"Well, I want you to know, we're not buying his company!" was Thomson's response, followed by a slammed receiver.

TD's CEO then dialled CFO Bob Kelly to tell him the same thing: "We aren't buying a U.S. broker!"

---

* The new building was a 50–50 partnership between TD and the Bronfman family of Seagram fame. Dick Thomson describes a meeting with Sam Bronfman, star architect Mies van der Rohe and Allen Lambert. Turning a plastic model of the project, Bronfman said he wanted the entrance of the building to be on King Street rather than Wellington. There was silence. According to Thomson, van der Rohe picked up the model and put it back where it was. "Mies looked at him, moved it back and said that's the way it will be." Thomson said Bronfman just smiled—not many people talked back to "Mr. Sam."

Kelly describes the moment in the politest of terms. "One day, sitting in my office, Dick Thomson called and he was very concerned and was not really supportive." According to Kelly, who spoke to me from his Manhattan office at Bank of New York Mellon in the fall of 2010, Thomson was thinking about other Canadian businesses that had taken the plunge into the States and failed. If the bank made a rotten acquisition, he reasoned, the odour would stick to him, the CEO, not an underling like Gray.

"To test you, Dick would sometimes appear negative," Robin Korthals says. Another retired executive recalls, "Dick was very hard on the deal. Dick was tough on numbers. He had tough standards, but he was a good boss."

Enter the diplomat. Over the next six or eight months, the soft-spoken, politically attuned future CEO, Charlie Baillie, worked on Dick Thomson, gently trying to persuade him that the Waterhouse acquisition was a good idea. Baillie had become president of the bank in 1995 after Korthals had left. He was in line to take over from Thomson as CEO, had already sampled discount brokerage and liked the business. As well, TD had gotten good at discount and by 1996 was making a very good profit from Green Line, giving him a sense of confidence about tackling the U.S.

"It's a rare instance where a Canadian would have superior experience," Baillie says. The bank didn't "get a chance to compete in the American market with a leg up very often."

Baillie knew the U.S. and he knew its scope and scale. He'd been to Harvard, and early in his career he had been posted by TD to New York. With typical dry wit, Baillie says he was considered by his superiors to be an "educated character," something relatively new to TD in the late 1960s. In New York, he was known as second agent of the bank, handling $25 million loans rather than the $25,000 ones he'd been in charge of in Toronto. These were corporate loans. Retail branch banking in the U.S., of the kind Ed Clark is engaged in now, was still years away.

While Dick Thomson enjoyed golfing and the social aspect of business and dealing with customers, Baillie was more introverted. A tireless traveller and history buff, he would in his retirement become one of Toronto's major philanthropists. Baillie led the fundraising, alongside the billionaire family of the late Kenneth Thomson (Thomson Reuters), for the redesign of the

Art Gallery of Ontario by superstar architect Frank Gehry. He is also an avid reader of American history, dropping names of Revolution-era characters like Aaron Burr and Alexander Hamilton like other guys might mention sports stars. In his high-pitched, quiet voice, Baillie would argue why he believed in scale in banking and viewed the U.S. as the place to get it.

He'd joined hands with Keith Gray in the late 1980s on the purchase of Gardiner Group, and as of 1990 had watched the earnings momentum accelerate at Green Line. For Baillie, buying Waterhouse was the way to go. He just had to get Thomson, a man who by his own admission saw banking as a local business, to understand. In the end, Baillie applied the right alchemy and won him over, clearing the path for Gray to make the purchase.

Thomson has a different interpretation of events. "I wasn't tough to get onside once I knew Waterhouse wanted to sell. If he wanted an offer he would have told him [Gray] he wanted an offer. And of course when he decided he wanted an offer, he did tell him. And he didn't go tell anyone else. So I think we handled it properly. We got it, without a competition. But Keith, he was not happy and neither was Robin. Maybe I made the mistake. Maybe we could have got it cheaper."

But when he okayed the purchase in 1996, the CEO wouldn't let Gray leave town without a warning, a dose of old school management, not the kind of thing you read in a case study at Harvard Business School, and certainly not the kind of tone Ed Clark demands in the new age, politically correct TD. "This bank has been around for 125 years. Don't you go out and screw it up," Gray says Thomson scolded him.

"I think it was probably after we bought it that I said that," Thomson says with a laugh.

One of the great parlour games of the workplace is complaining about your boss. But CEOs know things subordinates don't and face big-picture issues. When TD finally announced the Waterhouse purchase, Thomson recalls, "Two of our largest shareholders called and said they'd sell [their shares]. Three-quarters of a billion on a discount brokerage? Nobody made any money on a discount brokerage."

By now though, Gray had gotten over whatever apprehensions he'd had about the optics of a man in the discount business flying on the TD jet. He and Bob Kelly flew down to Florida on the private plane to do the detailed negotiations with Waterhouse. They met at Loxahatchee Golf Club, where Larry Waterhouse played. While there, who should walk in but Montague Black, Conrad's brother.

"Keith! What the hell are you doing here?" Monte yelled out. Black was on the board of the bank. He soon figured it out.

Gray, Waterhouse and Kelly went off to have their discussions in private in the Jack Nicklaus room, where they agreed on the basics of the deal, including the price. At one point, they took a break to go to Waterhouse's home for a drink.

Gray says Waterhouse had a "very nice home." But after selling his company to TD and pocketing $121 million USD worth of shares in the bank, Waterhouse built a new house. Gray adds, "They call it the TD Centre," nicknamed for the complex that includes the bank's skyscraper headquarters.

Once again, it appeared as though TD had paid a rich price. Waterhouse cost TD $38 a share or $715 million USD, at the time the largest acquisition in the history of the bank. In Canadian dollars, each Waterhouse account cost $1,300, indicating a steadily rising price for discount brokerage since TD had bought Gardiner in 1987. It was also about double what Gray thinks he could have purchased it for a couple of years earlier. However, what made it easier for TD was that Waterhouse was willing to take TD's stock as currency. Larry Waterhouse says Canadian bankers couldn't believe it.

"We have an interested seller who wants stock? You've got to be kidding me! They were in shock! They were ready to pay cash. You want stock?! Who would want our stock?! That was a joke when that happened. They fell on the floor. He wants stock?" Waterhouse says.

But taking stock as currency turned out to be a deft move. TD shares have increased in value many times over, the dividend has been raised numerous times since 1996, and Waterhouse has benefited from a significant increase in the value of the Canadian dollar. It turns out TD got a good deal too. Although it looked like the bank was overpaying, there was a hidden jewel inside the castle that would soon surprise everyone.

Gray and Kelly flew back to Toronto to get final approval from the TD board, while Waterhouse had to do the same with his directors.

Although he would end up with $121 million in TD stock, every now and again during the two-month due diligence process, Waterhouse "would get cold feet," in Gray's words. Due diligence is a period during which the purchaser gets to inspect the asset it is buying, in order to be satisfied it is getting what it is paying for, much like a house inspection. Because Waterhouse was a publicly traded company (as was TD), it was all done in a clandestine manner.

Due diligence took place in several rooms of what was then called the New York Marriott Financial Center Hotel, near the twin towers of the World Trade Center. A team of about a dozen people from TD camped out, along with advisors from the accounting firm Price Waterhouse, and began scrutinizing the business, going through the target company's books and proprietary financial information line by line, checking for problems that might have been overlooked during negotiations. Often, because of issues uncovered during due diligence, the price of a deal is adjusted. TD found nothing amiss.

One morning during the process, Larry Waterhouse phoned Keith Gray at about seven in the morning. "I'm downstairs in the lobby, I want to talk to you," he said. "We walked around for an hour or so," Gray recounts. "It was his baby he was selling."

Waterhouse was worried he wasn't getting full value for his firm's share in a consortium that owned a market-making firm called Knight/Trimark Group. It acted as the repository for the trades of discount brokers in the U.S., bringing them in electronically, consolidating them and then putting them on the market. Unbeknownst to TD, getting a stake in Knight/Trimark was akin to a lottery win. The bank, which was buying Waterhouse for shares, had valued the Knight/Trimark piece at just $3 million and Waterhouse wanted more.

"Why would I pay you any more? I don't even know what's in there," Gray asked.

"I'll keep it myself then."

"No, you're not keeping it. We're taking it. It's part of the deal. We're keeping it," Gray replied. "Thank God I said that!" he recounts.

Waterhouse let it drop. What a drop it was. In the end, Gray says TD valued

Waterhouse's share of Knight/Trimark at $7 million, a relatively meaningless increase given what the bank would eventually make from it. In the frothy equity market of the era, the bank sold it for $700 million, roughly what it paid in total for Waterhouse.

"I can't think of a transaction in North America that created more value," says Bob Kelly. "I can't think of a financial services trade that profitable.'"*

All the while, lawyers for each side were fighting. Twenty-five were gathered around the table in the offices of Simpson Thacher & Bartlett, TD's American law firm. At one point, the negotiations went on for eighteen hours straight.

"They had a kitchen that operated twenty-four hours a day. Many times, Larry Waterhouse and I had to go out into the hall—you withdraw, and you go back in again. I finally took our lawyer out and said, 'You're a prick,'" Gray recounts. "They would stand on a point of principle and we were trying to do business." Gray's belief is there's no need to create conflict when you're trying to do a deal. For lawyers he has a bit of advice: "Solve it, don't be confrontational"—as if Gray has never taken that tack himself.[†]

Gray says they finally signed at three in the morning. He got the first flight from New York back to Toronto. Within days, Gray (along with Thomson, Baillie and Kelly) flew from Toronto to LaGuardia Airport so Thomson could shake hands with Larry Waterhouse.

It was a huge moment for Gray because "a year before Dick Thomson was so adamantly against it."

"Keith never, ever gave up," says Korthals. "All the credit goes to Keith for that relationship [with Waterhouse] and winning his trust." And although Gray doesn't feel that he got any credit from Thomson at the time, his former CEO now says, "Keith Gray was the guy who made it happen." As another executive involved says, "He put a bear hug on Larry. You can't not like Keith."

Even though the Waterhouse transaction would become a steal, TD was

---

* TD increased its share in Knight/Trimark by buying other members of the consortium that owned it, the firms Kennedy Cabot and Jack White.

† Waterhouse says Gray is being self-serving in his recollection, and is playing good cop to his lawyer's bad cop role.

edgy. Frank Petrilli, who was running Waterhouse as its president, was asked by the bank to stay.‡ Describing TD's state of mind after the purchase, Petrilli says, "They were very nervous. How do they justify a stand-alone business in the U.S. with no explicit synergies to speak of?"

Petrilli remembers a meeting in New York with Charlie Baillie and Dick Thomson after the deal. Petrilli and Larry Waterhouse went over to see the two top executives at TD. "I'll never forget Charlie Baillie [saying] after the pleasantries, 'So tell me how we're going to beat Schwab?' I said, 'I can tell you how we're going to do it if you tell me how much I could spend.' We were fixated on: How do we catch Schwab? How do we catch Schwab?"

Branding and marketing were a problem. Waterhouse was not only going up against Schwab, but Fidelity as well. TD wasn't known for spending money on marketing at the time. Petrilli's marketing budget after being acquired by the bank would go from $3 million a year to $6 million, but it wouldn't be enough. Suddenly, the pressure of the Internet was upon him. "AOL had put a gun to our head," Petrilli recalls. The dominant Internet site of the era had told him there would be four icons on the site filled by his competitors, giving him two weeks to decide if he wanted one as well.

The price would be $25 million over two years for a "button" on the popular site. Customers were demanding it and Petrilli felt he had to match the others. His marketing team scurried to put together a business case to present to the bank, but it was not definitive. With just days left until the AOL deadline, Petrilli went with his gut. Flying up to Toronto to beg Charlie Baillie for $25 million—a significant sum at the time—he confessed he hadn't done a lot of research but argued this was a "frontier" and he needed the money within two days. Baillie said he'd give it to him, but coolly told Petrilli he would hold him accountable.

Petrilli also found that the initials TD didn't mean what they should in the U.S. He says they did polling and found people in football-crazy America

---

‡ In January of 2012, Petrilli became non-executive Chairman of E*TRADE, a company TD and TD Waterhouse looked at buying many years ago, but passed on. E*TRADE was hit hard during the financial crisis due to ties to the troubled mortgage market. Ironically, in 1999 Petrilli jumped ship to run E*TRADE, but after just a week, realized he had made a mistake; Charlie Baillie let him return to TD Waterhouse. In August 2012, Petrilli was appointed interim CEO of E*TRADE.

thought the letters "TD" referred to "touchdown." It was almost three years before the company added the initials to create the name "TD Waterhouse," a condition when the bank sold shares to the public.

Until mid-2011, Richard Neiman was the chief bank regulator in the state of New York, supervising almost 80 percent of the nation's foreign bank branch assets.* He was also once a TD employee, joining the fold while working for Waterhouse. He joked that people probably thought the initials in TD Waterhouse were the first two initials of Waterhouse's name, kind of like JP Morgan. All kidding aside, Neiman believes adding the "TD" initials were the bank's first step toward creating brand awareness in the United States.

From Neiman's office as regulator, a corner suite facing New York harbour, there is a postcard view of Governor's Island and the Staten Island Ferry. On a cloudless day, with sunlight shimmering off of the water, Neiman recalls taking a girl on the ferry when it cost fifteen cents a ride. "Now it's free!" he laughs. But the showpiece of the view from Neiman's old office is the Statue of Liberty, often the first glimpse of America by newcomers arriving by ship.

Neiman would go on to be president of TD Bank USA N.A., the company's first bank in the United States. It was the new name for Waterhouse National Bank, the other bonus TD had picked up in the acquisition. When Neiman left, TD Bank USA had $14 billion in assets, prior to any of Ed Clark's acquisitions. It was relatively modest, but a start for this newcomer to America.

"I wouldn't underestimate any of the opportunities TD could have in the U.S." Neiman says.

The acquisition of Waterhouse came just as one of the great phenomena of our time was coalescing. In addition to baby boomers working to bulk up their investments, by 1996 the Internet was moving into the public consciousness. The previous year had seen the spectacular initial public offering of stock in the Web browser Netscape. For the first time, surfing the Internet became simple and fun. Netscape brought users the World Wide Web, a way to navigate around the Internet and find websites of interest. Businesses soon twigged to the idea that they needed websites, electronic

---

* In May 2011, Neiman became vice-chairman of the global financial services regulatory practice at PricewaterhouseCoopers (PwC), the world's largest professional services firm.

brochures for their products and services. Websites could also be used to buy and sell, and eventually this would make do-it-yourself trading easy. However, high-speed access to the Internet would take several more years to develop. In the mid-1990s, people were still using dial-up access, and downloading a robust webpage with lots of photographs and detail was slow. But by the late 1990s, it was commonplace to be able to easily trade stocks and check your investments online.

Technology became something of an obsession for Gray in the early 1990s, perhaps a holdover from his experience with the enormous IBM mainframe he'd installed in Winnipeg years before. In 1994, the average cost to the bank per trade was $27. A year later, it had fallen to $24 and by 1996 the average internal cost of a trade was $20. Gray thought he could get it 25 percent lower, which would reduce overall operating costs by 10 percent. But he needed his bosses to commit to between $50 and $100 million for a new back office system to support the twenty-six offices across Canada. The stakes were rising.

In 1992, Green Line had introduced Telemax, a way to get market quotes and account information and place orders over the telephone. By using Telemax, a customer could also get an extra discount on the cost of a trade. Even though trading via the World Wide Web would be a few years away, in the same year, online access was introduced through a proprietary system called Micromax. By today's measures it was crude, but it allowed for access to online order entry, market quotations and investment accounts.

But when Green Line launched on the Net in 1995, it was one of only 10,000 websites worldwide, and ranked within the top 100.[26] Customers quickly became comfortable with online trading. Soon, ironically, these same customers would be buying and selling Internet stocks, making fortunes and then losing them. Any stock with a dotcom suffix was defying gravity, in spite of a lack of profits to justify its valuation. Companies were "valued" on their top lines (revenue), rather than their bottom lines, or earnings per share. Even Web domains, or website addresses, were being sold for insane amounts of money. It was like a land grab in the Wild West. Someone had the bright idea of registering the domain name "business.com." In the auction that followed, the owner sold the Web address for $7 million.

By 1998, day-trading houses would open to bypass even the discounters, where stock-obsessed individuals would gather in front of their own terminals to hook directly into the stock exchanges, trading in and out of Yahoo, Dell and Amazon forty or fifty times a day. Even Ringo Starr was doing testimonial commercials for Charles Schwab. He may have been the drummer in the greatest rock band ever, but when you saw Ringo shilling for Schwab, you couldn't be faulted for wondering how much he knew about investing. Many fans of day trading and dotcom mania ended up in a pile of broken dreams and ruined companies. On March 10, 2000, the tech-heavy stock exchange NASDAQ hit its zenith above 5,000. It has not been anywhere near that level since. On February 29, 2012, the exchange moved above 3,000 for the first time since December of 2000.

All through the haze of the tech stock boom of the late 90s, Green Line and its newly acquired Waterhouse saw spectacular growth. They stopped calling their businesses "discount brokerages," which sounded old-fashioned, and started calling them online brokers, which is what they became. It was also the right nomenclature when it came time to sell stock in an initial public offering, a watershed moment in the history of TD Bank.

Frank Petrilli says he kept trying to convince Charlie Baillie to take TD Waterhouse public. For starters, he says, if the company had a stock, it could use it as currency to make acquisitions, just as TD had done when buying Waterhouse. Second, if TD Waterhouse wanted to be noticed in the U.S., particularly by the media, it needed to have shares available to the public. The influential financial network CNBC wasn't interested in talking to a unit of TD Bank. "CNBC only wanted to talk to us if we were a publicly traded company," explains Petrilli. He claims he twice asked Baillie, whom he greatly admires, to do an initial public offering. He describes Baillie saying to him, "What part of NO don't you understand?" Baillie responds, laughing. "No, he made that up. We all remember it differently. When we wanted to buy Canada Trust, it really became important to have the cash. I'm not sure there had been a big lobby to take it public before. It would have made sense for them to be saying, 'Let's take it public,' because it improved the currency and so on. They could have pushed on it. They may well have said, 'Take it public,' and it didn't make much of an impression at that time."

Steve McDonald, a TD man who was sent down to New York to be the CEO of the bank's new U.S. property, had an office on the opposite corner from Petrilli's. They ran the company together but they had a tense relationship. McDonald, who left TD early in the Ed Clark years and is now a top executive at Scotiabank, says he saw the shares of Charles Schwab and E*TRADE rising. He remembers thinking their stock prices had become hard to believe.

As Petrilli had discovered, however, bringing up the notion of a public share sale of Waterhouse with the brass in Toronto was like hitting your head against a wall. McDonald recalls floating the idea of an IPO at a senior management meeting of a dozen or so executives. TD still had the flattest, most unbureaucratic management structure of any of the Canadian banks, perhaps because it was smaller. But McDonald got the same response as Petrilli had been getting—"It just got killed," he says. McDonald adds that Dick Thomson's response to the idea was, "That's just so contrary to anything we've done or want to do."

Thomson has no recollection of the conversation with McDonald. He says he was in favour of the IPO because the bank needed the money to buy Canada Trust. However, he concedes that when the idea was first raised, there were concerns about having the public as a minority partner. It would make cash transactions between the two public companies more complicated.

But McDonald and Petrilli kept at it, in spite of resistance from both Thomson and Baillie. In early 1999, McDonald bumped into Thomson, who was no longer chairman or CEO, but still a board member and one who continued to hold major sway. "I hear you're still working on that IPO for Waterhouse. Didn't I make myself clear?" Thomson chided him. McDonald had been dressed down, big time.

Clearly, Keith Gray was not the only executive who experienced Thomson's sharper edge. The third time Petrilli and McDonald asked for an IPO, a few months later, Baillie, who was now both chairman and CEO, said yes. He had waited, for his own reasons, and his timing was nearly perfect. It wasn't far off the height of the Internet bubble and TD Waterhouse was viewed as a play on Internet stocks, because people used the Net to trade. The bank sold one-eighth of the company to the public at a price of $24 a share, quickly raising $1.122 billion. (Baillie says he wanted to sell as much as 20 percent to the public, but the market was beginning to cool.) Suddenly, the $525 million U.S. (then $715 million CDN) purchase of Waterhouse the TD executives had fretted over was worth some $10 billion U.S. on the public market. Combined with the $700 million dividend from the sale of Knight/Trimark (some refer to it as Knight Trading), Charlie Baillie said the bank had "money in its jeans," close to $2 billion.* For most mortals and most companies, that's still a huge figure, but today deals involving that amount of money are common and many companies sit on much larger piles of cash. Although Apple may be an extreme example, its cash and cash-equivalent balance approached $100 billion in early 2012.

"We had our eye on Canada Trust. We knew that the owner, BAT [British American Tobacco] needed cash. You couldn't give them shares, it wouldn't work, we had to get a cash buildup if we were going to buy Canada Trust," Baillie recalls.

At that time, TD's market capitalization, or market value, was $24 billion, briefly making the plucky bank worth more than the titan of the Canadian financial industry, Royal Bank. It must have been a grim day around the offices of Royal. According to some who have worked there, the image Royal has of itself is that it is, and is destined always to be, number one, a sensibility sewn into the very cloth of the enterprise. Anything less is not acceptable.

Soon enough, however, tech stocks would crash and along with them, TD Waterhouse. Two years later, in November 2001, TD would privatize the company again, buying back the stock it had sold to the public for the bargain basement price of $9 a share, infuriating those who held TD Waterhouse. Shareholders of the bank, however, didn't mind.

In July 2012, TD Ameritrade, along with other firms, would come to the rescue of Knight Capital, the successor firm to Knight/Trimark, after a trading error resulted in a $400 million loss that threatened the company. TD Ameritrade contributed $40 million to its refinancing.

After the privatization, at Montague Black's funeral in 2002, Baillie saw Ross Johnson, the flamboyant Canadian buyer of RJR Nabisco*. Johnson asked

---

* Johnson was featured in the book *Barbarians at the Gate: The Fall of RJR Nabisco*, by Bryan Burnough and John Helyar.

Baillie if he'd seen Larry Waterhouse recently. Baillie said no, but recounted how Larry, who couldn't come to the TD Waterhouse "closing dinner," had sent two bottles of Château Le Pin, one of the world's most expensive red wines, costing in the thousands per bottle.

"I'd never had a bottle of Château Le Pin before," said Baillie, who as a wealthy, refined man could no doubt afford the occasional bottle.

"Neither had Larry till he met you," Johnson shot back, jokingly.

When told about the story, Waterhouse roars with laughter but corrects the record. He recalls that they were bottles of Château Petrus—also in the thousands per bottle.

\* \* \* \*

In spite of the growing emphasis on technology, new staff members at Green Line were never hired for technical competence. Gray was all about the soft skills, dealing with customers on the phone, solving their problems. Checking in on employees, Green Line management found the key concern was not salary, but lack of appreciation.

"One thing I think I am good at is judging people. I was respected because I could get things done through people," says Gray. As a result, TD staffers wanted to work for him. This was in contrast to the upper reaches of the bank. Gray contends that Robin Korthals was highly intelligent but "never stroked" his underlings.

"Robin was a hard guy to work for. Many guys couldn't work for him. I needed stroking," Gray admits. "I often wonder why I was allowed to continue on and be the entrepreneur I was." Looking back, he has come to the conclusion that he was "a necessary evil" just at the time when things started to get racier in the Canadian banking sphere. In the 1980s, banks, trust companies and brokerages were finally allowed to commingle. Allowing Gray to roar around and buy up discount brokerages to build on the Green Line platform (or at least not discouraging him from doing so) was a backhanded way to stroke him. However, he was given warning by the vice-chair of the bank, Bud McMorran, who jokingly called Gray by his legal first name, Willard.

"Hello, Willard. How are things in Wyoming?" McMorran would say, poking fun at him. Gray thinks he might owe his job to McMorran, who protected him inside the bank.* McMorran, perhaps wiser than Gray in the politics of the institution, thought he was starting to get too much attention outside of the bank. "You're getting your picture in the paper too much," he warned. "Dick doesn't like that."

Even though Thomson now praises Gray, there is a wound. "I never had a time in my career where Dick Thomson said, 'Good job.' I had many, many times when he gave me shit." Nonetheless, he would later say he respected Thomson, and appreciated that he let him keep his job and sent him to Harvard. Gray knows, however, that the combination of taking Waterhouse public and the sale of Knight/Trimark were crucial in providing the bank the capital to buy Canada Trust, bringing in Ed Clark. Few executives associated with the bank then or now disagree. "Those things combined made the TD Bank," Gray says.

Keith Gray had retired and was not at the bank when Ed Clark became CEO a few years later, but the shift could not have been more profound. The new boss could not have imagined the path of a Keith Gray, who started at a time when tellers kept revolvers at the ready and future executives often had little education. By the same token, Gray would have found Clark's academic pedigree utterly foreign. What they do have in common is focus and clarity of thought. Most important, they are doers. Clark would take the twentieth-century foundation built by Gray—and by Baillie, Thomson, Korthals and Lambert—and erect something entirely new.

---

* McMorran recalls a phone call he got from the upper reaches of the bank, from an executive growling about why the bank was paying the tab so Keith Gray could have a box at the Royal Winter Fair, a gathering of the horsey set. It turned out Gray had paid for the box himself to entertain customers.

# 6

# UNLIKELY BANK BOSS

*From PhD to Red Ed to Banker*

Dick Thomson's father was a top banker and Thomson lived at home during his first years working at TD. A customer once said to him, "You've got nice shoes for a bank clerk." Robin Korthals' father ran an oil refinery that bustled during the 30s and 40s, so much so that Korthals says he didn't experience the Great Depression. Charlie Baillie grew up the son of a medical doctor in a comfortable upper-middle-class environment. But Ed Clark is an odd duck in the banking world. In one sense, he wasn't of the right class to climb to the top of a Canadian bank. He didn't grow up on a struggling farm and join up as a clerk like Keith Gray, but he wasn't part of the upper crust either. He most certainly didn't go the MBA route.

Ed Clark grew up in Agincourt, a suburb of Toronto. His was a middle-class home, but it was bursting with first-class minds. His father was a nationally known university professor. His mother had an Ivy League education and earned her master's in economics at Columbia in New York in the 1930s. "So when I grew up the question was, where are you getting your PhD, not whether you were getting a PhD," Clark says.[27]

Clark was a sickly kid. As a boy of twelve, he was overweight and had severely flat feet. He couldn't walk very far, although he did for a time manage to play hockey as a goaltender. Operations on both legs kept him on crutches for one whole year of school. In his last year of high school, a virus attacked the sac surrounding his heart. He had to sleep seventeen or eighteen hours a day. As a result, he was forced to drop out around Christmas, missing much of his last year. His school passed him anyway and he was so bright he managed to become an Ontario Scholar. In his first year at the University of Toronto, he still had not fully recovered. He had to sleep three or four hours through the middle of the day in addition to a normal night's sleep.

Going to Harvard for his master's and doctorate, he finished first in his class, something he's self-conscious about and does not like to advertise. In spite of possessing a keen intellect, he has learned that to get along in this world, it's better to project an everyman image.

As an adult, Clark experienced more health problems. He had heart bypass surgery in his late forties. He had prostate cancer in his early fifties. In his early sixties, he had back surgery. As Gabriel García Márquez writes of a character in *Love in the Time of Cholera*, "He had always the iron constitution of the sickly."[28]

Clark agrees that illness can strengthen a person's will. "I've been in and out of hospitals my entire life and I think—there's no question in my case—that has framed my view of the world enormously," he says. His kids joke that he would be a complete egomaniac if he hadn't had so many things wrong with him. Illness, he says, humanizes its sufferers. "It makes you empathize with people. You certainly walk around with a view that bad things can happen to good people and life is not necessarily fair. And if you end up doing well maybe some of it has to do with you, but a lot has to do with a lot of good things going your way."

Anyone who says he is solely responsible for his own success clearly has to have his head examined, Clark asserts.

At the time of Clark's upbringing, Agincourt was a farming town that was morphing into a suburb. He says his friends would probably describe him as a "nerdy, normal kid." However, as former TD Chairman John Thompson said at Canada's Outstanding CEO of the Year Award dinner in February 2011, Clark is known around TD as a "dancing machine," at least at office events. Even as a kid on crutches he danced, and he fondly recalls school dances with live bands featuring the likes of transplanted Arkansas rocker Ronnie Hawkins.

Ed Clark comes by his smarts honestly. His father, Samuel Delbert Clark, known as Del, graduated from high school when he was sixteen. He got a PhD and his mentor was the famous Canadian scholar Harold Innis, who wrote a seminal book on the historical reliance of the country's economy on staples, what we would now call resources: fish, wood, furs, minerals, wheat. Clark's father wrote the introduction to Innis' *The Fur Trade in Canada* and went on to become the founder of Canadian sociology, building the department at the University of Toronto. In 1960, Clark Sr. went to teach at Berkeley in California, giving young Ed his first immersion in America. Berkeley was a centre of counterculture, which perhaps gave young Ed the touch of the leftie that surfaced later.

Clark's mother, Rosemary, a Catholic girl from Antigonish, Nova Scotia, came from a large family. Her mother died in childbirth with her seventh baby, when Rosemary was in her early teens. Her father remarried and there were another five kids. Progressive for his time, her father believed women should be educated. As a result, Clark's mother got a master's from Columbia and went to work for the Department of Labour in Ottawa.

Del and Rosemary met in the bar of the famed railroad hotel, the Château Laurier. They soon married, and Rosemary stopped working.

Ed Clark is the youngest of three siblings. His sister, Ellen, five years older, died at fifty-nine from kidney disease. Ed's brother, Samuel, two years older, who bears the father's name, chose an academic life, also in sociology. In spite of young Ed's impressive standings and scholarships, he faced bureaucratic obstacles. In high school, his guidance counsellor advised him against going into an academic course, in spite of the erudite air he breathed at home. After his time at Harvard, he was tested for a job in Ottawa. He delights in telling about the answer that came back: "We have never tested anyone [with] as low a score as this in the history of the Government of Canada. I would advise you not to join the Civil Service. You will not have a successful career."

Clark, however, is a powerful communicator, especially one on one. He doesn't see it that way, though, and confesses to fumbling lots of words. He says he surmounts verbal hurdles by being aware of his deficit and focusing intensely on what he has to say.

Although Clark likes to project "regular guy," the fourth floor of TD Bank's headquarters in Toronto is anything but regular. Notwithstanding the modern decor, the silence makes it feel a bit like visiting the Reading Room of the British Library. Colourful abstract paintings abound, accented by Inuit sculpture. Outside Clark's office, photographs of the famous surround his long-time assistant, Janis Dixon (who retired in 2011 after working for Clark for fourteen years). They include Bill Clinton and George W. Bush, who've been brought to town by TD to speak (with the help of TD's deputy chair, Frank McKenna, the former New Brunswick premier and Canadian ambassador to the U.S.). Inside Clark's office, a white Habitat for Humanity construction helmet is prominently displayed, a reminder of Clark's philanthropic commitment to that cause.

Clark talks about the three things a person can choose to emphasize in life: career, family and friends, and extracurricular activities. He claims that, with the kind of career he has had, he can't do all three, adding that a lot of people "cheat" on the second (family and friends) in order to do the first and third. He underlines that he has been married to his wife, Fran, for more than forty years, and his four adult kids all live within fifteen minutes of his home.

He and Fran met while both were at the University of Toronto. It was a blind date. A woman Clark had gone to high school with said to him one day, "I've met the woman that you're going to marry." Clark claims to have been "smitten" on the first outing. He says Fran initially told him to get lost, that she was interested in someone else, but eventually she came round and they started dating. By fourth year, he was heading off to Harvard and she to Montreal. After an all-nighter trying to muster his courage, he came to the conclusion that if she went to Montreal that would be the end of it, so he asked her to marry him. They got married and soon moved to Boston. The first half-year there was tough for Fran, with Clark deeply enmeshed in graduate school and Fran working as a bank teller. "She knew more about banking than I did back then," jokes Clark.

Soon they were expecting their first child and running out of money. Clark heard about a government program in Tanzania that needed a young economist. They moved to Tanzania and Clark worked at the Central Planning

Ministry. He confesses to having been "scared to death" when their son was born with just a midwife present. The young couple lived in Tanzania for two years before coming back to Boston.

Clark stayed home to look after the baby, writing his thesis at night and during the child's naptimes. After earning his doctorate in economics, Clark got offers to be a professor from Harvard and Stanford, but neither interested him. His ambivalence mystified his father, the famous academic. Here was Ed, shunning the family business.

Clark may be exhibiting false modesty when he states, "I don't have an academic mind." He says university types take something straightforward and make it complicated, while he does the opposite, taking complicated things and making them simple. "I guess I strongly believe that IQs are an overrated asset, a vastly overrated asset," he says.

He can resist the egghead label all he likes, but Clark is without a doubt an intellectual and about as sharp as they come. In the late 1970s, when the charismatic and cerebral Pierre Trudeau was prime minister, intellectuals were welcome in Ottawa and the capital was a fizzy place for young brainiacs. Clark wrote to various departments but got turned down by all of them. His father finally phoned someone in government and said, "I'm not asking you to get him a job, but surely there's one person that would actually interview him, you know. And then they can say they're not interested."

Michael Decter, a former public servant who once took an introductory economics course from Ed Clark at Harvard and now manages money in Toronto, says the story he heard is that Clark's father, while visiting the prime minister in his role as head of the Royal Society, complained directly to Trudeau. Del Clark reportedly said to the PM, "My son graduated top of his class at Harvard and can't even get an interview with your goddamned government."

Whatever happened, Clark got several interviews and several offers. On paper, as a result of his Tanzanian experience, where he headed up a staff of six economists, he looked like a "senior guy." What followed was a series of assignments for numerous departments and cabinet ministers.

Inflation was rampant in the 1970s, and Trudeau established something called the Anti-Inflation Board. Clark went to work there and headed up one side of the board, managing 150 people.[29] He started rubbing shoulders with executives from companies like IBM and Imperial Oil, all trying to figure out how to appease the government on prices. Soon he was at the Department of Finance, looking at the question "What if Quebec votes to separate?" At the time, countries in postwar Europe had not yet broken up. Czechoslovakia and Yugoslavia were still together and it would be a dozen years before the Soviet Union splintered. But the questions about Quebec were endless. What happens to the debt, the currency, borders? Clark was also sent to international economics conferences, often sitting next to a Nobel Laureate sent by the United States.

By 1979, he was anxious to work in the private sector, but the government wanted him to work in the energy department. He was told if he did so, he would get a one-year paid sabbatical. For his year off, Clark wanted to work in the private sector in France and learn French.

It was during this time, ironically, that Clark came into contact with the big banks, including TD. Dome Petroleum was in deep financial trouble, all the banks were on the hook and the federal government had to get involved. Clark's team would be dealing across the table with a prominent Toronto lawyer named Purdy Crawford, who was representing Dome. Working at the same firm and closely with Crawford was Brian Levitt. Clark had known Levitt since they were in their early twenties. In the 1990s, Crawford and Levitt would take turns being Clark's bosses at Canada Trust. In 2011, Levitt became Clark's boss again, as chairman of TD Bank.

In May 1979, the government changed. Trudeau was out, and a thirty-nine-year-old greenhorn prime minister named Joe Clark (no relation) was in. Ed Clark worked on Joe Clark's first and last budget. The document he helped create included a fatal eighteen-cent gasoline tax that sank the nine-month old Conservative government; Clark exited on a vote of non-confidence. Trudeau and the Liberals were soon back in power with a majority. Energy Minister Marc Lalonde asked Ed Clark, "Given your close association with the Conservatives, do you think you can actually serve me?" He said yes, and became Lalonde's assistant deputy minister of energy. Clark was in his early thirties at that point, with hair down over his ears, sporting a beard, and had an intellect that was always ready for an argument. "God, I feel sorry for the oil and gas industry now. I've got to tell you, I would have been up in arms against this guy!" Clark says of his younger self.

Clark became notorious for helping to pen the National Energy Program, an activist policy that enraged Alberta and the country's energy industry. Once the oil barons found out that the bureaucrat who'd devised this diabolical plan for the federal government was the same person who'd written a doctoral thesis about Tanzanian socialism, Clark had a nickname: Red Ed. John English, in his scholarly biography of Pierre Trudeau, quotes author Peter Foster on Calgary's reaction to Clark. Foster wrote that Clark assumed "a notoriety never before accorded any public servant" and that his thesis was "photocopied and passed around Calgary's Petroleum Club with 'selected quotations' highlighted in an angry yellow, felt-tip pen."[30] Clark claims that in Tanzania, the reaction was the opposite. There, he says, "I was called the running dog of imperialism."

There is no elaborate design on the cover of Clark's published thesis. It's yellow, with orange bars and plain type, looking vaguely like a canvas by Barnett Newman. The title isn't exactly catchy: *Socialist Development and Public Investment in Tanzania 1964–73*. It's dedicated to his mother and father.

Clark was just thirty-one when his thesis was published in 1978, but in it you can hear his distinctive and confident voice. While scholarly, it has colloquial touches, not far from the way he communicates now, more than three decades later. He was telling the world, with at times extraordinary authority, how Tanzania should reform its economy. As part of a University of Toronto project on the country, Clark, with the help of a grant from the Canada Council, had worked for Tanzania's central planning ministry from 1971 to 1973. "Central planning ministry" was probably all anyone in Calgary needed to hear.

It's not entirely clear from his thesis, however, where Clark comes down politically. He criticizes socialists. He criticizes capitalists. He criticizes the then socialist leader of Tanzania, Julius Nyerere. "It is my belief that socialist scholars in particular should devote more of their energy to analyzing the problems of socialist societies and the problems of transition to socialism and somewhat less to criticizing capitalist societies," Clark writes.

At the same time, he writes, "The rapid development of an industrial base producing intermediate and basic goods is as potentially damaging to the long-run socialist development of Tanzania . . . such a strategy will create an urban-oriented elite and a class structure almost as exploitative and unacceptable as one produced by capitalist development."[31]

Furthermore, he states "The commitment to equality, criticized by so many as being naïve, stands in stark contrast to most of the rest of the world's, both capitalist and many socialist countries' willingness to allow the few to enjoy so much, while the many enjoy so little."[32]

He goes on to say, "Anyone involved in radical politics cannot help but be dismayed at the way leftists devote so much of their energies to needless internal fights . . . one must be suspicious of socialist scholars who cart around the same intellectual baggage to every country proposing the same path to socialism for all. Surely it is absurd as the broken record of neo-classical economics ('emphasize primary exports, build a good climate for foreign investment, keep your tariffs low') which the international capitalist agencies have airlifted for so long, record player and all, to every third world country."[33]

And finally, "An investment strategy for Tanzania must have as its goal *growth with equality.*"[34]

These are the words of a pragmatist, not an ideologue. Clark's main thrust is that there needs to be more public investment in rural agricultural areas. Over 60 percent of the government's investment has to go into this, or 150 percent as much per capita in the poorest regions as in others. Change, he writes, will occur only with massive infusions of capital. Politics aside, was this an unconscious embryo in his thought process that would influence his later decision to expand into the U.S. during his tenure at TD? Capital talks. Go big or go home?

What is striking, given who Clark has become, is that the word he uses just as much as *socialism* is *strategy.* He keeps coming back to the country's economic strategy, and how it should be implemented. What the reader begins to understand is that an analytical mind was being formed, a mind obsessed with strategy. While card-carrying members of the Tea Party might draw a sharp breath when hearing about this banker's past, they would be missing one of his key points: "Indeed, people change over time, and it is easy for someone who was at the vanguard of revolution to tire of the hardships socialism inevitably imposes on the elite," Clark writes as he wraps up his arguments. "Socialism usually abolishes the marketplace as an effective disciplinary mechanism. However poor this mechanism is, it does serve to provide a degree of check on the actions of bureaucrats. By abolishing competition, without replacing it with democratic forms of control, socialist countries can run the risk of creating bureaucracies totally immune from the needs of the people."[35]

Clark's thesis made him toxic in Ottawa. Once a Conservative government came to power again, in September 1984, his days were numbered and he was eventually fired. Nearly three decades later, former prime minister Brian Mulroney says that during his time in Ottawa, he never met Ed Clark nor did he recall the details of Clark's firing: "I was brand new to Ottawa myself. I did not know the players."

However, he does admit that there was a "hurricane" of pressure from the Conservative party's Alberta caucus, which included powerful federal cabinet ministers Joe Clark and Don Mazankowski. There was also a fierce wind blowing in from Alberta's provincial government, headed by the "influential and respected" Peter Lougheed. Mulroney had campaigned on getting rid of the National Energy Program when he ran for prime minister in 1984 and had won big in the West. He had to deliver on that. "This [NEP] had been a symbol of alienation for Albertans for a long time. [Clark] was a pretty visible target," says Mulroney.

Ed Clark was by then in his late thirties with a young family. Mulroney concedes that Clark was a just civil servant doing what he was instructed to do by the government of the day. But others say it may not have helped Clark's cause that he was young, could be brash, and was little concerned with making enemies and more than willing to argue.

"Harvard doesn't produce small egos," says Michael Decter, who attended a few church-basement meetings of the Union for Radical Political Economics with Ed Clark while they were both at Harvard. Longtime Canadian business journalist and author Rod McQueen, in a 1993 profile in the *Financial*

*Post,* quotes Doug Smee, a former colleague of Clark's at the federal finance department. "Everybody either likes Ed Clark or doesn't like him," said Smee. "He's a very strong personality; he doesn't take any bullshit. He's always going forward and that puts people off because they can't take his opinions."[36]

Mulroney, surprisingly, comes to Clark's defence, saying that the young bureaucrat was not the true architect of the NEP and that he shouldn't have fired him. "The architect of the NEP was Pierre Elliott Trudeau and the chief executor of the policy was Marc Lalonde," he says. "This was a mistake I made as a new prime minister, lacking experience. Ed Clark became the symbol in this, in the absence of the two others."

Even though Clark was canned, his government experience was far from a write-off. Ottawa is where he got to know Purdy Crawford and deepened critical lifelong connections with people like Brian Levitt, with whom he worked on government legislation for crown corporations as well as parts of the National Energy Program. More broadly, it was during his time working for the federal government that he learned how to manage people and coax them to be better than they think they are.

Clark explains. "I do think the government experience was a tremendous experience for me in two things. One is, in government you don't have the traditional instruments of management—hiring, firing, promoting and rewarding. And so you actually have to learn to inspire, and I think that's important. But the other thing, ironically, is that in government you get used to multiple stakeholders and things going wrong. And so I think, as it turned out in the last few years, certainly, this has been a pretty confusing world for all of us, we've been pretty challenged, and so having that experience has turned out to be a positive for me."

Few people as they get older can resist the idea of making a bit more money. As much as Clark clearly relished intellectual challenges, he was no different. He needed a job and he headed to the place where the pay was better—Bay Street in Toronto. Mickey Cohen, who is now a director on the board of TD Ameritrade and a former TD Bank director, was Clark's boss at the Department of Energy when he wrote the NEP. "Lots of doors didn't open for Ed. Nobody's ever read his bloody thesis. But they saw the title," says

Cohen. "That first year for Ed was bad." Cohen also recalls that when Clark's name came up for hiring a lot of financial firms said, "Oh no, not you . . . the clients won't accept it."

It wouldn't be the last time Clark's connection with Purdy Crawford would pay off. Because of his work on the Dome Petroleum file with Crawford and an investment banker named Thomas Rahilly, Clark was asked whether he would like to work at Merrill Lynch. He was interested and met with Mike Sanderson, an American who'd just come over to run the Canadian operations. The out-of-work civil servant also went down to New York to meet more of the Merrill hiring squad. "I did explain to them who I was," Clark says, owning up to the "Red Ed" moniker.

Sanderson, however, didn't care, and in 1985 hired him as an investment banker, focusing on mergers and acquisitions, even though some say Merrill got pushback from Alberta when the province heard Clark was a serious candidate. By this time, Mickey Cohen had left Ottawa and was working for the Reichmann family, who owned Olympia and York. In addition to its massive real estate business, the Reichmanns' empire then included Gulf Canada and Hiram Walker.[37] "I used [Clark] extensively as an investment banker and he was terrific. He was the Ed then that you see now," Cohen says.

Clark alleges that he has not had any particular mentors (some might disagree), but that he has learned from every boss he's ever had, and every place he's worked. Merrill Lynch, while not a model he would choose to emulate, taught him many things. "It was a culture that taught you to go out, grow, create new business, and the guns should go out, not in, in an organization," he says.[38]

Within a few years, Clark was on the move again. Ignoring the advice of many, in 1988 he took a job running Morgan Financial Corporation, the last meaningful subsidiary of Financial Trustco.[39] Morgan was responsible for restructuring Financial Trustco Group, which had been the mastermind of the late Gerald Pencer, who went on to Cott Beverages fame.[40] Pencer was known far and wide as a creative but fast operator, principally criticized for aggressive accounting practices. He was a hard-driving outsider, and not the type to be embraced by the more conservative financial community. Pencer's approach at Financial Trustco had created a mess, particularly after a real estate–induced recession bubbled forth in the late 1980s and leaked into the early 1990s. Purdy Crawford says he was one of those who advised Clark to stay away from Pencer. "I advised him against it. But he did it. I was worried that he could get tarnished by the brush of Pencer."

"Every human being I knew said, 'Are you completely out of your mind?'" is what Clark told the *Globe and Mail*'s Sinclair Stewart in 2005. But the experience had an upside. "That's why I'm running TD Bank. Because I actually took the completely dumb decision to go to Financial Trustco," says Clark.[41]

Clark simply wanted to be the boss of something. As Mickey Cohen says, Clark is an operator who gets a kick out of running things. Purdy Crawford agrees. "Ed is a great doer, executor." He's also a big-brained guy, and smart people like control as much as they like challenges. For Clark, running Financial Trustco was like getting another PhD, but this time in how *not* to do things. "I think anybody who's had a good career in financial services has had things go wrong, and I saw *lots* of things go wrong."

Things went wrong almost immediately. There was a run on deposits. Clark told Rod McQueen in 1993 that he couldn't have foreseen how bad it was. "I may have been both naive and ignorant, but when you're outside a financial institution, it's very difficult to tell."[42]

When you're cleaning up a corporate mess and winding up a company's activities, you're also working your way out of a job. Within three years, Clark was looking for work again. He didn't have to look far because by this time he was über-connected. He'd gotten to know the CEO of Canada Trust, Peter Maurice, who'd been wooing him for a few years. And the CEO of Imasco, the parent of CT Financial's un-bank, Canada Trust, was none other than Purdy Crawford. Clark became CT Financial's chief operating officer in 1991 and moved up to take command as CEO in 1994. Canada Trust was where he'd learn to be a retail banker, from the company that had been irritating big banks like TD by teaching them how to do it.

"It's a complete switch," Clark said in an interview with the *Globe and Mail*'s Karen Howlett when the announcement of his hiring was made. "This almost sounds boring, compared to Morgan. When you get a shot at joining the Montreal Canadiens, who would ever turn that down? No one is a superstar in the Montreal Canadiens, but it's fun to play on a winning team."[43]

Clark is a big man, and he uses his size to his advantage. He's given to throwing his arm around people, bringing them in close, using the elemental power of human touch to persuade. TD CFO Colleen Johnston described a scene at a branch in New York City. Clark was getting a tour from Fred Graziano, one of the bank's top executives in the United States. Clark threw his arm around Graziano and said, "Fred, you're doing a fantastic job here." He then came in a little tighter and said, "I love what you're doing, Fred, but can you take some costs out?" Graziano then threw his arm around his real estate guy and hugged him a little tighter, Ed Clark style. "Jerry, you know, these branches, can we just build them a little cheaper?"

Clark is also not above using the "I'm just a country boy" routine. This was a favourite ploy in Keith Gray's arsenal, although at least in his case he actually *was* a country boy. Beware of those claiming soil under their fingernails, just as you'd be wary of those who claim they've never played pool.

John Pelton, a former colleague at Merrill Lynch and Financial Trustco, said of Clark in 1993, "He's completely fearless in business. He'll create an agenda even if none exists and then take control of it. He does not fail to take action in every circumstance."[44]

Michael Decter recounts an anecdote with relish. Driving to work in his Mercedes one morning, a chauffeur-driven Cadillac pulled up next to him at a red light. In the back seat, reading the newspaper, was none other than Ed Clark, by then CEO of TD—and a long way from radical economics meetings in church basements.

7

# BUYING CANADA TRUST, GETTING ED CLARK

*Charlie's Transformative Purchase*

Charlie Baillie prefers birds to golf. As one of his former executives and fond supporters laughingly says, "He is not a man of the people." While Baillie is unfailingly gentlemanly and generous, he is cerebral, making no claims whatsoever to being a people person like Ed Clark. Baillie has a cool persona and refined tastes in art, books, far-reaching travel and finely tailored clothes.

"Charlie's an analyst," Keith Gray says, marvelling at Baillie's ability to come to meetings with a stack of reports and busily scan and mark them while the discussion carries on, as though he had two brains operating in parallel.

Baillie is also a visionary. He may have taken a hit in 2002 for billions in soured media and telecom loans—the first time TD reported a loss since the 1955 merger—but he had, according to Clark, seen where the sector was going.

In 2000, Baillie told me in an interview for a documentary called *Titans,* based on Peter C. Newman's book of the same name, that he had wanted to run a large corporation ever since he was a young boy. He got his chance in 1995, becoming president of TD when Robin Korthals left, adding the CEO title in 1997 and the chairman's title a year later, which he kept into 2003.

Baillie's analytical mind had come to the conclusion that scale was crucial for success in banking. If you got bigger, you could spread your technology and network costs over a broader base. In Canada, that meant mergers of the big banks made sense. Beyond that, it meant planting the TD flag around the United States.

It had been decades since the last significant bank combinations in Canada. In the early 1960s, there was the marriage of the Imperial Bank and the Commerce Bank that created CIBC. Before that, there was the merger of the Bank of Toronto and the Dominion Bank in 1955 that had given birth to TD. Now, in the late 1990s, the Big Five banks were huge, with their tentacles reaching into all aspects of the economy. By and large, even though Canadians invested in them and liked their boring, stable ways, the banks were unpopular. No one liked the big fees they charged and people fumed when they saw how much money they made. They were also big employers. Mergers would mean closing branches and firing people. The banks were political dynamite.

It was early on the morning of January 23, 1998, when Royal Bank of Canada and Bank of Montreal announced their intention to combine. On Parliament Hill, the wily Jean Chrétien, a former TD director, was prime minister and Paul Martin, a future prime minister, was finance minister. The way the government found out about the merger is still a sore point. Martin and Chrétien did not hear the news from the banks. Without even considering the political or public policy implications, something Charlie Baillie and Ed Clark would likely have thought about first, the CEOs of Royal Bank and Bank of Montreal had charged ahead.

Jim Peterson, who was secretary of state for international financial institutions, was at home in bed early on that Monday morning when the phone rang. His wife, Heather, picked up the receiver. A family friend, Kevin Doyle, who had been editor of the weekly newsmagazine *Maclean's* but was now the bureau chief for Bloomberg News in Canada, was on the line. Somehow, shortly before the news was made public in the hours before the stock market opened, Doyle had gotten word that the two big banks were going to merge and called Peterson. He would not reveal who told him and his colleagues at Bloomberg. "They were very senior financial industry people," Doyle recalls. "They were the ones from whom we got the tip about the talks coming to fruition and that something was about to happen." When asked point blank whether the sources for the story were either of the two bank CEOs involved, Doyle says, "I can't go there."

As for Peterson's reaction, Doyle says, "It came as a surprise to him that something was actually happening without him or Paul Martin knowing, and I guess his reaction was to shout to Heather to call Paul."

Peterson was instructed by Martin to get into the office right away so they could deal with the situation. Peterson says he then also received a call from Royal Bank's head of government relations, asking where he could be reached in a couple of hours, presumably so the bank could finally give the government notice just before the news was made public and the market opened. RBC and BMO had committed a major faux pas: they had failed to give Ottawa a meaningful heads-up and they would regret it. Martin was furious: "It was clear that this was an attempt to pressure me. I wasn't going to be pressured. It backfired."[45]

What's more, the government had previously appointed an independent, non-partisan task force to look into the future of banking, and the out-of-the-blue deal between Royal and BMO had undermined the work of that group, which was set to report in a matter of months. Peterson recalls Martin telling the banks that if they wanted to merge, they had to make the case on their own to Canadians.

"Can you believe it? They didn't even call us first," a shocked Jean Chrétien told a retired banker on the morning the RBC–BMO deal was announced. The former banker asked Chrétien what the government would do. "I doubt we're going to approve it. But we're going to have to let them make their case," was the reply.

Chrétien, shrewd to the last vote, knew the political calculus. So did Paul Martin, who wanted to be prime minister himself one day. Mergers meant job cuts in smaller communities. What would a merger do for the average Canadian? Nothing. Charlie Baillie admits he was in awe of Chrétien's street smarts. You could not out-manoeuvre him. When TD joined in the merger sweepstakes a few months later with CIBC as a partner, Baillie recalls with a chuckle that he thought he had a strategy that would force Chrétien's hand on the proposals, even though, as finance minister, it was Martin's decision. They met secretly at an airport hotel. Baillie said to the prime minister that the bank would thrive if his government approved the deal. If you don't, we'll still be okay, the banker told him. But Baillie added that what bothered him was that ten years down the road, he might be talking to a prime minister who was no longer part of the G7. "He loves the G7. I've got him," Baillie recounts thinking.

There was, however, no outsmarting the *p'tit gars* from Shawinigan, who famously thought nothing of grabbing a protestor by the neck and choking him in front of television cameras.

"We shouldn't even be in the G7!" Chrétien retorted, dismissing Baillie's tactic. Chrétien told him the Europeans wanted to bring the Italians in, so the Americans had brought the Canadians in. Baillie was flabbergasted by how crafty Chrétien was.*

Paul Martin, with the support of Chrétien, deserves major credit for blocking the mergers. Had the deals gone through, Canada would likely have had two enormous banks during the financial crisis rather than five, thereby endangering the economy through their sheer size and interconnectedness. It's not inconceivable that one or more of the bulked-up banks would have become deeply involved in the U.S. subprime housing market, perhaps by buying a dodgy American financial institution, creating a banking crisis in Canada during the meltdown. Later, in 2002, the government also rejected a proposal to combine CIBC with Manulife, two companies that have since had their share of troubles. Had those two been able to join, they could have ended up creating double the grief.

"It raised the 'too big to fail' issue that we talk about today. If there had been mergers there would have been serious problems in Canada during the meltdown," says Scott Clark (no relation to Ed), who was deputy finance minister at the time. "We saved their bacon."

Politics aside, Paul Martin and the regulators still had a process to follow. The former prime minister recalls that the first file that landed on his desk as finance minister concerned the bankruptcy of what had been a major Canadian insurance company, Confederation Life. That was in 1994. Nine years before, in 1985, the country had experienced the failure of two

---

* Jean Chrétien did not respond to a request to be interviewed for this book.

banks in western Canada, the Northland Bank of Canada and the Canadian Commercial Bank. During the real estate crisis of the early 1990s, a once–blue chip company, Royal Trust, disintegrated and was bought in 1993 by Royal Bank. The prospect of bank failures was uppermost in Martin's mind.

The morning RBC and BMO announced their plan, Charlie Baillie held an emergency meeting of top management. Even though Dick Thomson was no longer CEO of TD, he had asked to attend. The discussion focused on two areas: whether the government would approve the merger, and how TD should react. The prevailing view was that the government would approve the deal because Bay Street was now "pricing it in" or seeing it as a foregone conclusion, given mergers and acquisitions in the financial sector in other parts of the world. There was a sense among the TD brass that this had now moved beyond the purview of the government. Such is the myopia of people in a cosseted bank tower. While banks are powerful, and no more so than in Canada, politicians still hold key cards. Sticking it to the banks would play well on Main Street.

Still, none of the banks wanted to be left out. TD, which was fifth largest, didn't relish the notion of being the only bank without a merger partner. It felt it needed to make a move. Although Charlie Baillie had stated the year before that his bank could still prosper if it didn't merge with another, the game had changed.[46] He was soon speaking with fellow Harvard Business School alumnus Peter Godsoe, chairman and CEO of Scotiabank. The view was that of the bank cultures available, it would be the best fit. It didn't take long, though, for those talks to fall apart. According to executives familiar with the discussions, neither Baillie nor Godsoe was ready to give up the reins, as one of them would have to do if their companies were combined.

"Charlie came back and reported it's a no go. Everything's social before it becomes financial," one executive says, meaning you have to iron out who would be boss and what the name of the new institution will be before you get down to the money side of the negotiations. Another executive says the idea was for Baillie and Godsoe to be co-CEOs, but was soon dismissed by a management committee of TD during an executive retreat at Langdon Hall, a luxurious inn about an hour's drive from Toronto.

TD's focus turned to CIBC, at the time the second-biggest bank in the country. To many, proposing a second merger was seen as a defensive move. By getting into bed with another bank, TD would put more pressure on the government to nix the RBC–BMO deal. Still, they had to put on a good act. Baillie, discreetly staying away from the banking district or his old-money Rosedale neighbourhood, paid a Saturday morning visit to the suburban kitchen of CIBC chairman and CEO Al Flood, to talk.[47] They made a deal and did intend to merge. TD would get virtually half of the combined bank, Flood would retire, Baillie would be chairman and CEO, and TD's green motif would survive, but the TD name would disappear (something that displeased retired chairman and president Allen Lambert).* When TD and CIBC announced their plans on April 17, 1998, less than three months after Royal and BMO announced theirs, the government suddenly had two big fat mergers to consider—something Scott Clark thinks the first two banks should have thought of before they made their announcement with guns a-blazing.

Martin said this was intolerable. If he approved both deals, there would be two huge banks, leaving Scotiabank and the National Bank (which was mainly focused on Quebec) as runts relative to the other two. The pressure, he said, would be too much for them. In the event of a crisis, two big banks could easily turn into just one big bank. Still, the finance department, the Competition Bureau and the Office of the Superintendent of Financial Institutions went through the process of looking at the implications for soundness of the system and competition, particularly in rural areas. Baillie, in a manner that's out of character, suggested Canada would look "Neanderthal" to the global business community if the government turned down the merger proposals.[48] TD and CIBC, in their press release, also had the gall to proclaim that their combination would be an "excellent fit." TD, at least, would soon find out otherwise.

There was certainly no shortage of bravado at the banks. As the two merger proposals lay stewing in the government pot, the governor of

---

* Lambert lived into his 90s and still went to his office every weekday until his death in 2002. Ex–vice chair Bud McMorran, who shared a retirement office with him, said Lambert started at the bank when he was 15 years old, a 75-year association with the company.

the Bank of Canada held a lunch with the country's major bank CEOs, something that occurred on a fairly regular basis. In addition to Governor Gordon Thiessen, central bank officials and the bank bosses, the others around the table in the Bank's dining room were Finance Minister Paul Martin and a few of his advisors and aides. The dishes were Bank of Canada dishes. The cutlery was Bank of Canada cutlery. There was no smoking allowed. But according to people who were present, Matthew Barrett, the dashing and daring chairman and CEO of Bank of Montreal, lit up anyway, only to find there were no ashtrays. At one point, the bankers were told in no uncertain terms that if they were to make any headway with their merger proposals, it would be up to them to convince Canadians that the deals were in the public interest. It was then that the top bankers in the country began arguing amongst themselves about whether mergers were in the public interest or not. Royal and BMO led the charge, Scotiabank and Quebec-based National Bank argued the opposite. "They seemed oblivious to the fact that they were having this basic disagreement among themselves in front of the governor of the Bank of Canada and the minister of finance, who would eventually have to make the decision," said someone who was in the room. The government people sat dumbfounded, watching and listening to the most powerful businessmen in the country engage in a catfight. "It was quite a scene. We enjoyed ourselves immensely," says one witness. Paul Martin confirms that tempers flared. "It got [a] little steamy. Words were spoken."

Almost a year after the first two banks made their intentions known, Paul Martin announced his decision, a verdict that the prime minister supported. On December 14, 1998, he gave a speech outlining the federal government's reasons for rejecting both proposals: "They are not in the best interests of Canadians. The mergers would lead to an unacceptable concentration of economic power in the hands of fewer, very large banks. They would result in a significant reduction in competition." Another worry was what would happen if one of the bigger merged banks found itself in difficulty. Would the government then have to amend foreign ownership restrictions to allow a company from outside of the country to rescue a Canadian bank?

Scott Clark says he informed Royal Bank's CEO, John Cleghorn, that the Royal–BMO proposal had been quashed. Cleghorn, Clark says, seemed shocked and wanted to hear it from the minister himself. Amazed at what he perceived to be the bankers' ignorance of the political process, Clark recalls the story that Cleghorn and Barrett had floated their merger notion at a Bank of Montreal Christmas cocktail party.[49] "Never make decisions over eggnog," the former deputy minister says, laughing.

Rejection, however, was one of the best things that ever happened to TD. At a luxurious corporate retreat north of Toronto now called the Kingbridge Centre (then a CIBC training facility that had originally been built as a high-end spa), top employees of both Toronto-Dominion and CIBC had hunkered down, trying to get to know one another. It had all the hallmarks of a disaster.

"CIBC felt gigantic and blobby to us," recalled a former TD executive. Another described some of the CIBC team as not very familiar with banking, many of them having come from the investment banking or deal-making side of the firm through the bank's acquisition of Wood Gundy. Yet another remarked on what appeared to be a high-expense culture at CIBC, perhaps an indication of jealousy on the TD side, but certainly a culture clash: "They had a resort. We didn't. We drove North American automobiles, they didn't. Most of us had never seen food like that at a bank event."

There were a lot of blank stares across the room. In one session on the first day, the CIBC people were busy preaching their corporate values. Dan Marinangeli, TD's outspoken CFO at the time, hit the wall. A big man, who often dressed as if ready for a *GQ* photo shoot, he listened impatiently. "I think Dan just kind of reached his limit and he said, 'Maybe this is out of line, but we run a bank and I don't know what you people are talking about,'" said one witness. Another recalled that Marinangeli was even more blunt and "ruffled a few feathers."

Whatever CIBC thought of them, the TD gang had an inside joke: "We run a bank, what do you do?" But it came down to the fact that, according to a former executive, at the time, TD "didn't know how to be in an institution that large. It was very apparent very early that we were a different animal than CIBC."

Steve McDonald, now a top executive at Bank of Nova Scotia, would have been the one to oversee the integration of the two banks. He says that when the two companies went through an exercise of declaring what they each stood for and what they saw in the other, CIBC said to TD, "You're too much into the numbers, the ROE (return on equity), shareholder return." That left the TDers somewhat mystified, given that's why they were in business.

"I was getting so nervous," says McDonald. "On paper, it was the best thing I'd ever seen. [But] we couldn't even carry on a conversation. It's something I learned indelibly for the rest of my career. Do not underestimate the importance of culture."

Part of the story has the ring of a spy novel. Once TD figured out its proposal to combine with CIBC would be turned down by Ottawa, it thought it had a duty as a publicly traded company to inform the markets. This was material information, but the government had not announced its decision yet. The bank didn't think it could scoop the government with an official release of the news. Instead, a decision was made to leak it to one of the major newspapers. According to one former executive, two TD types went to the extraordinary length of making their way through the underground concourse that connects much of Toronto's financial district, ending up at a pay phone under the Bank of Montreal. It was from there they made the call, informing a member of the press that the deals were dead.

The strategic Charlie Baillie was already on the move. Once summoned by the department of finance, he got a lift down to Ottawa on the CIBC jet. While on the flight, Baillie says, he suggested to Al Flood that once they were told they had been turned down, they might each ask for a private five-minute chat with Paul Martin. When it came time for his five minutes, Baillie says he popped the question to Martin about Canada Trust: Would it be okay if TD bought it?

"He said, 'Fine.' And I said, 'Are you sure? Do you want to think about it?' And he said, 'No, as long as it's not one of the (Big) Five,'" Baillie recounts. Martin remembers the situation differently. He says he "didn't have any trouble with TD doing it 'cause the TD was a small bank. There was a difference between the TD making that bid and another bank. The only issue I had to address was could TD do it, and I had no trouble."

TD had been eyeing Canada Trust for years. In the early 90s, Dick Thomson and Robin Korthals looked seriously at it, but the bank couldn't afford it. Thomson says that at one point TD actually offered $32 per share for Canada Trust and that he told Purdy Crawford he could become chairman of the bank. But ultimately, the owners wanted "$36 or $38" and Thomson felt that was too expensive. Others say Thomson would have been too cautious to make such a big acquisition, and that he held the view that the British didn't really want to sell so it was a waste of time to try. As well, before the merger plans were announced, Charlie Baillie had gone to Ottawa with André Bérard, the CEO of National Bank, to make a pitch for Canada Trust. TD and the Quebec-based bank had hatched what they thought was a politically savvy plan to split Canada Trust's branches. National would get the ones in Quebec, TD the rest. "We never heard back," Baillie recalls. He was also skeptical about whether Ottawa would give the CT transaction the okay, because TD had information that CIBC had made a play for Canada Trust but had been turned down.

This time, though, it was different. TD was the smallest of the Big Five, and that worked to its advantage. Since getting the nod from Paul Martin, Charlie Baillie and one of his vice-chairs, Bill Brock, had been working on a deal. Jim Peterson got a call in the spring of 1999 from Baillie, who said, "Here's what we want to do." Peterson let him know what the political concerns were, mainly branch closings.

Paul Martin also says he was afraid that the Americans would buy Canada Trust and was nervous about "the backdoor importation of American regulations," which he saw as weak compared with Canada's. Martin says that, at the time, the Brits and the Americans were engaging in regulatory weakening to entice financial institutions. Each country was trying to ensure the dominance of its financial centre, London versus New York, and loosening rules to attract more foreign players. "I remember being personally quite concerned that if an American bank had taken over Canada Trust at that time that that could be an Achilles heel for the Canadian banking system," Martin says.

Imasco, controlled by the British firm BAT, owned almost all of Canada Trust. It was therefore conceivable that a U.S. bank could buy Canada Trust. With the government onside, TD needed to strike a deal with BAT.

Charlie Baillie's emissary to the BAT brass in London was Bill Brock. Brock looks like the archetypal bank executive. Once a vice-chairman of the bank, he refers to himself as "the invisible executive," an irony given that he has the shoulders, chest and height of a lineman. Now well into his seventies, Brock sports a head of thick white hair that shows no sign of thinning and a full face that blushes easily. Another one of the select group of MBAs hired in 1963 who shot to the upper levels of the bank, Brock experienced his pivotal moment at TD just as his career was coming to a close. As Charlie Baillie's virtual number two at the time, Brock was dispatched along with another TD banker, Mark Wheaton, to the U.K. to negotiate the purchase of Canada Trust from BAT. Brock reckons he made at least a dozen trips in three months.

Brock says that before making its pitch TD got legal and tax advice indicating the bank should propose to BAT that it buy the rest of Imasco it didn't already own for cash, pre-sell Canada Trust to TD for cash as well and then dispose of its additional holdings such as Shoppers Drug Mart to others. Fortunately, BAT wanted to bust up Imasco and it wanted cash, not shares, for anything it sold. That put TD at a distinct advantage versus the other big banks. Thanks to the sale of shares of TD Waterhouse to the public and the sale of the hidden bonus company, Knight/Trimark, within that transaction, TD had an extra $2 billion under its mattress. All those years of slogging by Keith Gray had positioned the bank to make its most transformational deal.

"Waterhouse doesn't look like a bad investment now," Brock says with a tone of understatement.

Canada Trust would cost the bank just under $8 billion. TD did issue shares and a small amount of debt, but the bulk of the proceeds for the purchase came from the bank's considerable war chest at the time.[50] Had BAT been willing to take stock, Baillie says all the banks would have bid for it.

"There was no beauty contest," Purdy Crawford says—meaning no other bidders.* For BAT, sources confirmed, the deal was beneficial "tax-wise," giving "no-cost gravy" to the seller.

---

* Brian Levitt, who was CEO of Imasco at the time and is now TD's chairman, says it would be misleading to say there were no other bidders. Charlie Baillie concurs with Crawford that TD was the sole bidder. Paul Martin says Finance officials told him that no other banks had shown interest.

\* \* \* \*

Trust companies have all but disappeared from public view, either the victims of financial failure or absorbed by the banks in takeovers. But for years, Canadians had their choice of essentially two retail bank systems. There were the big chartered banks, which to this day exist as a protected oligopoly, with a stranglehold on financial services in Canada. They are solid, immensely profitable, and by most people's standards, dull. Until the late 1990s, however, there was an alternative. With names like Royal Trust, Canada Trust, Montreal Trust, National Trust and lots more, some with just a branch or two, trust companies peppered the commercial streets of the country. You could go to one, open a deposit account, buy a GIC, get a mortgage, and often get better deals than at the big banks. These trusts were often controlled by families or, in the case of Canada Trust, the conglomerate Imasco. By 2000 though, they had in large part vanished.

Canada Trust, the convenience store of banking that TD bought in 2000, had similar roots to the bank that purchased it. It was established in 1864 in London in southwestern Ontario. That was nine years after the founding of the Bank of Toronto and just a few years prior to when the Dominion Bank opened for business. Canada Trust was initially called the Huron & Erie Savings and Loan Society, and acted as a co-operative pool for lending to farmers, much like TD was a rural bank hanging its shingle in farm towns. Keith Gray says that TD banked the farmers so they'd buy booze—no coincidence since the president of the Bank of Toronto in 1864 was none other than George Gooderham of the famous distillery family. Bit by bit, over the years Canada Trust gobbled up other financial institutions until 1989, when it finally merged with Canada Permanent, a company whose name you still occasionally see chiselled into the cement of buildings in the financial core of cities. That deal made Canada Trust the country's sixth-largest financial institution and it was good to its owners. The original shares in Huron & Erie went for $50 each. Thirteen years later, in 1873, they were going for $130 apiece. By 1989, an original share would be worth $6,000. Canada Trust itself came into being in 1901 as a subsidiary of Huron & Erie, its largest shareholder.[51]

By the time Ed Clark got to Canada Trust in 1991, it was already legendary in Canadian financial services. It was the un-bank. For some fifteen years, it had been tweaking the prim noses of Canada's banking elite. The by-product of some eighteen mergers since its founding, Canada Trust had pioneered the idea of staying open beyond the now unfathomably inconvenient bankers' hours of ten a.m. to three p.m. Looking back, who could possibly have done any banking in those days? For sure, they were slower times. In the 1960s, merchants even closed up on Wednesday afternoons, a consolation prize for being open on Saturdays. Being open on a Sunday was unthinkable.

Fast-forward fifty years. In the 24/7 world we live in now, many people eat their lunch at their desks, with nary a second to run out and stand in line in a bank. In the early 1970s, Peter Maurice, a young computer-minded buck at Canada Trust who would later become CEO and be involved in bringing Ed Clark into the fold, suggested to an old-timer at the company that Canada Trust should be competing more fiercely with the banks. The senior fellow said simply, "Son, we are farting against thunder."

That would change. Canada Trust saw the work world was shifting. Women were employed outside of the home. Families seemed to need two incomes in an inflationary world. Everyone was busier. Customers needed a bank with hours that suited new lifestyles and a new reality. Out of that thinking came a memorable marketing slogan in 1976: "Eight to Eight, Six Days Straight." In his history of Canada Trust, *The Trust Builders*, Philip Smith chronicles the slow rollout of what was then a revolutionary step for a staid industry. But more than that, the folks at Canada Trust acted like the underdog, and it worked. Chairman and CEO Merv Lahn was the driving force. CT tried everything and no *shtick* was too corny. As Keith Gray would say when he was building TD's Green Line, "Corn sells." Ed Clark's take: "Canada Trust was a marketing department with a bank attached to it."

To get attention, Canada Trust brought in steel bands, organized car give-aways, had celebrity endorsements and even put a small airplane in a branch one day.[52] Among the big names associating themselves with the company was the fists-first hockey star Eddie Shack of the Toronto Maple Leafs.[53] Shack was an exciting player given to breakout rushes up the ice, not to mention spirited brawls. His most prominent feature was perhaps his major league nose. Put it all together and he was a crowd favourite. Being popular and showing you were "down-to-earth" were the name of the Canada Trust game and Shack was on the roster.

So was Canadian actor Lorne Greene. Greene was perhaps the best-known face on American television for a time, famous for his starring role as Ben Cartwright in the hit show *Bonanza*. To Canadians of a certain vintage, he was also known as "the Voice of Doom," a nickname he got after a gig as a radio news announcer for the Canadian Broadcasting Corporation during World War Two. At the time Canada Trust approached him, Greene was producing a nature series, and as a way to capitalize on a growing sense of the public's interest in the environment, the company sponsored the show.[54] It was replete with Greene's bass voice providing the narration.

Its best-known publicity stunt, however, involved none other than country and western droner Johnny Cash. In 1983, Canada Trust was trying to promote its bank machines, newfangled gizmos that would soon make waiting in line for a teller ancient history. A group of marketing types was sitting around brainstorming about names. Philip Smith, in his history of Canada Trust, writes that "Casheteria" was one name they threw out. The groaner "Harvey Wallbanker" was another. At one point, "Johnny Cash" came up.[55]

"That's good. A jailbird drug addict," Peter Maurice remembers reacting caustically. But soon the group agreed there was something to the Johnny Cash idea. As luck would have it, the singer with the signature monotone voice, famous for "Folsom Prison Blues" and "A Boy Named Sue," was performing north of London, Ontario. Someone from Canada Trust went to the show and pitched Cash's manager or agent.[56] Eventually, Cash signed on, and when Canada Trust began rolling out its bank machines, Johnny and his wife, June Carter, would roll into town and give concerts. It was the kind of thing the uptight banks wouldn't dare try.

There was no end to the cheekiness of this company. Next on its list was the burn-your-mortgage contest. The people who ruled Canada Trust ran the place like entrepreneurs. They didn't operate like custodians, as did their counterparts at the top of the big banks, where gobs of money were often made in spite of second-rate service. The big banks had more to lose, and many of their bosses lived in fear of driving their profit machines into the proverbial ditch—and did so on plenty of occasions (like the fiascos of Dome Petroleum, the Latin American debt, and Olympia & York, to name but a few). These big companies and their bosses had the nameplates, the reputations and the prized seats at the table of Canadian high society. They were, however, losing market share and it was driving them crazy. CT was able to reduce the paper flow associated with its operations. Theirs was a simpler business than that of the banks and they used the advantage to the fullest. In a delicious bit of irony, a TD executive phoned Peter Maurice at Canada Trust and said he was doing his annual planning and he needed to know how much market share Canada Trust was going to take from TD that year so he could get his numbers right. On a much later occasion, Maurice recalls, Dick Thomson pointed his finger at him and said, "We were stupid to let you do whatever you did. I want you to know right now whatever you're going to do, we're going to copy."

When Canada Trust began to expand, it did so in "cells."[57] Executives looked at maps, traffic flows. This was a page out of the development of Holiday Inn. Its founder, Kemmons Wilson, would pilot his private plane over the highways that ringed American cities. When he'd fly over a cloverleaf jammed with cars he'd say, "Let's put one right there." Wilson's ways were soon copied by anyone who wanted to survive in the motel business.[58] Canada Trust was the same. It would innovate and the banks would copy.

By the time Ed Clark arrived in 1991, Canada Trust was, in effect, Canada's sixth major bank and was viewed as a catch by many major players in the Canadian business community. Imasco had bought Canada Trust just months after it had been bought by another aggressive company, Genstar Corp., which had a wide range of interests, including cement. Canada Trust had also been in the crosshairs of Manulife, which held almost 30 percent of its shares. Ironically, Genstar had been the training ground for one of Canada's most daring CEOs, Manulife's Dominic D'Alessandro, who went on to purchase John Hancock Financial Services, at the time (2004) the priciest foreign takeover by a Canadian company and certainly the largest investment by a Canadian company in the United States until Ed Clark settled into buying American banks for TD.

On the Friday before the August long weekend in 1999, Secretary of State for International Financial Institutions Jim Peterson got another call from Charlie Baillie about buying Canada Trust. "We're going to do it on the Monday or Tuesday," Baillie told him. Ottawa was ready, unlike when RBC and BMO had blindsided the government the previous year. "We worked hand in glove with Charlie. It was a co-operative effort rather than a take it or leave it," Peterson says.

On August 3, 1999, Baillie announced his play for Canada Trust, and with the capital from Keith Gray's discount brokerage business, he had the financial ammo to do it. The $8 billion deal closed on February 1, 2000, the forty-fifth anniversary of the merger of the Bank of Toronto and the Dominion Bank.

"It was a huge price," says Robin Korthals, adding that a chance like that comes once in a generation. In retrospect, Purdy Crawford thinks the price TD paid was low, given the people it got in the deal. Another executive says that while the jury is still out on whether the bank's recent expansion to the U.S. will be successful, that's not the case when it comes to the Canada Trust purchase: "That was an unbelievable turning point—one of the most successful bank acquisitions in history, a life-changing experience for the bank."

Arguably one of the best assets TD bought was management, most notably Ed Clark. Insiders insist there was no quid pro quo that Clark would get the CEO job at TD when the deal was announced, but it wasn't long before Baillie recognized who his successor would be. In fact, Baillie says Clark told him he thought he should leave, but he and Brian Levitt convinced Clark to stay, saying it would be good for morale. The two others who were in line for Baillie's job would soon leave TD. Bob Kelly was by now vice-chairman and Steve McDonald CEO of TD Waterhouse. (Kelly went on to run Bank of New York Mellon for four years* and McDonald is co-CEO of Global Banking and Markets at Scotiabank.)

Little did the banks know that Ed Clark, a political animal if there ever was

---

* In 2010, Kelly was on the shortlist to be CEO of Bank of America. He stayed at BNY Mellon, but resigned in August 2011 over a disagreement with the board on how to manage the company.

one, was making very regular trips to Ottawa during the year of the merger proposals. Scott Clark, then deputy minister of finance, who had known Ed Clark for years because the latter had hired him, recalls Ed coming to the nation's capital with spreadsheets under his arm outlining what branches the combining banks would have to sell in order to meet competition guidelines. "He's saying, 'I'll buy them.' I think Canada Trust was nice, but I think he felt that the banks looked down on him and he didn't like that part. He wanted to show he could play in the same league as these guys play."

Ed Clark would get that chance very soon. The plan for the integration of TD and Canada Trust would call for a three-year process. Baillie says the approach was to bring the Canada Trust people onside as soon as possible. "Why don't you be the champion of the TD people and I'll be the champion of the Canada Trust people?" Baillie says he suggested to Clark. "Ed calls it plaid, the two colours," a melding of TD's green with Canada Trust's orange.

At the first Monday morning meeting between Baillie and the top executives, the Canada Trust people were edgy, wondering if they'd be welcomed. Someone brought up credit cards, and Baillie said to CT's Bernard Dorval (who is today chairman of TD Insurance), "Bernie, what do you think of that?" The people from Canada Trust knew from that point on they were part of the team.

Many TD top guns, however, quickly came to the conclusion that it was a reverse takeover by Canada Trust and resented Baillie. After all, the bank was adopting CT's banking model, which it (rightly) thought to be better than its own. "Canada Trust priced so that every customer was profitable," Clark told Baillie. At TD, 80 percent of its customers were not profitable for the bank. Canada Trust, which made every customer feel important, was a revelation for Baillie.

Canada Trust "had the best CEO in the country. But he wasn't a 'banker,' whatever that means," cries Mickey Cohen. "He hadn't been a teller when he was young!" Cohen describes a board meeting where Charlie Baillie said, "I think we can do this deal and I think I found my successor." Cohen says, "It was an astonishingly insightful and courageous thing—Charlie coming back and recognizing real cream when he saw it."

Still, Clark caused friction, as he had elsewhere. One former executive, who admires his intelligence and what he's done for TD, says Clark suffers from smartest-kid-in-the-class syndrome. He is said to give off the vibe, "I don't need *your* smarts. I have them in spades. I need people who can execute."

Those who were about to be let go figured it out pretty quickly. A former top executive said there was a call from a colleague saying, "I've just received a visit from two of Ed's guys 'cause Ed sent them to tell me how to do my job." This was a signal you were going to "get toasted."

"I knew it was like putting a lion in a sheep pen when Ed went there," Peter Maurice says. Forty-nine hundred layoffs were announced. As difficult as it was, this was not unusual given the size of the companies that were combining.*

The Canada Trust acquisition, while suppressing the share price of TD for a number of years because of the market's view that it had paid a hefty price tag, catapulted the company into the premier ranks of banking in Canada. It did, however, take time for the investment community to grasp what had happened. As with all Canadian banks, a huge chunk of TD's earning horsepower now lay in its formidable retail banking franchise, a switch from the 55 percent reliance on wholesale banking under Robin Korthals and Dick Thomson. Retail means residential mortgages, personal loans and credit cards. As one top banker likes to say, the mortgage business "pays the overhead. It keeps the lights on." Besides, because of conservative lending policies and practices in Canada, mortgages have been a safe and steady business for the banks. The shift to more of a storefront culture intensified the chatter around Bay Street that it was Canada Trust that had actually taken over TD.

Eight months after the deal closed, Clark made a PowerPoint presentation to investors and financial analysts. On the bottom of page three, the future was laid out. "Our Vision: To be the best retail bank in North America." He stated the same goal in an interview with *Maclean's* in November of 1999.[59] Even though he had a couple years of settling in and getting TD back on track after its telecom and media-related loan losses in 2002, you could guess where Ed Clark was headed: America.

---

* Ultimately, 3,100 positions were lost as a result of the Canada Trust deal. According to the 2000 annual report, TD had 30,636 employees. After it bought Canada Trust, it had 44,798. Now it has approximately 85,000.

# 8

# OBSESSED WITH THE U.S. OF A.

*The Spotty Record of Canadian Business*

Until the spring of 2011, Royal Bank of Canada was in torment. Its U.S. retail bank was a failure and for a time, barely a board meeting went by without an internal debate about whether the bank should sell the division or keep it. Nothing could signal the perils of trying to beat American bankers at their own game more than the highly anticipated announcement that came from RBC in June of 2011: it was getting out. After a decade of trying to be a retail banker in the southeastern United States and spending about $5 billion, Royal was tired of losing money and sold its operations to the U.S. bank PNC Financial for $3.62 billion. Compared with Royal Bank, which is enormously profitable overall, the U.S. retail division was puny, but it had taken on outsized proportions in the eyes of analysts, investors and the media and had become a distraction. Besides, the bank figured it had better places to put its money.

Incursions into the U.S. market are like forbidden fruit for Canada's banks—extremely tempting, but fraught with risk. Canada is easy pickings for the Americans, but it's a limited market of 34 million people. The U.S. is almost ten times the size, has a go-go business attitude and a culture that until the meltdown was comfortable with borrowing lots of money. As well, there are thousands of regional banks that can theoretically be bolted onto a Canadian bank. The experience for Canadians in the U.S., however, has been less than satisfactory. The first major foray, ironically, was by an American who was at the time the CEO of Bank of Montreal. In 1984, Bill Mulholland bought Harris Bankcorp in the Chicago area. Almost three decades later, BMO was still trying to make something of the franchise. Critics say it didn't go into the market in a big enough way, and hasn't been able to compete with the huge U.S. banks.

In December 2010, however, current CEO Bill Downe caught the market by surprise. BMO would pay $4.1 billion to buy a bank called Marshall & Ilsley (M&I) of Milwaukee. Aside from some smaller purchases since Mulholland's day, this was the first significant step BMO had taken to make its U.S. retail banking operation something with enough scale to be meaningful. Upon closing, it would have some 688 branches in the United States. It was sizeable, but its branch count was still only about half the number that TD has in the U.S. As of the end of January 2012, BMO was making $152 million per quarter on its U.S. retail bank, a little over 40 percent of what TD was earning. Bank of Montreal had made the leap, but it hadn't quite made it over to the other side. Downe, in a veiled dig at TD, would argue BMO paid a cheap, post-crisis price for M&I that would allow his bank to achieve 15 percent return on equity within three to five years, almost double TD's ROE in the U.S. at the time. Unlike TD, however, as of 2012, BMO was not revealing the return on equity for its U.S. division. "Good returns within the banking industry should be above 15 percent," Downe said at the time, adding that when BMO acquired another bank, it had a "hurdle rate" that required the investment to ultimately return more than that amount.[60]

Although not a bank deal, Manulife's transformative purchase of John Hancock Financial Services Inc. for $15 billion no doubt left Canada's bank bosses feeling jealous. Curiously, Manulife's boss at the time was a former banker. Dominic D'Alessandro had been CFO of Royal Bank and CEO of the small Quebec-based Laurentian Bank. Although the acquisition was viewed for several years afterward as a company-making purchase, in the years following the financial crisis the Hancock division in the U.S. started to create problems for Manulife. There were even suggestions that it should be sold.

Some forgotten history is that at TD, there were stirrings in the early 1960s about getting involved in retail banking in the United States. In 1963, six years after joining the bank, Dick Thomson became the assistant to the president and chairman, Allen Lambert. It was an extraordinary break for Thomson. He says Lambert gave him complete access to his files. When appropriate, he even let the young assistant sit in on meetings. His instructions to Thomson were vague: Go around the bank and meet people and talk to them. Then, in the spring of 1964, Lambert said to him, "I've had talks with David Rockefeller. We're looking at whether we can work together. I'd like you to be in charge of this."

In the 1960s, the name Rockefeller was like combining the names Bill Gates and Warren Buffett. Measured in today's dollars, the Rockefellers were far richer and their legacy far greater. They were the family behind Exxon. They had created New York's Museum of Modern Art and were huge cultural benefactors to many other institutions. David Rockefeller ran Chase Manhattan Bank, today part of JPMorgan Chase. His brother Nelson was governor of New York, and became vice-president of the United States. Another brother, Winthrop, was governor of Arkansas.

Lambert's instructions to Thomson were to go to New York to observe Chase's operations. After that, someone from Chase would come to Toronto to observe TD. The plan was for each bank to buy 10 percent of the other. In New York, Thomson had access to major executives at Chase. TD had a representative office in NYC, mainly to lend money to brokerages on a short-term basis. (Charlie Baillie would work in that office a few years later.) What Thomson learned was that U.S. banks centred all their loans at their headquarters. TD started doing the same, opening a national accounts office. Without this step, Thomson says, TD wouldn't have started lending to the cable television business. TD eventually became the world's largest lender to the cable industry.

What Thomson and TD soon discovered was that David Rockefeller really wanted to buy TD Bank. The U.S. tycoon was friendly with Prime Minister Lester Pearson, who had been Canada's man at the United Nations and won the Nobel Peace Prize for his work around the Suez Crisis in the 1950s. "David was going to see his buddy Lester Pearson," Thomson says. TD president and chairman Allen Lambert phoned up Walter Gordon, the finance minister, to give him a heads-up, telling Gordon he was going to have a visitor who wanted to buy TD Bank. Rockefeller had a pleasant meeting with Pearson, who finished by saying, "I'd like you to meet Walter Gordon and I'll take you to his office."

When Rockefeller got to the office of Pearson's staunchly nationalist finance minister, Gordon politely informed the richest man in the world, "I want to tell you that I'm introducing a bill in Parliament that restricts your ownership to 10 percent."* Gordon was closing the door to foreign ownership of Canadian banks.†

Some more forgotten history is that before BMO bought Harris in Chicago in 1984, TD and CIBC tried their hands at branch banking in California. Recounts Dick Thomson, "In 1971, TD purchased three retail branches and later added another for a total of four. In 1983, we sold them to a Japanese bank. They were in Los Angeles and San Francisco. We learned that you must start big and not small." He adds that the Americans' propensity for litigation makes it more challenging acquiring businesses there.

Before Ed Clark came along, Charlie Baillie had his eye on U.S. regional banks as potential targets for TD's expansion. At one point, he wanted to buy Northern Trust, a Chicago-based bank that serves wealthy clients. It has paid a dividend uninterrupted since 1896. Had it been purchased in 1978, it would have increased in value by 5,204 percent as of August 31, 2012. Baillie says that back then Northern Trust had corporate customers that were growing faster than TD was. As a result, there was excess demand for loans that would have allowed TD to get into a lot of lending. With TD, Northern would have had the muscle to lend more and Baillie was keen. Thomson, he says, was interested as well.

Ultimately, though, TD shied away because accounting for the purchase would have meant a significant hit to earnings. Also, banks were more expensive than discount brokers. The latter could also give TD synergies it wouldn't get with a bank. In the end, the notion of buying Northern Trust was scrapped. Baillie, however, never lost his taste for a regional bank in the

---

* The ownership restriction for the major, or Schedule 1, banks, would later be raised to 20 percent of voting shares and 30 percent of non-voting. Any holding over 10 percent requires ministerial approval. The intent of the *Bank Act* is that the shares be widely held.

† Politics aside, it would be a cornerstone of Canada's policy toward bank mergers, an issue that would come up more than thirty years later for TD and would lead to the purchase of Canada Trust.

U.S. But Thomson was at the time essentially uncomfortable with the United States when it came to retail banking, preferring to stick to corporate and institutional work outside the country.

"Dick was kind of a build guy, not a buy guy," Mickey Cohen says. "There's no way Dick Thomson was going retail in the United States." Cohen is now one of five directors on TD Ameritrade's board. The feeling was, he says, "The U.S. is death. We're not going over there."

"Banking is a local business," Thomson has said as late as 2009. The market for Canadian banks is here in Canada, he argued. Canada's banks are the pillars of most people's portfolios. They've always paid their dividends. Not one of them trimmed or cut their payout during the financial crisis, and the last time any did so was during the Great Depression. As one senior investment banker says, "They're run for their dividends." Thomson, still a shareholder, would have rather seen a dividend increase than the bank buying this and that in the U.S.

In many ways, it's hard to argue with Dick Thomson. He may have forgotten more about banking than Ed Clark ever knew. He ran TD for an astonishing number of years and was highly successful. In 1967, Allen Lambert made him chief general manager before Thomson had turned thirty-five. In 1972, Lambert, who remained chairman, made Thomson president at thirty-nine. In 1977, he added the CEO title and in 1978 consolidated his power as chairman. Thomson remained CEO until 1997 and chairman until 1998 and stayed on the board into the early years of Ed Clark's tenure. Including his time as chief general manager—essentially the person running the bank—Thomson had a remarkable thirty-year run at the top, a streak unheard of today. "It was my bank," he says proudly.

"Dick was a great banker and Dick was a great businessman," says Cohen. But many who worked with him will say Thomson was a very cautious, conservative banker (not necessarily a bad thing, given what's gone on in banking circles in recent years). By 2011, Thomson's mind would change about southward expansion given Ed Clark's ambitious foray into the U.S.

Charles Baillie looked at the world differently. Baillie had worked for the bank in New York on a couple of occasions. He was more comfortable with the U.S. than his predecessor and saw it as ripe. After all, the Canadian government was unfriendly to in-country mergers. You had to go elsewhere to grow. Elsewhere was the United States.

TD thought it had two aces in its pocket. When Keith Gray bought Waterhouse, it also got a banking licence for the United States. Waterhouse National Bank was TD's first retail bank in the United States. Richard Neiman, the lawyer (and former regulator of banks in the state of New York) who helped Larry Waterhouse set up the bank, says that initially TD didn't know how the bank could be utilized.

After the Canada Trust acquisition, TD had another piece of the U.S. banking puzzle. Neiman says Canada Trust was in possession of a thrift charter. Thrifts are savings associations in the United States that provide financial services with a focus on residential mortgages. The idea, under Charlie Baillie, was to use the charter in an arrangement with Walmart, so that TD could introduce electronic consumer banking into a select number of Walmart stores. But the bank was not able to receive approval from the regulator, the Office of Thrift Supervision (OTS).

"Walmart is such a lightning rod. It's feared by unions. It's feared by community bankers," Neiman says. The regulators were concerned Walmart would control the relationship, while community banks were worried that the retail behemoth would do to banking what Home Depot had done to local hardware stores.

Neiman says he will never forget the day when he filed for Walmart approval on behalf of TD. "It was September 11, 2001. I was in Washington in the Senate Building. We filed it that morning and were going to brief members of the senate banking committee that morning and then we were evacuated." TD's case was lost in the dust of 9/11 and the bank was denied access to Walmart. Ironically, this made the bank think about having its own branches instead of simply electronic or virtual banking.

Ed Clark already knew something about U.S. banking. His learning process began in the late 1980s when Peter Maurice, Canada Trust CEO, was scouting to buy a bank in the United States.

London's old Canada Trust Headquarters—formerly the Huron & Erie—

is a well-preserved Art Deco building completed in 1931. Now in his seventies, and retired since fifty-seven, Maurice is friendly and talkative. He is short, of medium build, and sports a crew cut. One of those who picked Ed Clark as his successor, Maurice was not trained in finance or as a banker. Describing himself as from the "wrong side of the tracks" in London, he studied engineering after a brief stint in geology. His competitive advantage was being a computer geek before there were many computer geeks. Philip Smith writes that Maurice was one of the first executives to have a computer in his office.[61]

By the mid-1980s, Maurice had decided, "I wanted to go into the United States. I'm going to find a place in the U.S. to buy." Sometime around then, Ed Clark came to see him at Canada Trust. Clark was looking for a job. Maurice says he had no idea Clark had been fired by Brian Mulroney's government for his association with the reviled National Energy Program. After about twenty minutes, Maurice, a self-described libertarian, says it dawned on him that he was talking to "Red Ed."

The interview didn't go anywhere, but a couple of years later, while Clark was working as an investment banker at Merrill Lynch Canada, Maurice took him on a trip to the U.S. as an advisor or a sounding board. The two visited all the major Wall Street banks, scouring for a possible acquisition for Canada Trust, a beachhead bank. During that time, he says he and Clark spent a lot of time talking about retail banking and how it was superior to wholesale and better than providing banking services to corporations and institutions.

As for geographical targets, Maurice says he was not comfortable buying in Florida, describing it as a "drug culture" (As of September 1, 2012, TD had 172 branches there). He preferred to find something in northern New York State. Maurice ultimately found his quarry fifty kilometres from Toronto across Lake Ontario in Rochester, the home of Kodak. First Federal Savings was in big trouble, as were many so-called Savings & Loans (S&Ls) in the U.S. in the late 1980s.

He went to see First Federal in 1986, but its executives said the bank was not interested in being acquired. As Keith Gray had demonstrated with Waterhouse, acquisitions can take years to orchestrate. Maurice's response was, "Okay, but if you have to be acquired, we are your least dangerous owner."

It took four years, but eventually First Federal caved and Maurice bought it in 1990. Those were simpler times. Like Keith Gray with Waterhouse, Maurice didn't even use an investment bank to make the purchase, even though he had previously been surveying the territory with Ed Clark. To Maurice, it was a bargain. People told him he was stealing the company.

The problem at the Rochester outfit was as old as the hills in banking: a balance sheet mismatch—borrowing short, lending long. First Federal was handing out thirty-five-year, fixed-rate open mortgages but was funding itself with short-term money. When Paul Volcker, chairman of the Federal Reserve Board, raised interest rates to sky-high levels, the mismatch was gaping and scores of S&Ls suffocated. Suddenly, First Federal found itself having to pay double-digit interest rates on money people loaned to it, but had mortgages that were paying only single digits. The lesson is: If you're going to lend long term, then you need long-term funding—five-year mortgages, five-year funding.

Maurice injected $300 million into the Rochester S&L. Among other things, the purchase of First Federal gave Canada Trust exposure to metro New York with thirty-five branches. So while TD shareholders might think Ed Clark's adventures in the U.S. with Banknorth and Commerce Bank were his first experiences in American banking, they were not. Peter Maurice had introduced him to it and he would learn valuable lessons.

When Clark took over from Maurice as CEO of Canada Trust in 1994, First Federal posed a problem. It wasn't big enough. Brian Levitt, who was CEO of Imasco and Clark's boss, said the corporate structure of Imasco meant that it could not raise capital easily. This would be another issue for First Federal. As the 2008 financial crisis had taught everyone, banks need to be able to raise money in the stock markets quickly. Because of Imasco, Canada Trust was capital constrained, so expanding First Federal of Rochester into something with sufficient scale beyond the roughly 120 branches it had would be tricky. Clark, at the behest of Imasco, sold the U.S. bank in 1995 for $1 billion.

"I learned in the U.S. things move quite fast," Clark says, thinking back on First Federal. The plan was to make more acquisitions in two or three years, but in the States windows of opportunity don't stay open very long. Anyone who's capable climbs through those windows. There were also special risks associated with the mortgage business in the United States (i.e., in some states people can walk away from their mortgages, a lopsided contract that favours the homeowner, not the bank).

The biggest lesson Clark took from First Federal, though, was that in order to succeed in the United States you had to "go big or go home."

\* \* \* \*

John Thompson, Brian Levitt's predecessor as chairman of TD, has a head of white hair, a ruddy complexion and the short but strong build of someone who you could easily imagine in the fullback position on a football field. He has such a healthy dose of self-confidence that he seems to have no need to express it. Instead, what comes across is a kindly, wise air, nothing showy.

Thompson's term as chairman was supposed to wrap up at the end of December 2010 but he stayed around longer than planned, despite suffering from fatigue and asthma. When the bank made its announcement about Brian Levitt succeeding him, Levitt's wife had just been diagnosed as terminally ill. She died in February 2011, shortly after Levitt's term was to begin and not long after Ed Clark was honoured as CEO of the year (Levitt was in attendance that night). Thompson stuck around to help Levitt and the bank through the transition, "for the right reasons," Thompson said.

John Thompson has been on the board of TD Bank since 1988, making for a twenty-five-year run when he departs in 2013. He has a singularly unique take on the modern history and evolution of the bank.

Indeed, he has been a director during the terms of three of TD's CEOs. Dick Thomson, he says, was a superb corporate lender, looking Canada's captains of industry in the eye and deciding whether to lend them money or not. Thomson loved visiting clients and it would not be unusual for him before leaving a meeting to roll up his sleeves and write up a term sheet for a loan. Thomson was also a serial returner of capital to shareholders in the form of better dividends.

Today, under Ed Clark, Thompson says, TD is not sacrificing its payout to shareholders, but it's also looking to grow, not only in underpenetrated parts of Canada like Quebec, but also in the United States. Clark wants to ensure that when diminishing returns set in as the bank maxes out domestic market share, growth will come from somewhere else, ergo the U.S. market.

Charlie Baillie's tenure as CEO, in between Dick Thomson's and Ed Clark's, was someplace in between. Thompson gives Baillie credit for buying Canada Trust, which he calls a brilliant move. Baillie, he says, was outward looking, having worked in New York.

John Thompson was invited to join the board in the late 1980s by Dick Thomson because he ran IBM's operations in Canada. Banks were highly dependent on the IBMs of the world. If, among other things, transaction and record-keeping technology was not up to date, the banks were vulnerable. Thompson also knew his parent company in the U.S., where as vice-chairman he was number two at Big Blue. He worked there for thirteen years in one of the most complex multinationals in the world. "I wasn't afraid of going into the States," he says. "They weren't as good as our branches, right? And so from a retail point of view, I wasn't nervous."

The caveats were twofold. First was picking the right target. Canada's population is highly concentrated in cities. The U.S., however, has thousands of small towns. Every one of those little towns has shopping centres. You can think you're buying a retail bank but it turns out to be commercial and you end up owning a lot of real estate. "You need to be very careful that you know what you're buying and that it fits your strategic advantage," Thompson explains, which in TD's case was retail strength and customer service.

Thompson also says you have to focus on a fairly narrow area at the beginning to build up enough presence so you don't become marginalized. You'll get taken out if you can't become a mainstay player. He says a bigger bank can outmarket you—you can't advertise because you're spread too thin.

Although Clark's stated goal in 1999 and 2000 to become the best retail bank in North America may have sounded to some like he was already focused on taking the bank south of the border, Clark said he wasn't even thinking about expanding into the United States when he first got to the bank. "It wasn't [my goal] at all at the time," he said. He said TD was embroiled in one of the most embarrassing episodes in its modern history. The bank had outsized exposure to the telecommunications and media industries, being the fourth-largest lender to telecom in the world, while it was only the fortieth-largest bank, "risks that were pretty high relative to its balance sheet," Clark says. When he took the helm at the end of 2002, the bank was more focused, he says, on exiting businesses than on entering them. The so-called wholesale and corporate lending side—the part that involved complex, potentially high-risk financial products—had been 55 percent of the bank's income in 1999. "I was gradually dismantling those sources," Clark recalled. (Charlie Baillie would graciously fall on his sword and take a $2.925 billion provision for credit losses in order to clear the decks for Clark to take over. Most of the problem loans recovered and Clark was the beneficiary of this turnaround.) As a result of the risk being downsized, the bank's growth profile was also suddenly downsized. "So then you had to say, 'Well, then, where am I going to grow?'"

Clark and his associates then spent a year going across the United States, meeting with people and looking at various locations. The advantage he had was a capital base that duplicated every three years, thanks to the strength of TD's core Canadian business. The debate about whether the U.S. was a good place to put that burgeoning capital soon landed on the board table. The discussion kicked off with words from chairman of the board John Thompson. With the bank's directors assembled, Thompson turned to Clark and told him that he wasn't being paid to simply preside over a mature company, that he had to have a growth strategy. Clark avows that in the bank's 150-year history, the feeling has always been that standing still as an institution usually means going backwards. The board understood that there was going to be a short-term cost, he says.

Tim Hockey, according to Clark, was the strongest proponent among the executives. Hockey was a Canada Trust alumnus and a fierce Clark loyalist. Among other things, he now runs TD's biggest and most profitable division, the Canadian retail bank TD Canada Trust, and is one of a small group of contenders for Clark's job when he steps down as CEO.

Clark knew that Canadians and Americans do business differently, that you have to be more explicit with people in the U.S. than in Canada. "You can't hint that you'd like people to do something. You have to say: I *absolutely want* you to do this."

At a reception after TD's 2010 purchase of South Financial Group of Greenville, South Carolina, an elderly member of the Greenville business community came up to Clark. Grabbing the CEO's hand, the man said, "At least you're not a Yankee." "They don't like Yankees," Clark says with a laugh. Working in the U.S. you have to adapt your approach and speaking style because there is a "more rapid and ferocious counterattack from your competitors than in Canada," he explains.

\* \* \* \*

Brian Levitt is very tall and a bit stooped, with a scholarly air and a vague resemblance to the actor Alan Arkin, only Levitt still has hair. You could mistake him for a literature professor padding around the halls of academia rather than stewarding the board of one of the world's most successful banks. He displays a wry wit, wisecracking that we had met at "Ed's bar mitzvah," code for Canada's Outstanding CEO of the Year Award dinner honouring Clark in February of 2011 at the Royal Ontario Museum.

An intellectual with business and legal cred, Levitt has known Clark since their early twenties. Both were born in 1947, the second year of the baby boom. They met around the time they finished their undergraduate work at the University of Toronto in the late 1960s. Levitt was looking for a job. Clark was on the interview panel. Thus began a forty-year friendship and on-again off-again business association and partnership in which they worked for each other. After Clark returned to Canada from Harvard, the two worked together at the Anti-Inflation Board. As a lawyer, Levitt says he even helped Clark draft some of the notorious National Energy Program material. Then in the 90s, Levitt was CEO of Imasco, which made him Clark's boss when the latter was running Canada Trust. Simply put, the roots are old and deep.

Now Levitt is Clark's boss again, having taken over as chairman of TD in 2011. The plan is that Levitt will still be there when Clark leaves. By working with Clark for the next few years, the succession, in theory, will be seamless. Levitt's ascension to the chairmanship also completes what many believe to have been a reverse takeover of TD by CT. With Levitt now chairing the board, it certainly looks once and for all as though the guppy—albeit a big guppy—dined on the whale.

The mark of a strong board chair is that he or she has independence from management and can fire the CEO if necessary. While there is not a shred of a suggestion that this would ever be necessary with a superstar like Ed Clark, it's a considerable corporate governance issue, like making sure you have enough lifeboats on an ocean liner. Recognizing this protection measure exists is one of the key reasons Canadian banks stopped the practice of having the CEO also be the chairman of the board. At TD, the dual roles ended when Ed Clark took over as CEO from Charlie Baillie. Levitt says his relationship with Clark is one of mutual trust, built up over decades of working for each other.

He explains, "That means we have completely open communication. There's nothing we can't talk about. There's no reason to think that because John [Thompson] is not here anymore that he's going to start hiding things. I've worked for him. He's worked for me. I sold Canada Trust when he was CEO 'cause that was the right thing to do for Imasco shareholders." Levitt says they are both focused on doing the right thing and if they come to logger-heads, they have been through enough together. "We know that it's not personal," he says. But could Levitt muster the gumption to fire Clark if he had to? "Yeah, I could do that. Because it's not personal," he asserts.

One wonders how their relationship could not have a very large personal component after forty years. It would be the ultimate in compartmentalizing; not everyone buys that this is possible. "You've now got one of Ed's best friends as his boss," says a former executive.

Levitt knows Clark's history as well as anyone does, meaning he understands Clark's experience with banking in the United States prior to his time at TD. As he explains, "What's important for the future story, when the TD decides to go back into the U.S. in retail, two things are important in terms of why it's successful. That it was *the* strategy, not one of many strategies, so it got real focus and CEO oversight." The second thing, he says, is that Clark had studied U.S. retail financial services, so he already had an undergraduate degree. Clark, he says, understood what was different about the American business environment. "We learned all that during the First

Federal period. Ed had been to school on all this stuff so he went back in with his eyes open."

At TD, Clark also had a balance sheet genius on staff—Al Jette, who'd been with him at Canada Trust. Jette knew from his molecular analysis of assets and liabilities when companies had "gaps," a mismatch in their funding and lending—borrowing short term and lending long term. Levitt says Jette learned from First Federal, which did all sorts of things he wouldn't have done.

TD was not about to set up branches in China and India. The U.S. was the bull's-eye in its targeted strategy. Once he made the decision to go back, Clark would be ready. Over the next half dozen years, he would invest some $19 billion U.S. of shareholders' money south of the border, giving him more branches in the United States than in Canada.

# 9

# TD'S BUDDING U.S. EMPIRE

*Buying in New England*

Bill Ryan was not impressed with Ed Clark. Here was Ryan, sitting at the bar in a New York restaurant, getting jerked around by some Canadian who was an hour late for their meeting. The CEO of New England's Banknorth had made a good name for himself in American banking, building up his bank throughout Red Sox Nation. He didn't need this. "We definitely got off to a bad start," Clark admits.

William J. Ryan Sr. was born in 1943 in New York City. After attending Catholic schools, he ended up working for Allstate. In the early eighties, he was drawn to New England to work for a series of banks. In 1989, Ryan was wooed to become president of Peoples Heritage Bank after it got into trouble. He would either be able to turn it around or, as he put it, he would go down in flames with it. In 1990, when his boss retired, Ryan took the top spot and continued to nurse the company back to health. By 1993, Bill Ryan was ready to do what he became famous for—acquisitions. He aggressively went after banks that had found themselves crippled like Peoples Heritage. By 2003, Peoples Heritage morphed into Banknorth after it took the name of a Vermont bank it acquired. It had gone from a bank with $2 billion in assets to one with more than $29 billion.* Now retired, Ryan says he tells his friends, "How overconfident can a young man be?"

---

* Almost $30 billion in assets made Banknorth a medium-sized bank in the U.S. Anything over $100 billion is considered big. As of July 1, 2012, TD Bank Group had $806 billion. JPMorgan Chase had approximately $2 trillion.

As Banknorth got larger, it probably grew as much as it could without taking outsized risks to get into the next logical market, which was New York City and vicinity. After discussions with some of his Wall Street friends, Ryan took their advice and started thinking about a bigger bank that could help offset the risk associated with trying to grow to the next level. He looked around at banks in the U.S., but realized that the American banks all had their "pimples and warts." Canada popped into his mind—common border, common language—so he touched base with his Wall Street contacts again, advising that if any Canadian banks were looking to come south, he might be interested. One day, he got a call from the investment bank Goldman Sachs. The message was, "There's a fellow by the name of Ed Clark who runs Toronto-Dominion Bank, the second-largest bank in Canada. And he'd like to have dinner with you."

"In my eyes, it [selling the bank] was my last big decision," says Ryan, "certainly the biggest decision I would ever make. So I didn't want to rush anything. So I really was trying to find reasons *not* to like Ed Clark."

He found a reason before they met. Clark flew to New York and Ryan drove up from Portland, Maine. The dinner was scheduled for 6:30 p.m. Trying to make a good impression, Ryan got there a bit early. Soon it was seven o'clock and no Ed Clark. Then it was 7:30 and still no Ed Clark. "So here he is an hour late. Now I don't like him and I've never met him before," Ryan says with a laugh.

When Clark showed up, he blamed the weather for his delay. At first, Ryan wasn't buying it. He did not know Ed Clark at all. Ryan's stock in trade was familiarizing himself with bank CEOs in his region, particularly those who might someday want to sell their bank to him. Normally, before getting to the stage of a dinner like this, he would have met a bank CEO several times.

TD's chief financial officer Colleen Johnston, who had started working at the bank in early 2004, just about six months before the acquisition of Banknorth, makes this assessment of Bill Ryan: "He knew the height and weight and grandchildren of every CEO in his footprint. He was very charming, he had a good business relationship with people out there. That's what smart acquirers do. Things don't come at you out of left field. Bill Ryan was fantastic at that."

Ryan doesn't disagree. His approach is reminiscent of Keith Gray's multi-year, dogged pursuit of Larry Waterhouse. Ryan says he would put himself in the shoes of the CEOs he was going to see for the first time, men who didn't know Bill Ryan from Adam.

"First meeting or two, I would never bring up the fact that maybe they should sell to us," Ryan says. Instead, he'd ask about their families and their kids, leaving the bank owners dumbfounded. Most everyone else was throwing money at them, and here was this guy Ryan asking about their families. "A lot of times, we would part company and the CEO would say, 'Thanks Bill, but we're not selling.' And then a year later when they decided [to sell], the first call they'd make would be to me," Ryan recounts.

With this modus operandi, Ryan was a road warrior. He would drive about 80,000 kilometres a year, visiting the owners of smaller banks in New England, sometimes motoring three hours just to have coffee. "I spent a lot of time in my car. Knew the words of every song on the radio."

Although he did not know the height and weight of Ed Clark, he had done some snooping. Via investment banks like the now defunct Lehman Brothers, he'd do reconnaissance of sorts on the Canadian banks. Then he'd phone up some Canadian bankers and play dumb, so he could get a bit more intelligence on who was good north of the border. As Colleen Johnston says, when you're doing stock transactions, the target wants to do as much due diligence on the acquirer as vice versa. But for Ryan, there was a more personal reason than getting a pile of TD stock. "Whoever I sold the bank to, I was still going to live in Maine. That's my home," he says. He didn't want people in his town pointing a finger at him and saying, There goes that dummy Bill Ryan who sold the bank to that big company that came in and tore up the community. "You kind of kiss a lot of frogs to find your prince," Ryan explains.

At the other end, TD was doing its own surveillance on the U.S., with the help of Goldman Sachs. David Livingston was the head of corporate development at TD then. It was his job to research and select targets. Livingston is tall and very slim, with a cropped, beatnik-like grey beard. After spending twenty-nine years at the bank, Livingston spent several years as CEO of the government agency Infrastructure Ontario before becoming chief of staff to Premier Dalton McGuinty in May 2012.

"When it becomes known that you want to do something, there's no end to the number of calls you get," he says with a sigh. "We looked at tons of different possibilities." TD looked at all the banks of any size on the eastern seaboard, Livingston says. That included Key Bank; SunTrust; BB&T; North Fork Bank on Long Island; M&T, based in Buffalo; and even M&I, a Midwest bank recently purchased by Bank of Montreal.

"It wasn't like I woke up one day and said, 'Gee, let's do that one.' You can't do something like that and have not at least satisfied yourself that you've looked at everything," he explains. That means in-depth analysis—footprint, management, balance sheet, income statement, annual reports.

"Not everybody's going to take your call," he says. As for Banknorth, they happened to hit them at a time when they were open to a transaction.

The hurdle with the first out-of-country transaction is that it's usually expensive because there is not a lot of what executives like to call "synergies"— a polite term for cutting. If you're not combining with anything else in the same market, you can't cut costs by eliminating duplication. But TD liked New England, Banknorth had scale, and Bill Ryan, the CEO, had been through a baptism of fire during his early years at the bank (1989–90), seeing the institution through a troubled period. TD also liked that Banknorth was acquisitive. "We weren't there to buy a bank and then do nothing," Livingston says.

Ed Clark, for his part, says TD kept asking, "Who is the best banker in the northeast?" and everyone would cite Bill Ryan. Everyone kept saying Ryan was a straight up guy, a good guy, with great people skills.

TD's biggest fear in buying a bank in the United States was that there would be a huge cultural clash. Equally worrisome was teaming up with someone who didn't appreciate risk the way TD did. The last thing Clark wanted to do was blow it on his first big acquisition in the U.S. What he liked about Ryan was that the American had been through trying times and had come out on the other side.

"He had all the scars of a guy that said, 'I am never going back there again,'" Clark recalls, meaning Ryan had an appreciation of what could go wrong.

Ultimately, TD kept Ryan's management team, as it would do with Meloche Monnex insurance, as well as with subsequent purchases like South Financial Group, Commerce Bank, and most recently Chrysler Financial.

Clark also seemed entranced with the market potential beyond New England. Ryan told Clark that within the Hartford to Philadelphia area there were 40 million people. "So you can almost see his eyes light up," he recalls. Ryan says that when he told TD's board in Toronto that one day "we could probably be a $100 billion company in America," the directors snickered. "I just had the sense they thought I was BSing a little bit."

If anyone who followed Canadian banks had aimed a dart at a map of the United States, one of the last states they might have targeted for a regional bank purchase might well have been Maine. The northernmost state on the U.S. eastern seaboard is known as a vacation spot in the summer, particularly for those looking to escape the suffocating heat of New York City. The coast is rugged, dented with coves full of lobster traps. There's L.L. Bean, known far and wide for its mail order business of outdoorsy clothes and gear. There are potato farms as well, but a lot of Maine is woods, backwoods. The winters are fierce, and there's not a large population. Mainers are classic New Englanders, diehard Red Sox fans. They're sturdy, tough and a bit flinty, in some ways as close to Canadian as one can get.

New England was not widely viewed as a growth area. Clark, however, had other reasons for going there. "First, it's physically close," he says. TD didn't want a footprint that was too far away, like California, where management would wearily say, "I'm too tired, I don't want to go all the way down to see them."

The bank set up a shuttle between Toronto and Portland, Maine. A flight would go out Monday and an executive could go for the day, or stay all week until another flight home on Friday. From Clark's viewpoint, the proximity was strategic. Clark laughs. "We said we probably will understand a Mainer or will understand someone from Boston. I think it was a great bridgehead."

From the woods and coves of Maine, a little bank had grown up, and by 2004 had become, according to *Forbes,* the best-managed bank in the United States. Banknorth had not always been called that. In 1978, its predecessor, Heritage Savings Bank, consisted of just three bank branches in Rockland, Maine. It had a mere $100 million in assets. When bankers talk about their firms' assets, they are generally talking about loans.* They are the bedrock on which a bank makes money. A bank is a factory that makes loans, and the loans are supposed to make the bank money based on the spread, the difference between what the bank pays a customer for deposits and what it gets for lending money.

The guys running Heritage were consolidators. They saw that the U.S. banking system was riddled with pint-size banks, thousands of them. There is a historical reason for this. The U.S. was founded, in part, on the philosophy of decentralized power, and that extended to its banking system, leading to a proliferation of community banks.

Bit by bit, though, this is changing and the overall number of banks in the United States is shrinking. The people running Heritage were part of the group doing the shrinking. They started vacuuming up little banks to make something bigger, an entity with economies of scale that could be more profitable. By 1986, Heritage had been renamed Peoples Heritage and it sold shares to the public. With the money from the share sale, it continued to buy banks in Maine, New Hampshire and Vermont. One of the banks it acquired in Vermont was called Banknorth. It turns out management liked that name, so they named the whole group Banknorth.

Each time they bought a bank, however, it was not without pain for someone. Back-office jobs that were redundant disappeared—accounting, marketing, and human resources. In the early 1990s, it looked like Peoples Heritage was on the ropes, with its stock down to $2 a share as the company dealt with a raft of bad loans. But eventually, the acquisition machine carried on, so much so that the COO, Peter Verrill, who was there when the process started in 1978, told an investor conference in 2005 that the company did not have an organic growth strategy. It was a buyer of banks, plain and simple.

Once Banknorth had almost $30 billion in assets, it was large enough to attract the attention of TD. Banknorth had the foothold, TD had the capital,

---

* Assets of a bank can also include real estate, investments in other entities, or securities such as bonds. Loans, however, are the main assets, and the key question is whether they are good or bad loans. Banks are often highly levered, or indebted themselves, which amplifies the impact of bad loans.

Verrill says. Between the two, they could expand in the U.S., particularly into faster-growing areas. TD would acquire 51 percent of Banknorth, a cautious way to start. Banknorth shares would still trade on the U.S. stock market and Banknorth would use those shares as currency to acquire more banks in New England and beyond. When it came to negotiations, Banknorth's COO Peter Verrill and TD's head of corporate development, David Livingston, did the heavy lifting.

"They would kind of do the grunt work . . . get within a range," Bill Ryan recalls. Then, at the end of the day, he says, "I told Ed what our number was," which was in the same ballpark as TD's.

As usual, negotiations took place secretly. Verrill recalls being in Toronto on the Canada Day weekend of 2004. Toronto had emptied out for the first long weekend of the summer. "I can remember the holiday I went up to see David, it was your independence day," he says. Livingston remembers that there was no traffic.

The complicating factor was that TD was buying only 51 percent. Initially, according to Ryan, Clark was interested in less than that but Ryan argued, "There will be a fight over who's really running the place." With just 51 percent, there was also an out, if necessary, and it wouldn't leave quite as much egg on TD's face. "We could pull out if we had to. But that wasn't really our main thought," says John Thompson.

There was no specific understanding at that point that TD would ultimately take full ownership, as it did a couple of years later, although it was widely expected to do so unless the acquisition was a complete disaster. In that worst-case scenario, with just 51 percent TD hadn't tied up too much capital. Some would say that, with a price tag of $5.1 billion, TD had overpaid, as usual. Still, it was a beachhead.

Acquisitions sound easy. CEOs get a big splash in the newspaper. They get to be big shots, making deals in fine restaurants, toasting with fine wine. But most big acquisitions end in failure. AOL combining with Time Warner is the classic example, at the time the richest deal ever, at least on paper. It was the fat belly of the Internet craze, about to burst.

According to Verrill, the acquisition is just the beginning. Then you have to make it work. Each company has a different culture. Each has different processes. They can have different computer systems. Six to eight months is the quickest possible timeframe to weld one bank to another. For bigger deals, it may take a year to eighteen months to get everyone on the same operating system, or platform. Banknorth's rule of thumb was that whatever company it bought, it would immediately migrate everything to its own platform. Our show, our platform was the Banknorth way. In Verrill's view, the culture would become unified a lot faster that way. On this point, he took issue with TD's approach when it bought Banknorth. Perhaps they were being polite Canadians, but Verrill was mystified why TD kept the Banknorth name, branding the banks as TD Banknorth.

"I said, 'Don't do that! Call this TD Bank. Get over this culture shock.' Because when we used to acquire banks we did that, and it hurt at first—but I tell you, it was less painful than maintaining a separate name, a separate culture and then having to do it four or five years later. To me that was just a more honest way to do it, 'cause that's what eventually you were going to do."

Bill Ryan says he and Ed Clark were the ones responsible for hanging onto the name TD Banknorth. "If you immediately changed the name to a Canadian company that nobody knows much about, you're risking the wrath of the customers saying, 'Who are they? We don't know. They're foreigners. Oh, my God, this is terrible,'" Ryan recalls. A misguided soul at TD even wanted to change Boston Garden to "Toronto-Dominion Garden." The suggestion was overruled. It's called TD Garden now.

Ryan found working for Clark relatively easy, claiming that, a year or two away from retirement, he didn't have anything to prove. Nonetheless, he was a bit surprised about how involved Clark wanted to be. "He's a strong manager. He likes to get into things on a daily basis, so we had a lot of calls." Was Clark micromanaging? "Oh, sure," says Ryan without hesitation. "I'd get off the phone and say, 'Jesus, why does this guy want to get involved to the Nth degree in all of those things?'"

David Livingston can't say enough good things about Ed Clark, particularly as a negotiator. "He always knows what the best deal is and he constantly pushes on every term because that's what he gets paid for. I can't imagine that he's ever missed anything. Everything gets negotiated, you don't just blow by any terms. You want the best. You know the best. Ed's not big on tradeoffs. Unless you've walked away once, you don't know that you've gone too far. I consider him a mentor." Livingston says Clark is incredibly smart, engaging, quick on his feet and a nice guy. "And he uses all of those things."

Once TD controlled Banknorth, Ryan said to Clark, "Ed, now you kind of own New England." Did he want to make moves into New York and New Jersey? The answer was yes, so Ryan was back in his Caddy making courtesy calls. Two banks came up for sale—first Hudson United and then Interchange. In both cases, the executives wanted to retire and move to Florida.

With Hudson United, the deposits per branch were about double what competitors had. But Ryan said its costs were astronomical because they were "kind of running individual franchises; they were kind of mediocre." He and the TD brass thought they could go in there and convert them within ninety days. Interchange, on the other hand, came to him. When the CEO, who was looking to retire, saw the Hudson United deal, he rang Ryan. "I'm sixty-eight years old," the man said, "and it's time." Interchange was small—only $1.6 billion in assets—but it was right next door to Hudson.

The Hudson United purchase, however, raised eyebrows. One of the best-known banking attorneys in the United States said privately that he had no idea why TD wanted Hudson United. Others have said it was the worst piece of banking garbage in America. Another well-known New York–based bank had passed on the deal. Peter Verrill admits Hudson was not without its problems. The industry knew about the bank's loan problems, its high leverage and involvement in mortgage-backed securities, which would become the lepers of the financial world just a few years later. People were saying, "Do Banknorth and TD know what they're doing?" The company was viewed as being strong at sales and acquisitions, but not quite as astute on the slog required to run a bank. In the end, the price was $1.9 billion USD ($2.2 billion CDN), a lot of money to mere mortals, but not enough to do any real damage to the Canadian acquirer.

For Banknorth and TD, though, Hudson United was worth something strategically. As Verrill said in a presentation to investors and analysts in

September 2005, it was a way to break out of New England. There were not many more acquisitions left for Banknorth to make on its home turf. Hudson United filled out Connecticut, particularly in the highly populated wealthy areas that are bedroom communities for New York financial types. It also took Banknorth into suburban New York, New Jersey and the Philadelphia area. The latter would prove to be critical a few years down the line, with the purchase of Commerce Bank. It was like building a railroad, one piece of track at a time. Instead of going from the Atlantic to the Pacific, the bank was going from Maine down the whole eastern seaboard to the Sunshine State. With Hudson United folded into Banknorth, TD now had 590 branches in eight states.

As for what's achievable for TD long term in the U.S, Ryan is loath to guess, but after talking about more than 1,300 branches the bank already has in America, he hardly misses a beat. "I can't imagine that you can't double that over the next several years," he says. His caveat is that no one knows the impact of technology. He says we don't know how many more people will use ATMs, or smartphones and tablets, forgoing branches. Retired but still speaking as though he is part of the bank, Ryan says, "I can certainly see us doubling our customer base," which is different from simply adding branches.

Soon enough, TD would do both.

# 10

# AVOIDING SUBPRIME

*Ed Clark Stays Out of Trouble*

The last year of Charlie Baillie's reign at TD was not pleasant. The dotcom mania that helped fuel the IPO of TD Waterhouse had a dark side. The stock index most heavily weighted with technology companies, the NASDAQ in the United States, had peaked in March of 2000 at more than 5,000 points. Companies like the now defunct Nortel Networks had been flying close to the sun. Just two months before, perhaps indicating the end was near, AOL and Time Warner announced their ill-fated merger, a combination of old and new media. "Convergence" is what they called it.

From there, it was a one-way trip downward for almost all tech companies. Apple's astonishing journey into orbit notwithstanding, the NASDAQ has not returned to those levels since 2000. The collapse in technology stocks was exacerbated by the recession that followed the terrorist attacks of September 11, 2001. It was grim, and TD's heavy lending to both the telecom and media sectors made 2002 a very rough year indeed.

Baillie swallowed hard and took almost $3 billion in provisions for credit losses. The result was TD's first loss in the modern history of the bank, since the merger of 1955. It was an embarrassment and he said so at the time. Nine years later, Baillie would simply say it was "really tough" and that Ed Clark encouraged him to take the write-offs. Clark's view, according to Baillie, was that investors and analysts had already priced in the loss so it was as though the bank was getting a free write-off. Perhaps, but Baillie was of the mind that most of the bad loans would recover and now says that the bank should have stuck with them. (He was right: all of the loans except for one eventually recovered.) He says Scotiabank had a similar portfolio and did not take write-downs. Baillie, however, was leaving his post and, being a devoted reader of political history, he did the honourable thing, clearing the decks for the new man. The bad loans have now been largely forgotten in the context of all the good he did for the bank, like buying Canada Trust, but they are most surely an ugly blemish on Baillie's otherwise sterling record.

When Ed Clark took over as CEO in December 2002, he began his own deck-clearing process. Building the best bank in North America and going after the U.S. retail market may have been his ultimate goal, but he wanted to sell some things first. His head of corporate development, David Livingston, held a yard sale of discount brokerages that Keith Gray had bought outside of North America. After the Waterhouse purchase, Gray, with Baillie's blessing, had been trying to build TD's online brokerage business in places like Australia, the U.K. and Hong Kong. In fact, in Gray's last presentation to the board before he retired, he laid out a plan to expand throughout Europe and Asia, including Taiwan, Singapore and India. Clark wasn't interested. He thought the business was too fragmented and assigned Livingston the job of unloading the scattered operations.

What Clark was also not interested in was highly engineered financial products. After the dotcom implosion and the recession of 2001–02, Americans were fed up with the stock market. They were turning to hard assets like real estate. Encouragement came from the U.S. Federal Reserve, which had lowered its key interest rate drastically in order to juice up the economy. Between sugar-coated interest rates and the American tradition of being able to deduct your mortgage interest from your taxes, people loaded up on debt. Banks and other operators were handing out mortgages like leaflets. Even if you had no income and no assets, you could get a mortgage. If you had no documents you could get a mortgage. Just show up with a pulse, and sign on the dotted line. These were known as subprime mortgages, loans for people who under normal circumstances should not get loans.

The housing market boomed and banks boomed right along with it. Something else that boomed was financial engineering. So-called mortgage-backed securities had been around for a while. Constructing them involved putting many mortgages of differing risk together to make a bond that was then sold off to investors. In theory, the mortgage holders could be relied upon to make their monthly payments and all those payments put together would form the stream of cash paid out to the bond holder.

But the highly incentivized wizards of Wall Street always come up with a new twist. They started piling up these mortgage bonds into supersized bonds. They could then sell those to even bigger investors, mainly banks around the world. Investors would buy them because the firms that assign credit ratings to bonds, agencies like Moody's and Standard & Poor's, had given the issuers of the bonds top marks in return for fees. It was a glaring conflict of interest that had been overlooked for years. Sure, some mortgages would go bad, the rationale went, but there would be enough in those pools that the bad ones wouldn't spoil the bunch. That, of course, turned out to be terribly wrong. As Steve Forbes, chairman of Forbes Media, said in a speech in New York in the fall of 2009, it's like the *E. coli* spinach scare. Most of the spinach is okay, but are you going to take a chance and eat it while there's a heightened risk of contamination?

Beyond the über-bonds, which were known as collateralized debt obligations (CDOs), there were even more arcane products. There were synthetic CDOs backed by derivatives, not even by real securities.* There were CDOs backed by other CDOs, known as CDOs squared, all devised by math whizzes with computer models.[62] As the world's investors became more exposed to real estate between 2002 and 2007, these so-called structured products got manufactured at a faster and faster pace, shoved out the door by investment banks to clients like pension funds and banks around the world.

---

* A derivative is a financial product taken from an underlying security. In the case of mortgage-backed securities, there are products called credit default swaps, insurance contracts on the likelihood the issuer of the debt will default. One party pays a premium to the other for insurance and if there's a default, the other side has to pay up. Those bets were also packaged up and sold.

The other gross assumption was that housing prices would continue to rise. As Warren Buffett has said, "You only learn who has been swimming naked when the tide goes out."[63] When housing prices started to fall in late 2006 and early 2007, the tide was beginning to recede. Many of those who'd taken out mortgages in the United States had been enticed by so-called teaser rates. These were the equivalent of the drug pusher telling the junkie-to-be that the first hit is free. Eventually teaser rates gave way to real, much higher rates. In many cases, people had to renew at higher rates at the same time as their home prices were beginning to fall. Many had also used their homes as credit cards. Lofty house prices had allowed them to take out home equity loans based on the value of their real estate. As housing prices sank, these borrowers had less equity in their homes. Eventually, for many, there would be negative equity, meaning the house was worth less than the mortgage on it.

Mortgage bonds and the products that were created from them were suddenly viewed as infected. No one knew for sure what was in these "structured products." Banks, which lend money to each other constantly to fund each other's various operations, suddenly didn't trust who they were lending to because loans were often backstopped by these mortgage-backed securities. In July 2007, word got out that this was happening and stock markets started to crater. It was the beginning of a credit crunch that would lead to the collapse of banks in 2008 and 2009. Governments would have to bail out financial institutions worldwide and spend trillions to stimulate their economies. It was a race to avoid a second Great Depression. What we got instead was a Great Recession. Throughout 2011, the United States still struggled to create jobs, with unemployment stubbornly above 9 percent. The global economy would soon be experiencing the second round of the crisis, with sovereign debt calamities in countries like Greece, Ireland, Spain, Portugal, Italy and even the United States, where the national debt load has become too high and the possibility of default looms.* The financial sector had become too smart

---

* In the case of the United States, political squabbling over whether to raise the country's so-called debt ceiling pushed that country to the brink of a technical default on its debt in the summer of 2011. Although the U.S. has severe long-term debt issues, its short- and medium-term issues were not anywhere near as severe as those of Greece, Ireland, Italy or other peripheral countries in the Euro Zone.

by half, devising engineered products with much of the sales tied to perverse bonus and compensation incentives.

It's said the mark of a truly smart person is not being afraid to say he or she doesn't understand something. That's what Ed Clark said about subprime mortgage-related structured products in 2005. This was Clark's epiphany and perhaps his most important decision as CEO. It was his view that these products were far too complicated for anyone to understand, and if he didn't understand them, TD was clearing out any exposure and not buying them. He no doubt resisted pressure from within saying he was being too conservative. But by being a prudent banker and distancing himself from subprime-related structured products, Clark would position TD as one of the strongest banks on the planet.

Purdy Crawford, Clark's old boss at Canada Trust, pinpoints Clark's best quality: "He's smart as hell, of course. I think it's judgment—plus getting good people around him."

Crawford says he knows a lot of people tried to talk Clark into buying what turned out to be toxic asset-backed commercial paper. Third-party asset-backed commercial paper, or ABCP, as it became known, was Canada's own brush with subprime chaos. Commercial paper is a financial product that allows issuers to borrow money and lenders to park money for a set number of days—for periods less than a year. Government-issue treasury bills provide a similar function, but are backed by governments. Commercial paper is not. It's backed by creditworthy corporations that need to borrow. In the case of ABCP, assets such as consumer loans and credit card receivables were pooled together like mortgages to create a stream of cash that could be paid out to an investor. The paper was also backed by synthetic assets, or derivatives, making it highly complex. Most importantly, assets and liabilities were not properly matched.[64] Once again, however, a credit rating agency, this time Canada's DBRS, gave the ABCP a top rating.†

Unfortunately for those in Canada who had invested $32 billion in ABCP, the market for it froze up along with the credit crunch. Commercial paper

---

† The controversy around many rating agencies is that they have been conflicted. Issuers of bonds pay them for ratings. Defending themselves, the agencies say they are only giving an opinion. Still, many large investors will not buy or are prevented from buying a security unless it has a top rating.

that matured could not be rolled over into a new investment. Holders were stuck and couldn't get their money. Ironically, it was Purdy Crawford who was recruited, in his late seventies, to help solve the ABCP crisis and restructure the market, a daunting task.

Clark would be forced to swallow some medicine, even though he and the bank were not sick. The Bank of Canada, involved in finding a solution to the ABCP crisis, asked TD to participate to show solidarity among all the Canadian banks. Clark balked, but ultimately played along because the country's central bank had requested his participation for the good of the financial system.

It's possible Ed Clark is being disingenuous about structured products. He is probably one of the few people actually smart enough to understand them. What is more probable is that he saw the heightened risk profile they presented, isolated mishaps came to his attention, or maybe he thought there wouldn't be enough people in his organization who could properly understand them. Whatever the truth is, he avoided them. He does, however, say that he wishes he'd got out of them even sooner. "Oh, my God, that was close!" he exclaims, like someone who manages to get the car safely in the garage after narrowly avoiding a bad crash.

These complex products would have been under the umbrella of TD's wholesale or investment banking division. Clark proudly said in the summer of 2010 that when he arrived at TD, the bank's earnings were 55 percent wholesale. Nothing gave him more pleasure, it seemed, than the fact that this was no longer the case. By the end of 2010, just 10 percent of the earnings were from wholesale. Give me simplicity, Clark was saying. Give me old-fashioned retail-branch banking that's easy to understand.

That's not to say the crisis was easy for Clark. He claims he was still up at two in the morning writing notes to himself or rising at five a.m. to check what had happened overnight.* As well, during the crisis, the bank went to the equity and bond markets to bulk up its capital cushion when it could.

Astonishingly, TD still made $3.8 billion profit during 2008, the worst year of the meltdown. This was at a time when foreign banks were either failing or

---

* These days, Clark says that before going to sleep, he lies in bed with his iPad reading the *Economist,* the *Financial Times* and other publications to prepare for the next morning.

requiring oxygen in the form of capital injections from governments. To be fair, of the big five Canadian banks, all except one were profitable throughout the crisis of 2008–09. CIBC had a loss in 2008, but was back in the black in 2009. The other four made combined profits of more than $13 billion in 2008, and the five together earned $16 billion in 2009, with Royal Bank leading the pack in both years. In addition to having stable national deposit bases for funding and a legal shield protecting them from foreign takeovers, Canadian banks have been the beneficiaries of other factors. They are less interconnected and complex than their U.S. counterparts. They have been more rigorously supervised and have been required to hold more (and higher quality) capital than banks elsewhere. The latter factor has made them more resilient. Canadian banks also typically hold loans (a large portion of which are residential mortgages) to maturity on their balance sheets, providing an incentive to lend prudently.[65] Conversely, U.S. banks packaged up their mortgages into structured credit products and sold them to investors. Arguably, by offloading those loans they were less concerned about their performance. Still steady on its feet, when opportunity presented itself, even with an economic system in peril, TD was ready to take advantage and buy distressed assets. There would be plenty, in particular one in the U.S. that would be entirely unexpected and perhaps as transformational as the Canada Trust acquisition had been for TD in Canada.

# THE $8.5 BILLION WOUNDED DUCK

## *How TD Landed in Manhattan*

Within two kilometres of Vernon Hill's New Jersey mansion and in two directions, there are TD Bank branches. It can only be galling to Hill, the man who conceived of and built those bank branches, and to his wife, Shirley, the interior decorator who designed them, sparing no expense.

"I did all the site acquisitions. So I know every site, I know all the stories, I know how we bought it, when we bought it, why we bought it," Hill says defiantly.

Perhaps as an emotional defence against one of the greatest hurts of his life, Hill also sees the branches as a reminder of TD's "top of the market" purchase of his beloved Commerce Bancorp, Inc. (operating as Commerce Bank, NA) in October 2007. It was an acquisition that suddenly put TD on the U.S. map for real, in particular in Manhattan. As owner of 5 percent of the shares, Hill walked away with $400 million, but only after a painful resignation from the bank he'd founded and built.

"They paid us $8.5 billion. It gives me the chance to do it all over again and better," says Hill, still nursing the wound years later.

The $400 million is only part of a fortune that includes being a partner in thirty-three Burger Kings, a developer of some 2,000 real estate sites that house the likes of CVS drugstores and McDonald's, and a re-entry into banking via Metro Bank (he plans to build 200 branches in England—a country he says has not had a new bank since 1830). A dog lover, Hill is also now chairman of a burgeoning pet insurance business called Petplan.

The community of Moorestown, New Jersey, is about half an hour from the bustle, grit and grime of Philadelphia. Founded by Quakers in 1682, it's what Norman Rockwell might have had in mind when he thought of a town—slow-moving rural America. Moorestown's main street, coincidentally called Main Street, has tall trees giving shade to the huge, rambling wood-frame houses typical of New England and the mid-Atlantic states. It must also be one of the few Main Streets on which a billionaire lives in one of the largest and most expensive homes in the United States. There are few in Canada to match it.

Vernon Hill's Villa Collina is hidden from view. A long laneway leads to a huge set of black wrought iron gates, the kind you'd find at a palace. Once through the gates, there are a few hundred metres of a winding lane through trees before the home appears. It is long and grey, with multiple wings a few stories high. On either side of the driveway are reflecting pools, eight in all, each lower than the other with gentle waterfalls cascading from one to the next. White lion statues overlook the property and there is a large fountain in front of the house.

The design of the home bears the influence of sixteenth-century Italian architect Andrea Palladio, whose work was also the inspiration for Thomas Jefferson's Monticello in Virginia. In the foyer, there is a soaring ceiling with an enormous chandelier made of Murano glass. An eggshell-white marble staircase curves upward. It was made in Venice and shipped over during the twenty-three months it took to build the mansion, which sits on eighteen hectares (44 acres).

At the back, there is a modest vineyard that produced sixty-six cases of wine in one season. From the terrace, there is a vista of magnificent gardens. In the distance, someone is working on the plants. Hill brushes off the question about the size of the home. *Fortune* magazine puts it at 4,700 square metres (50,000 sq. ft.).[66] Inside, there is a solarium they call "Limonia" that can host 150 people for dinner.

The house is spectacular and beautiful thanks to the design supervision of Shirley. Everything appears brand new. While getting drinks in the kitchen, Hill confesses he doesn't know how to use the coffee machine and the housekeeper is not there to help.

Hill wears glasses and has a stutter. It doesn't take him long to get riled. "TD didn't build shit" sums up his take on the Canadian bank. He wears his hurt on his sleeve. How could he not? The entrepreneur who built the company that could very well define TD's level of success in the United States is surrounded by the Barbarians from Toronto who came down and plundered what he built site by site, beginning with the nine-person branch where he started out in 1973 in his late twenties. When it comes to retail banking, Hill makes Ed Clark look like a rank amateur. Hill built it. Clark bought it.

To Hill, banking and Burger Kings may as well be the same business. It's all retail, and it's all about customer service. As he said in a Harvard Business School case study, Commerce Bank was a cult, and he wanted "whack jobs" working for him, people who did nutty things to provide show-stopping customer service.[67] Dogs were welcome in Hill's banks, any *shtick* to get you in the door. Welcome to what he calls "retail-tainment"—a term TD has now taken for its own.

You can see Hill's masterworks very close to his home. The TD branch in Moorestown, next to McChesney's Funeral Home and across from the First Baptist Church, sits on a large, manicured plot of land. There are at least twenty parking spots for customers. There are four lanes, no fewer, sitting next to the building where you can cruise through in your car to do your banking. It's not unusual for U.S. banks to have drive-thrus, but four is noteworthy. Out front, there are park benches. Inside, there are more staffers than customers—three tellers at the ready and no rope lineup like at airport security. Off to the side in a cubicle-free area are other bank employees ready to help you with a loan. In the corner sits a "Penny Arcade," one of the $40,000 coin-counting machines that made Commerce famous and make Hill beam with pride. He sneers at TD's new policy of charging non-customers for coin counting.

"The whole point of the machine is to get customers who don't bank with you to come in and use the machine and switch. They got it completely reversed," he says, shaking his head. Entrepreneurs like him, he says, are the only people who wouldn't balk at spending millions on these coin-counting machines. Banks, he says, only understand cost cutting, not investing. "Name me any bank committee in the world that would say, go spend $4 million to make more friends."

It's no surprise that Ed Clark disagrees with Hill. TD's CEO says his U.S. staff like the idea of giving the bank's customers a deal on coin rolling.

Anyone else can get the same deal if they open an account, he says. He cites an example of a man worth $100 million who came in and rolled his coins while Clark was there. The multimillionaire was not a TD customer but was entranced with the Penny Arcade. "He thought that was the biggest cat's ass he'd ever seen," Clark recounts with relish, saying the man then opened an account, putting paid to Hill's argument.

This branch in Moorestown makes the competing PNC branch across the street look shabby. A plain brick house, the competitor has no landscaping and does not have a welcoming vibe. There are only four customer-parking spots, each one sternly warning parkers that there's a thirty-minute maximum. There is another parking spot reserved for the owner of the property. To be fair, down the road is a branch of Susquehanna Bank. Its landscaping and parking rival TD's, but its hours are shorter: TD is open seven days, Susquehanna six, and TD is open longer each day.

At the lowest end of the aesthetic spectrum in Moorestown is the bank owned by Wells Fargo. It looks like a place where you'd pick up an urn full of ashes. Etched below the roof is the name Burlington County Trust Company. Wells Fargo has stuck up a cheap, modern sign right above the door, with no respect for the historical nature of the building. It looks about as welcoming as a Brink's truck.

Vernon Hill was raised in suburban Washington, DC, the oldest of six kids. His father worked in a bank and young Vernon worked there as a kid after school. His dad convinced him he should study business at Wharton, so he became an undergraduate in 1963, working at two banks while studying. By nineteen he was senior lending officer. The joke was that if you wanted a loan, you had to wait till noon when Vernon got out of school.

After four years at Wharton, Hill found himself in the real estate development business and his first client was McDonald's. His familiarity with fast food would greatly influence how he thinks banks should operate. The service should be able to be replicated with predictable results, but most important, every customer has value. He was twenty-seven when he started Commerce Bank. On July 29, 1973, the first office opened with nine employees. To get started, he had raised $1.5 million.

"In America, we have a culture of starting new banks, and I literally woke up one morning and said, 'Let's go start a new bank,'" Hill reminisces. He is also quick to repeat what he's told others about that initial capital infusion. If you'd held onto your investment, you would have made 470 times your money. "That happens to be 47,000 percent."

Like flipping burgers, he approached banking with an elegant simplicity. He came up with the neat analysis that anyone can make loans, but only banks can take deposits. So he built a deposit machine. "We were then, and to a large extent are now, the outliers, the low-rate payer." His view was that people will sacrifice a few basis points of interest if they are treated well. He has the audacity to liken his old Commerce to being the Apple of banking. "Apple products cost more, not less, but who cares?"

By focusing on deposit taking, coin-counting machines and dog biscuits, Commerce had expanded to twenty-seven branches by 1991, all of them built from scratch. "Customers conclude that if you love my dog, you love me too," he says. "I don't believe great retailers ever have been built by acquisitions," he adds, in a direct dig at TD.

In 1991–92, when other banks faced credit problems, Hill kept building out his branch network. "So while everybody else was retrenching, we were going crazy building branches." The store count grew 18 to 20 percent per year, ultimately getting to 444 branches by October 2007, with close to $50 billion in assets, "all on the New York effect." Commerce grew the most in the metro New York area, a move that would turn Hill's property into a jackpot for TD, allowing the Canadian bank to penetrate one of the richest markets in the world faster than it ever dreamed.

"Very similar to going to Mars," Hill says about entering New York City, casting his mind back to just before 9/11 when Commerce was about to open its first branch in Manhattan. "How can this little bank from New Jersey compete against Chase?" was the talk in New York banking circles. The chatter was that New Yorkers didn't give a damn about service.

Before moving into New York, Hill was spending $3 million to build each branch, including the price of the land. In the Big Apple, he was spending $3 million, but he also had to pay New York City rents. Still, as an old hand at real estate deals, he went for location. He had prime spots up and down Broadway, not to mention other choice corners all over town. "The best site is always worth the money," he says, adding that Commerce always took the best corner, always went for high ceilings.

On being told that TD is looking to take at least 30 percent out of the cost of each new branch, Hill goes into rant mode. "They're accountants by nature and they love to count beans. I'm not a bean counter, I'm a business builder," he says, adding that TD's growth will slow over time. "TD's culture is to count, measure and quantify everything."

"Building branches on a large scale in a retail network is not a talent that banks have. Have they destroyed our model? No, they haven't totally destroyed our model. But have they made it more bank-like? Absolutely." He complains that banks like TD are about lots of meetings, lots of policy, lots of procedure, with compliance officers and auditors running the place. "Entrepreneurs don't care about all that stuff. Bureaucrats do."

One wonders whether Hill wishes he'd been more interested in bureaucratic matters. TD was able to buy the bank he built because Hill attracted the attention of U.S. banking regulators in 2006. He was never found to have done anything illegal, but the regulatory concerns were twofold. Commerce's deposits kept growing, but its loan department never kept up. That meant the bank had to rely on bond investments to make a return on its mountain of deposits. This became a problem when the so-called yield curve became inverted. Normally, short-term money yields a lower interest rate than long-term money. When the yield curve is inverted, short-term rates are higher than long-term rates. It's often a warning that a recession is on the way, because people perceive short-term risk to be high and want to be compensated for it. Although Commerce could get more short-term return on its bonds than before, the flip in the yield curve meant it had to rely on those very short-term returns, something that made regulators edgy. As well, by the end of 2007, Commerce had $46 billion in deposits but had only lent out $17.6 billion, so it wasn't making much money from lending. Its return on equity was a meagre 4.8 percent. It had been dropping steadily from more than 18 percent in 2003.[68]

In addition, one of the oversight bodies, the Office of the Comptroller of the Currency (OCC), became concerned about alleged inappropriate related-party transactions between various business interests of Hill's and the bank, such as leases for land and bank premises.[69] As well, Commerce Bancorp Inc.'s 2007 annual report describes a golf club whose principal owner was Hill receiving payments from the bank in the hundreds of thousands of dollars per year between 2005 and 2007. There were also regulatory concerns about transactions between the bank and family members, in particular Hill's wife, Shirley, who was the interior decorator for the branches. Her company, according to the filing with the SEC, received $24.5 million in payments between 2005 and 2007. Hill maintains that any related-party transactions had the approval of Commerce's board of directors.

"They started on a witch hunt," Hill says of the regulators. "Some would say I became the next target in America," hinting that perhaps some powerful New York banking interests wanted him out of the business. If true, those same New York bankers were not successful in knocking out a threat. They now have TD as a competitor instead.

Hill says the regulators were keeping him on a leash. "Their weapon was not giving us new branch approvals, which the regulators in America use as a way to extort from the banks, not just us in particular; it's one of their infamous extortion weapons." Leaving Commerce in 2007 was his decision, he says. "It wasn't worth the fight any longer. It was better for the shareholders, better for the bank, and better for me, and it certainly turned out to be much better the way the world went." No charges were ever brought against him.

"Welcome to America," he says with a laugh, befuddled by the process that resulted in the end of his career with the bank he founded. Hill did, however, sign a consent order allowing regulators to monitor related-party transactions at any banks with which he is associated in the future.[70] "If I do related-party transactions with banks, it has to be approved by the boards, which it always had been at Commerce. It was a complete surrender by the OCC," he says.*

---

\* On November 17, 2008, more than a year after TD announced it was buying Commerce Bank and more than seven months after the deal closed, the Office of the Comptroller of the Currency, a division of the U.S. Treasury, announced that it had "entered into a consent cease and desist order with Vernon I. Hill, II,

With Hill gone from Commerce after regulatory actions in connection with the bank on June 28, 2007, the bank was in flux and the board and management were advised to find a buyer with deep pockets. Bharat Masrani, Ed Clark's top executive in the United States, who was running Banknorth out of Portland, Maine, phoned Bob Falese, who was the CEO at Commerce after Vernon Hill left: "Hey Bob, I don't know you. Here's my name, here's my number, and if you want a solution, make sure you call me." A few weeks later, Falese contacted Masrani, telling him that he was the first guy to call.

For Falese it was an excruciating time. He had originally been Vernon Hill's banker before he went to work for him at Commerce in 1992. They took pride in their bank. It was like a first-class 7-Eleven, and Commerce staffers would fall all over themselves to keep customers happy. If a company doing business with Commerce did its payroll in the evening and it was late, the branch in question would stay open simply to accommodate that one customer. They call it "high touch" service. As a customer, you weren't dealing with an institution.

Falese expresses admiration for Hill's talents. "He was a terrific entrepreneur," one of the smartest, most exciting people with whom he'd ever been associated. "I thoroughly enjoyed my experience with him. He was challenging. He was fun. It was hard to argue with his success. I know the lower level employees had a very high regard for him. He built the bank from nothing. He worked tirelessly. It's unfortunate it ended for him the way it did. So if I sound like I'm a fan, I am."

At Commerce, the executive team and the board were trying to decide what to do. They had some big long-term investors. They all wrestled with the question of whether to continue to build the business, which would have required a large capital infusion, or sell it. They decided to sell and

---

former Chairman & CEO of Commerce Bank, N.A., Philadelphia, PA. The Order places restrictions on Mr. Hill's future real estate transactions with any associated insured depository institution, holding company or any of their subsidiaries or affiliates. Mr. Hill must report all future transactions to the board and the audit committee of the institution involved in the transaction. Additionally, when Mr. Hill is an officer, director or major shareholder, he must obtain an opinion that the transaction is fair from an independent accounting or other firm with appropriate expertise."

hired Goldman Sachs to find a buyer. Goldman had represented TD as well. Suddenly, a bank Ed Clark had been eyeing since his Canada Trust days was on the block.

"We got lucky," Clark says modestly. "Anyone that tells you that I'm just smart and that's why I do well, then you know they are not that smart."[71]

Clark saw Commerce Bank as the Canada Trust of the United States. He wanted it and could check off a lot of the required boxes. The Canadian dollar was climbing to par with the American dollar for the first time in thirty years, TD's share price was in the neighbourhood of $70 and Clark's bank was not infected with subprime exposure. The only problem was that the banking system was getting chest pains, the warning signals of the cardiac arrest that was to come in the financial world. The subprime mortgage calamity in the United States was already staring bankers in the face in the fall of 2007. The reprehensible practice of lending to anyone who was vaguely conscious was finally exposed for what it was. Even Ed Clark, who had kept TD out of the products associated with that market, had no idea of the financial superbug that was yet to come. On the day of the announcement of the Commerce purchase, Clark told the world it was his view the subprime debacle would last another six months. He was smart, but not smart enough to predict that in six months it would just be the beginning of a hellish slide.

"A great franchise became available unexpectedly. Now many of you heard me say that I expect the current market turmoil to continue for another six months or so, but you may well be asking, why now? Why not wait until we move a little further through this cycle? Well, there's one simple answer—sometimes you just don't get to choose your timing," Clark said on the conference call to analysts and investors on October 2, 2007.

"This was one that it would be very tough to take a pass on, it was such a perfect fit with TD," said CFO Colleen Johnston. As part of the protocol of keeping transactions a secret until a deal is announced, the bank assigned the Commerce purchase the code name "Cardinal."

"What are the qualities of the Commerce that make it such an attractive target? Well, simply put, it is the TD Canada Trust of the United States. In short, we believe that Commerce can do for TD's U.S. growth strategy what Canada Trust's acquisition did for TD in Canada," Clark said on the call.

With Banknorth, Clark was buying acquisition prowess—twenty-seven acquisitions over fifteen years. With Commerce, he was buying an established champion of retail banking that knew how to grow via building new branches and luring deposits away from other banks.

"Really, they're more than just bankers; they're retailers who get banking," Clark said in maximum sales mode. Former CEO Dick Thomson got a phone call that day from the former president of Citigroup, Robert Willumstad. "Dick, you guys have bought one great bank. It's the best retail operation in this country," Willumstad told Thomson.

From a financial point of view, Vernon Hill's business model of pulling in lots of deposits but not lending out too much money turned out to be the perfect cushion for a bumpy time. Just one third of Commerce's deposits were tied to loans. That had posed a question for regulators: How could Commerce's model sustain itself long term? Fair enough, but in the short term, ironically, it made TD's purchase a relatively safe bet for the size. Because there hadn't been much lending, there wasn't a big issue of problem loans. TD planned to use that fat deposit base to make plenty of loans later.

"We had to find another growth engine. We've got that growth engine," Clark said in a TV interview. [72]

Clark wasn't interested in competing against Goldman Sachs or other investment banks in the United States. That was pointless. What TD could offer, and in even a bigger way now, was retail banking. He not only had New England, with Commerce he now had branches in New York City, throughout New Jersey, the Philadelphia area and Florida. Manhattan, though, was the big score. Buying elsewhere would not get Clark the media attention he would get from having the TD shield all over New York City. If he'd bought in Seattle, CNBC wouldn't have cared. He'd soon be getting lots of free media exposure simply because of TD's New York City presence.

"The acquisition of Commerce was the kind of game changer that Canada Trust had been back in 2000," Colleen Johnston says.

Before the game could really be played, there would be months of angst until the deal closed. Eight-and-a-half billion dollars was just a bit more than TD had paid for Canada Trust. The problem now for TD was that the wheels were coming off the financial system and the economy.

The Commerce acquisition would not close until March 31, 2008, six months later. March would be the month when Bear Stearns evaporated and the world at large started to realize something extremely serious was happening. Bear had survived the Great Depression and was known for being a sharp-elbowed, no-nonsense player on Wall Street. Its longtime chairman and CEO, Alan C. "Ace" Greenberg, famously wrote a book called *Memos from the Chairman,* in which he commanded employees to stop buying paper clips. The firm, he argued, would get enough paper clips via documents sent to it by other companies. Be cheap in the good times, was the message, and Bear will survive the bad times. Unfortunately, by the time of the real estate craze of 2002–06, a new cadre had taken over from Greenberg at Bear Stearns and had leveraged the firm up to between thirty to forty times its capital. That meant for every dollar it had, Bear Stearns was borrowing $30 or $40. Through this leverage, gains would be greatly amplified, but so would losses. When the losses hit, Bear found it couldn't get people willing to lend to it in the critical overnight markets, and within a matter of days it collapsed, only to be bought by JPMorgan Chase for a paltry $2 a share (later to be raised to $10) in a weekend deal orchestrated and backed by the Federal Reserve in an attempt to calm global markets. Sitting in his Madison Avenue office two weeks later, the octogenarian Greenberg appeared on the verge of tears, his beloved firm ruined.

"You play the hand you're dealt," he said sadly.

By the deal's closing date, the financial world had not calmed down. It was worsening by orders of magnitude. In an interview with Clark on the executive floor of TD Bank that day, the questions turned to the macro situation. Clark was asked for his worst-case scenario, given the stunning liquidity crisis just witnessed at Bear. He indicated that TD had modelled for a total shutdown of the markets, meaning the bank couldn't borrow for the next six months, a case of zero liquidity. "We survive it, we do well," was his calm reply.

It turns out he was right. When Lehman Brothers collapsed on September 15, 2008, with tentacles spread much more deeply through the global financial system than Bear Stearns had, the result was exactly what Clark had described. Markets virtually came to a standstill. There were no buyers for anything, other than paper issued by the U.S. Treasury. In fact, there was such a rush into the safety of government-backed bonds that the yield on treasuries was either negligible or slightly negative. People were willing to get nothing for their money, or once inflation was factored in, actually pay the government for the privilege of making sure their money was safe.

Even though he'd been correct that TD could survive the kind of liquidity freeze created by Lehman's demise, it was cold comfort to Clark. The financial system was not functioning and he confessed to fitful sleeps in the weeks after the failure of Bear. "I have not developed the skill that lets you sleep all the way through the night. I think this is probably among the most stressful periods that bank CEOs have ever faced. I'm usually awake at two o'clock in the morning writing some notes to myself," he recounts.[73]

In September 2008, it looked as if the global economy would die of the interconnected shocks resulting from the failure of Lehman Brothers and insurance giant AIG. Americans would soon face an official rate of 10 percent unemployment. The unofficial rate would be in the high teens. Small banks would fail each week for months. Big banks had to suspend dividends and were forced to take billions of dollars from the U.S. Treasury to ensure they had enough capital. There was a rash of rescue takeovers—JPMorgan had bought Bear Stearns and later Washington Mutual. Bank of America suddenly found itself the new owner of Merrill Lynch, and Wachovia fell into the arms of Wells Fargo. It was chaos, and no one knew how it would end. The effect: a crash in asset prices everywhere, posing a particular problem for TD as it moved to finalize its purchase of Commerce Bank.

\* \* \* \*

Late afternoon atop the TD Tower, a friendly butler named John appears to greet guests. From the waiting room, there is a northern view of the city that includes the new Frank Gehry–designed Art Gallery of Ontario, spearheaded by former CEO Charlie Baillie. A black and white portrait of Baillie, and one of his predecessor, Dick Thomson, hang on the wall. On another wall, from a distance, a large painting looks like it might be a Jackson Pollock, but it is by the celebrated Canadian Abstract Expressionist Jean-Paul Riopelle. The chairs are from the Mies van der Rohe era, medium-brown leather. Fresh daisies sit in a vase on a table.

Right on schedule, Colleen Johnston, a petite, fit woman in her early fifties with short blonde hair, strides into the room. Johnston is highly regarded in the banking community, so much so that Ed Clark once asked her to sit in for him at a meeting with the governor of the Bank of Canada and the other major bank CEOs. In 2012, she was named Canada's CFO of the Year. As usual, she is cheerful and friendly. She has just returned from climbing Mt. Kilimanjaro in Tanzania, the highest peak in Africa.

Johnston describes the peril that TD faced after it said it was buying Commerce. There was time lag between the announcement of the deal in October of 2007 and the closing six months later. By March 2008, the dilemma for TD was one of accounting. "You have to 'fair value' the balance sheet when you close the deal," Johnston says. It's mathematical gymnastics, but a bank's capital or buffer against losses (which regulators eye closely) is critical. In this case, "fair value" involved an accounting concept known as "goodwill," defined as the difference between what is paid for a company and what the tangible assets are worth. (Intangible assets include a company's name, brand and reputation.)

Between October 2, 2007, and March 31, 2008, when the deal closed, asset prices fell dramatically but the purchase price remained the same. For example, if the purchase price was $100 and the fair value of the assets was $30, then the goodwill is $70 and $70 has to be carried on the balance sheet and is deducted from the bank's capital. If assets fell even more, say to a fair value of just $10, the purchase price is still $100. In that scenario, the good-will then becomes $90. It's then a bigger deduction from the bank's capital and the bank might have to shore it up by various means, preferably by issuing common shares, the most risk-absorbent form of capital.* Issuing shares,

---

however, means diluting the holdings of existing shareholders. It also wasn't a great time to issue debt, given that the world was deleveraging, or trying to shuck debt. Fortunately, TD's capital ratios were "very acceptable" at the time, Johnston says.

When the deal closed, TD's securities portfolio was worth $1.5 billion less because certain securities were deemed to have lost fair value and the bank had to account for that. In November 2008, because of the gravity of the crisis, TD sensed investors might be more comfortable if it raised more money and the bank did sell common shares to fortify its core regulatory capital level. Even though TD could get only $39.50 a share, at least it could raise money in a dead market. A year before, its shares had been worth $70.

"Ed—and he was absolutely right—he said, 'You know, we've just got to do it,'" Johnston recalls. During the crisis in fiscal 2009, TD raised almost $5 billion of qualifying so-called Tier 1 regulatory capital—the highest quality and most permanent form of capital—a testament to investors' confidence in the bank when others outside of Canada were failing.

Once the acquisition closed, the integration began and there was a black eye. It came in the so-called "batch processing," computer mumbo-jumbo for posting people's bank accounts. It was supposed to occur over a weekend but it wasn't contained. It bled over into the week and it was an embarrassment for the bank that had boasted about smooth integrations in the past. The hurdle was that Commerce was a seven-day a week bank.

"Branches, they were live and running on Saturdays and Sundays, so your window to do all this work was very, very narrow," says John Davies, who supervised the systems integration, as he'd done in the TD Canada Trust deal. When Canada Trust was folded into the TD system, he was able to split it up regionally and CT was open only five days a week.

"That was a big thing, to flip those 400 [Commerce] branches in one weekend," Davies recalls. In all, he spent two years in the U.S. to make the integration work. While he was in New Jersey, many senior people at Commerce came to him to get a read on the TD people. "You were almost like the father confessor," recalls Davies, who is now retired and works with a charity that trains seeing-eye dogs.

In addition to Ed Clark's prior knowledge of U.S banking from his Canada Trust days and the operation in Rochester, TD's team had developed more of an understanding of the picture from Banknorth. They realized they were buying an American bank and they claim they tried to respect the culture and not say, "We just bought you guys for $8 billion," so they should do it their way.

"It was not overbearing," the former Commerce CEO says of TD's approach. TD knew it was operating in the U.S. under U.S. regulations and was sensitive to what its new customers would accept.

It was also tricky because Commerce customers were Commerce loyalists—fans, as Vernon Hill called them. Americans, Ed Clark says, don't stick with the same bank from birth, accepting subpar service, like Canadians do. TD had to tread carefully to minimize the number of lost accounts.

The integration was also more complicated than most in that it was a three-way combination—TD in Toronto, Commerce in New Jersey and Banknorth in Portland. The plan was relatively simple. Banknorth knew how to integrate banks from the endless number it had bought under Bill Ryan. When TD bought Commerce, it would do the back office the Banknorth way, but the front of store would still be the happy face of Commerce, preserving its strength. As for TD, the man in charge of the whole U.S. operation would be Bharat Masrani, who would move from Portland to Vernon Hill's old office in Cherry Hill, New Jersey.*

The sale to TD, as healthy as it was, "was the death of an institution, in a sense," Bob Falese says. This made it a bittersweet transaction. "It was a good thing for the shareholders and employees, okay? But it was also a bit of a funeral. It was the thirtieth anniversary of the founding of the bank the day Vernon Hill stepped down."

In spite of Hill's departure, the bank still had an anniversary party. In an age when the media and investors obsess about whether Apple can go on without Steve Jobs, it turns out institutions are more important than individuals, even the ones who create them.

---

* Across the street from Masrani's office is a Burger King. Many wonder if it is one of Vernon Hill's. Hill says it is not.

"The world didn't come crashing down. We changed colours, but kept operating as we had in the past," says Fred Graziano, a Commerce banker who became Bharat Masrani's number two man.

At the end of the week in June 2011 that saw RBC leave U.S. retail banking with its tail between its legs, Vernon Hill is asked how he thinks TD would do in the United States long term. "Certainly they're going to do better in America now with Commerce than with the crap they had," he replies. Will they be there in ten years? "Definitely," he says, "'cause they have Commerce as a core."

But Hill practically loses it when he hears Ed Clark is planning to get rid of the marble floors that his wife Shirley tailored for the Commerce branches. Clark says the marble floors get scuffed, look ugly and are not good for branches "because they're stupid. There's stupid retailing and there's good retailing. Marble deteriorates faster and looks worse than much cheaper flooring. So that's not smart retailing." New branches are also 30 percent cheaper without marble floors, and Clark admits he wants to take those costs down another 30 percent.

"They don't have enough money to take out all the marble floors. You could tell Ed I said that," Hill fumes, adding it's the dumbest thing he's ever heard. "We've got branches that were built in 1975 still got the same floors, but Ed thinks they scuff. I wanna live long enough to see Ed Clark take out all the marble."

He and Shirley wonder aloud whether the TD boss has ever been to Rome to see how the marble has held up over the years. Hill still has his loyalists, he says, who let him know what's going on in the branches he built.

"I have been doing this a little longer than Ed Clark has," he boasts, although he claims to know little about the TD CEO's past. Surely Clark's Harvard pedigree would get him off on the wrong foot with Hill. The deposed boss of Commerce talks with scorn about when he once spoke to Harvard MBA students, one of whom asked him what kind of research and focus groups Hill and his team had done before choosing the signature colour for the bank, red. Hill says he told the student that he and his squad laid out all the newspapers for the week on the floor, and none of the other banks had red in their designs or ads, so that's how it was done. No focus groups, no Harvard overthinking. Hill, like Larry Waterhouse, was intimately involved in marketing and advertising, coming up with the line "America's Most Convenient Bank."

After his brush with regulators, the unstoppable Vernon Hill is back in banking. In addition to establishing a Commerce clone in the U.K. called Metro Bank, he is co-founder and a shareholder in thirty-three branches in Central Pennsylvania, courtesy of the fact that, back in the day, Commerce had franchised that region to another company so it was not part of what was sold to TD.

"They're going to expand on the east coast," he says defiantly. He's also bought into and acts as a consultant to a small bank in Philadelphia, Republic Bank, with twelve offices in the metro area. "Hopefully, the two will get together and we'll take back all our market share from Ed Clark while he's taking out the marble floors."

Is he serious about taking on TD? "Why wouldn't I? I didn't mind taking on Chase. The fact that the competitor's large is not really an issue."

Even Hill softly gives Ed Clark some credit. For a bank guy, Clark has done okay, he concedes. He can't resist one last jab, though. Hill's Yorkshire terrier, Duffy, runs out into the garden to pee. Hill picks him up and says he always takes the pooch on his frequent business trips to the U.K. "I guess he's small enough you can take him in the cabin of the plane," I volunteer.

"I have my own plane," Hills fires back, without missing a beat. "A G5. I made a lot of bucks in my life. Probably a lot more than Ed Clark will ever make."*

That may be true. But what is certain is that without buying Commerce, TD Bank would not be the force it is today in the U.S., particularly in Manhattan, where it had no presence until early 2008. As of 2012, it is the number five bank in New York City, gunning to be number three by 2015, a market that has somewhere between half and two-thirds the deposits of all of Canada. In the metropolitan New York region, that would be the equivalent of almost *all* the deposits in Canada.

---

* Hill has fractional ownership of a private aircraft through a company called NetJets. The G5 model by Gulfstream costs in the range of $50 to $70 million.

Ed Clark has put a pile of chips on the old Red, White and Blue. Branchwise, TD's presence in America is now bigger than in Canada, where it took 150 years to build the business brick by brick—in part because of the accidental purchase of Vernon Hill's Commerce Bank.

# 12

# THEY'RE NOT BRANCHES, THEY'RE STORES!

*Culture, Culture, Culture*

Visiting a five-year old "store" on Route 73 in Mount Laurel, New Jersey, manager Kim Palermo doesn't seem like one of Vernon Hill's "whack jobs." If she is, she hides it well. Palermo is friendly, showing off an automated teller machine that also spits out postage stamps. This kind of service seems normal to her and it's yet another leaf from the book of Vernon Hill. There are also public restrooms in the bank, just in case a Starbucks or McDonald's isn't handy. Palermo opened this branch in 2006. The Penny Arcade sits there looking a bit like a Wurlitzer jukebox. For non-customers, the automated coin-counting service will cost you 6 percent of what you pour into it, a bad move by TD if you listen to Hill.

Forget old-style banking like the branch in rural Ontario where Keith Gray worked in the 1950s with a manager who read the sports section all day and locked the doors from noon till one. This is retail. The idea to call branches "stores" was the brainwave of—who else?—Vernon Hill. TD kept many of his notions. Its use of his line "America's Most Convenient Bank" tortures Vernon Hill to this day. "The best way to describe us is that we are retailers that happen to be in banking," Bharat Masrani, Ed Clark's chief point man in the United States, says.

It sounds a bit like Keith Gray's mission statement at Green Line: "We're order takers. That's all we are."

Born in Uganda of South Asian heritage, Bharat Masrani started his career with TD in 1987 as a commercial lending trainee. Twenty-five years later, after stops in corporate banking, discount brokerage, a stint as chief risk officer, and time in the UK and India for the bank, he sits atop what TD believes is its future hothouse. Now logging time in the U.S., he may also have the best résumé of the possible successors to Ed Clark. If Masrani gets the CEO job in Toronto, he would be the first person of non-European origin to hold such a position in the world of Canadian banking. He is said by some (not all) to be Ed Clark's intellectual equal and of like mind. Critics, however, say he is anything but entrepreneurial, given his previous employment as chief risk officer.

"TD Bank, America's Most Convenient Bank" is the brand, and as hokey and chirpy as it might seem to old-style pinstriped bankers at King and Bay, TD means it. Its bankers now wear pins emblazoned with the company logo, something that's more Rotary Club than National Club—the wood-panelled, leather-wingbacked clubhouse of the financial elite in Toronto.

What TD has done differently from other Canadian businesses that have tried to penetrate the United States is that it has embraced the American way of doing things. The U.S., at its core, *is* more Rotary Club, as is Canada for that matter. TD bought Commerce Bank for its culture and, for the most part, it has kept it intact (although there are rumblings this may change).

Fred Graziano, Masrani's right-hand man, has been a Commerce Bank man since 1992, and now oversees the entire retail bank and 27,000 people. (For the record, although he's had to live with the question since he was a little kid, he's no relation to the boxer Rocky Graziano, who he thinks may have taken on the name.) He says that Bharat Masrani has the view that the model is easy to explain, but tough to implement. Graziano refers to a book called *212°: The Extra Degree,* one in a long line of inspirational business books designed to capture a market of corporate leaders. Excellence is all about that little bit extra. At 211 degrees Fahrenheit, water is just hot. At 212 degrees, it boils, produces steam and can power a train. The difference is only one degree, but the result can be astonishing.

He gives an example from his corporate lending background. A competitor would not do something simple for a client, like issuing 3,000 American

Express gift cards that the company would give to employees for the holidays. "The branch manager looked at it and said, 'You know, this is a lot of work, a lot of hours.' *What do I get out of it?* was the attitude of the competing bank." Instead, Graziano and Commerce said yes, delivered the cards, and got a $20 million deposit in the branch.

Graziano says that despite the Canadian takeover, he is still operating stores the way he did when he started in 1992. TD let Commerce run the way it always did, with much the same management. Ed Clark had made it clear that he bought Commerce for the model, and that model was going to survive the acquisition. "I'm sitting here living proof that it is and we're operating and executing it every day," Graziano declares.

No one who goes to New York City these days misses the point. In the metropolis emblematic of finance and banking, there's a new shingle on corner after corner, challenging the old incumbents like JPMorgan Chase, Citigroup and Bank of America that still call their outlets branches. TD Bank "stores" have sprung up like dandelions in New York City. They're everywhere, and they look brand new. In addition to the corporate slogan, signs also boast "Maine to Florida with 1,000 plus Locations," "Open 7 Days. Legendary Service. Hassle-Free Banking," and "Time Is On Your Side. Open Early. Open Late."

There is also "We Don't Nickel and Dime You. We Count Them for Free," in reference to the now famous coin-counting machines. If they went much further with the corny slogans, it would be a bit like Honest Ed's gaudy discount emporium on Bloor Street in Toronto: "Don't just stand there! Come in and buy something!"

The bank has also used name-brand showbiz personalities to flog its shield in the U.S. Wearing his grim *Law & Order* face, Sam Waterston has long been associated with TD Ameritrade. To advertise its long hours, TD has used the morning show duo of Regis Philbin and Kelly Ripa. In one commercial, a bird handler is standing with a huge owl between Ripa and the now retired Philbin. The owl, of course, likes TD because it's open late. From December 2008, another spot shows Regis at his shrink's office on a TD green couch, saying, "Regis doesn't like change. Change makes Regis nervous." It's a spoof on the rebranding of Commerce Bank to TD. There's yet another ad with Regis and Kelly riffing off of the problem of getting lost in voice mail when you call customer service. The promise and punch line from the ad is that you'll always get a real person on the line at TD, 24/7.

It's reminiscent of the old Canada Trust days of Johnny Cash machines and mortgage bonfires. But it's more than that. TD is so confident about how much better its offering is than other banks that it repeatedly (Clark says it in every interview) promises to steal market share if it establishes a store on a corner where there are already three U.S. competitors, simply because its branch is open longer and its employees are now conditioned to wow customers.

In fact, "WOW" is the mantra, a Vernon Hill mantra. In the U.S., they even measure the WOW factor somewhat scientifically with what they call CWI, the Customer WOW Index. The idea of "WOW" is to go further, to do something for the customer so that the person tells you, "*Wow,* you went beyond the call of duty."

In sleepy old Canada, the bank doesn't call it a WOW Index, at least not yet. Rather, it's the banal sounding "customer experience index" (CEI), like something the ciphers at some consultancy devised after endless billable hours. Either way, it's the same thing. Thousands of customers are surveyed each week. The bank then takes the number of happy customers and subtracts the number of unhappy ones to get the index number. When the bank refers to customers who like TD, it means those people who would take the next step of recommending the bank to their friends. Typical for any garden-variety retail chain, "stores" are "mystery shopped," meaning a TD person will anonymously troll the branches like an ordinary customer to look for deficiencies in the service.

"This guy was a very good businessman in the sense that he invented a very good model," Ed Clark says about Vernon Hill, whom he has not met. Clark admits to a bias since it was a similar model to what he had been running at Canada Trust. While doing due diligence, before signing on the dotted line to buy the bank, Clark was walking around Commerce stores with minders assigned to him. He told them he wanted to go into the coffee room to talk to workers who didn't want him there. He asked the employees what they would do if he gave them a magic wand. "Hire more good people" came the response.

Clark was instantly impressed, saying that 90 percent of other bank employees would answer, "Give me more deposits." As Clark explains, Hill had embedded in the whole organization the notion that people make a difference.

Still, investors can only hear so much about WOW. At a certain point they want to see the results. As of the end of July 2012, the highly watched number in TD's U.S. division is the ROE, or return on equity. It is stuck at 6.4 percent, something about which TD's top bankers can get a bit defensive. Adjusted for unusual or one-time items, it sits at 8.1 percent.* According to TD's third-quarter 2012 report, its cost of equity is 9 percent. While it's earning money in the United States, it's not earning at a rate higher than what it costs the bank to raise equity for its investment activities. On April 17, 2012, US Bancorp, one of the banks TD considers its peer in the American market, posted return on equity of just over 16 percent in its most recent quarter. On the same day, at a TD investor event, Bharat Masrani reiterated that his division would earn $1.6 billion in 2013, up from $1.3 in 2012. Five days before, a BMO Capital Markets analyst estimated that "despite almost flawless execution," because of the price TD paid to enter the U.S. market, it would take between $2.1 and $2.7 billion for the bank's U.S. division to generate returns of 12 to 15 percent, "unrealistic over the next three to five years."[74] Colleen Johnston said in a May 24, 2012, interview that over that time period, double-digit returns in the United States would probably be achievable.[75] Double-digit, though, could mean 10 percent, not 12 to 15 percent. While TD has achieved considerable scale and visibility in the U.S., the bank has yet to deliver meaningful returns there. Because of post-crisis regulatory requirements, such returns may be challenging to achieve.

\* \* \* \*

---

* While it does not have retail banking in the U.S., Bank of Nova Scotia has significant retail operations in Latin America, the Caribbean and now Asia. In the third quarter of 2012, $448 million or 30.7% of its core earnings came from this unit. Scotiabank's return on equity from this division was 11.7%, substantially better than TD's in the U.S.

Building a business with branches, or stores, requires intense focus on detail. Fred Graziano obsesses about eliminating clutter, making each location look like the next. TD has picked up on Vernon Hill's fanaticism about the stores. First and foremost, Colleen Johnston says, it's all about location, then the size of the branch, the parking, the signage, the "egress" or the ease with which customers can get in and out. What are the traffic patterns and directions at rush hour? Are there medians to cross and turns required? Again, it brings to mind David Halberstam's description of Holiday Inn founder Kemmons Wilson. Instead of enjoying the vacation, Wilson was measuring motel rooms, looking at locations, suddenly stricken with the brilliant notion that road-side sleep joints could be much more pleasant than the depressing motels he and his family had checked into after cruising down the new Eisenhower-era Interstate. His obsessing over these things ruined a family holiday.

Johnston boasts that TD is superb at "branching," clearly a new word (shouldn't it be "storing," as in stores?). As for the number of years for a new branch to break even, Johnston says it will take "several." Keith Gray stands by the number five. Fred Graziano says three. When pressed on what "several" means, Johnston says between three and five years. The cost is also high. She says that the price of building a branch in the United States is a multiple of what it costs in Canada. TD, she says, rarely owns the real estate.

Even Larry Waterhouse has noticed TD's "branching." Before he became famous for his discount brokerage, he was a banker. For ten years, Waterhouse worked for Chemical Bank, bought by Chase Manhattan years ago. He ran his own branch, which in banking meant you had arrived. From his home in Florida, he watches the bank's branch expansion with abiding interest, not the least of which is his family's enormous stock holding, but also because branch banking is in his blood. "I'm a branch guy. I think it's the smartest thing they can do. *Stores,* as they now call them—I hate that word!"

Waterhouse describes a branch he uses in Jupiter, Florida. "It looks like it cost $10 million. I've never seen a branch like this in my entire life. It's humongous. It's huge and it's gorgeous. Every time I go past there I say, 'What are they doing with my money!'"

But he seems to like TD's retail strategy in the United States. "If you can open a thousand of them, open them." TD already has just over 1,300 branches in the U.S., and is working toward 2,000.

At the time of the purchase, though, Commerce employees were edgy, concerned the distinguishing factors of their bank would be lost when the TD shark finished swallowing it. Among the symbolic things they fretted about, Colleen Johnston recalls, was the Commerce lapel pin. TD said to them, "Yes, you're retiring your Commerce pin, but welcome to your bigger family." Now everyone wears a TD pin.

It's not just about pins. Apparently ties are cause for concern as well. On the day of a conference call in 2011, it was about half an hour before the senior executive team would be "on," and the head of TD Securities, Bob Dorrance, reportedly said, "Oh, my goodness, I'm not wearing a green tie!" Green is like the bank's national flag and not being dressed properly would be like forgetting to salute. Dorrance asked whether Ed Clark had another green tie he could borrow. Clark did not, so Dorrance ran back to his office to search for one. As a result, the conference call started late.

From the bank's viewpoint, it may be as simple as whoever has the best store wins. From the best location, to the best hours, to the best parking, to a washroom if you need one, to service you didn't expect, TD is trying to replicate that model up and down the eastern seaboard, creating a refuge for disgruntled customers of other banks. Ed Clark likes to say that Canadians will put up with poor retail service and bad banking out of sheer inertia. Americans won't. "They say, I'm out of here. And then they look across the street and there's this beautiful branch and it's got a greeter in front [who says], 'Why don't you do this and we'll give you an umbrella. Got any kids? Why don't we give you some toys for your kids.' And you've got a customer."

On April 17, 2012, half a dozen of the bank's top executives presented at an investor event in Toronto that included questions from the audience. One of the last ones was directed at Ed Clark, who sat in an oversized green leather armchair with a large faux fireplace roaring behind him. The questioner wanted to know, given all the rosy talk from the bank about its opportunities in the face of economic and regulatory uncertainty, why TD's share price was currently languishing. Clark admitted it was uncertainty among investors about the bank's U.S. expansion. "People have huge doubts about whether this U.S strategy will work or not," he explains. He said he understood that point of view. "The United States has been a troubled land here. And there have been more examples of people going down into that troubled land and losing, than there have been successful."

Clark concluded, however, by saying that his own substantial shareholding in the bank indicates he is a believer in the long-term prospects of TD in the U.S., and that over time, it will outpace other Canadian banks because of its investment in the United States.

# 13

# THE MOST TRADES IN THE WORLD

*From Green Line to Waterhouse to TD Ameritrade*

It must have felt unlucky at the time, but Fred Tomczyk may be one of the luckiest CEOs in the financial services sector. He took over as chief executive of TD Ameritrade in October of 2008, just as the global economy looked like it was at death's door. "Lehman went down and Merrill Lynch got [forcibly] sold I think a week before I took over," he says, laughing. "I took over in the midst of all that." TD Ameritrade's stock, like every other stock in the world, proceeded to crash in half.

Tomczyk had already been chief operating officer for a year, and previously in his career had run a life insurance company, so he could point to time in the corner office. He was also an Ed Clark guy, having come from Canada Trust. Tall, with the well-built frame that harkens back to his days as a defenceman on the Cornell hockey team, Tomczyk is in his late fifties. He was good enough on the ice, he says, to have just squeaked into professional-level hockey, had he not also made the dean's list in the undergraduate business school. From St. Catharines in the Niagara region of Ontario, he started in banking at Bank of Montreal, became a chartered accountant with Coopers & Lybrand, which he "couldn't stand," and over the years made his way into the insurance business, becoming CEO of London Life in 1995 at the age of forty-one. The insurance company became the object of Royal Bank's affections, an acquisition target that was ultimately purchased by Great West Life, part of the Power Corporation empire of the billionaire Desmarais family. He could have stayed on, but got plucked by Ed Clark, who was then running Canada Trust. The conversation with Clark was short: Tomczyk was initially offered a job to which he said no. Clark asked him what he wanted out of a job.

"So I told him, and he says, 'Okay, here's my organization. If I did this, this, and this, and gave you this job would you come?' And I said, 'Okay, you've answered all my questions.' We never even talked about compensation till the last second."

Tomczyk may run an online brokerage company, but he knows banking. When TD bought Canada Trust, Tomczyk ran the branches during the conversion. What he now runs for Clark is a very large investment of TD Bank's in the United States. It is very different from the retail banking system. TD Ameritrade is an online brokerage and wealth management business stretching the four directions of the compass in America. It is the prominent offspring of Keith Gray's TD Waterhouse creation, now sporting almost 355,000 trades per day, the most of any brokerage in the world, including the pioneering Charles Schwab and Fidelity. When Gray started Green Line in 1984, 1,000 trades per day would have been a dream come true.

Unknown to its investor customers, TD Ameritrade has another role in life. It feeds gobs of money into the TD Bank apparatus in the United States. Gone are the days of discount brokerages just being order takers, such as it was in Gray's day. Gone even are the early halcyon days of online brokerage, which was coming into fashion in the last years of Gray's career. Electronic stock trades have become totally commoditized. They are cheap.

Although Ameritrade has always been known as a shop for active traders, it has gone through the equivalent of an identity change. It is now what they call in the business an "asset gatherer." Sure, they say, make your trades with us, but put all your assets under our roof, your stocks, and bonds and cash—whatever. As a result, TD Ameritrade's assets under management as of June 30, 2012, were some $455 billion, even in an uncertain market.

It's that last asset class—the cash—that most excites Fred Tomczyk, and no doubt Ed Clark. Like an anthropologist who has figured out the human species, Tomczyk confidently says that most people keep somewhere between 15 and 20 percent of their assets in cash. It's what they're comfortable doing.

They don't want every cent invested all the time so that cash is just sitting there. It turns out that such a pile is very useful to TD Bank in the United States. In fact, somewhere around $60 billion a year is "swept" from those TD Ameritrade accounts into TD banks in America.

In the parlance of banking, this is what is known as "cheap funding." TD Bank branches, or stores, can then use that money to make loans, perhaps car loans via TD's late 2010 purchase of Chrysler Financial. In 2012, TD Ameritrade earned 140 basis points (or 1.4 percent) by providing that funding to TD Bank. Even better, though, is that TD, as a 45 percent shareholder in Ameritrade, is eligible for 45 percent of the 140 basis points. It is a financial arrangement with an elegant circularity to it.

"They look at it as almost like their cost of funds," Tomczyk says, adding that it's a better rate for TD than if the bank had to raise that funding in the market. For a bank "to have stable deposit funding is worth a lot," he says, and it would be dear to the risk management ventricle of Ed Clark's heart.

"This got proven out in the crisis," Tomczyk says.

It's like those millions in cash sitting in the rural branches of TD in Canada. Keith Gray calls it cold money. It's not "hot," like funds that zip in and out of high-rolling hedge funds, or what happened at Lehman Brothers and Bear Stearns, which depended on money they borrowed overnight, twenty-four-hour money. That kind of high-temperature money can lead to trouble.

Since Tomczyk became CEO, the amount of cash he's pumped into TD bank accounts has grown from $15 billion to $60 billion. Over time, the amount TD Ameritrade can sweep into TD Bank accounts will only grow. Tomczyk says his goal is to grow assets at a rate of 7 to 11 percent per year. "So say 9 percent," he estimates. At that rate, assets will double in about eight years. "TD Ameritrade moved from being purely an active trader shop. Today you would say, 'Jeez, they're gathering assets at a higher rate than anybody else,'" he explains.

The next phase of the journey is to do more with TD Bank. "We're going to start working with Bharat's group to originate accounts and assets for TD Ameritrade out of his network of branches," Tomczyk predicts. As well, TD Ameritrade will try to sell its customers on getting their mortgages or lines of credit from TD Bank. "The vision is all about the integrated financial institution. There's no other financial institution that can do that," Tomczyk explains matter-of-factly, without a trace of the hubris that Ed Clark flags as a bank's greatest vulnerability.

Charles Schwab is a much bigger company than TD Ameritrade. It has $1.83 trillion in assets and its market capitalization is double TD Ameritrade's. As Tomczyk points out, however, Schwab does not have a relationship with a bank, nor do Fidelity, E*TRADE or Scottrade, the other major players in the sector.

TD Ameritrade is now the favourite cousin of TD Bank. Put another way, it's an in-law that gets along with the family very well. If it wanted to, it could also give TD bragging rights versus Royal Bank, with which it was comparable in market value at the beginning of September 2011. RBC has long been the largest and most valuable bank in Canada. Maintaining that position is very important to the culture of Royal, but TD has been creeping up on it for a long time. If you add in TD's stake in Ameritrade, its market value as of the spring of 2012 would be on par with RBC's.

A couple of years into his tenure as CEO, Ed Clark was trying to figure out what to do with TD Waterhouse in the United States, so he went through the options. Schwab was too big to buy, Fidelity wasn't selling and, although online brokerage wasn't his first love, Clark was loath to sell his property because TD Waterhouse was making money and it kept the bank's two-letter name prominent in the U.S. For a solution, TD came up with a novel way to stay in the business: get bigger but don't pay to do so. TD Waterhouse would combine with Ameritrade, swapping its stake in Waterhouse for a major share in the newly combined company. At first, TD would have 32 percent of TD Ameritrade, a piece that would grow with time to 45 percent. Even though it doesn't own more than half of the merged entity, the bank is far and away the largest shareholder. It has five seats on the board and chooses the CEO. It is virtual control.

It would not, however, be an easy negotiation requiring a couple of years of on-again, off-again discussions. "That one was off as much as it was on," says David Livingston, who was involved as the head of corporate development at TD at the time.

The principal at the other end of the line was an entrepreneur by the name of Joe Ricketts. On May 1, 1975, the day the U.S. Securities and Exchange Commission banned fixed brokerage commissions, Ricketts started a firm called First Omaha Securities, a discount brokerage for do-it-yourself investors that became Ameritrade. As a result of building that business, Ricketts is a billionaire who made it to the *Forbes* 400 Richest People in America list. In addition to a sprawling ranch in the western United States, he owns a palatial apartment in New York City at the Mandarin Oriental, near Central Park and Columbus Circle, that reportedly cost close to $30 million in 2006.[76] Most recently, he got a producer credit on a film directed by Robert Redford about Abraham Lincoln. Politically, Ricketts is far right wing. Someone who knows him jokingly says that Joe probably thinks the Tea Party is a bunch of communists. It is amusing to think that this arch-conservative was negotiating the sale of his company to none other than a guy who was once known as "Red Ed." Clark, however, doesn't see the humour.

"You and three other journalists spend all their time on that particular topic," he complains, ever so slightly losing his usual cool. "When I go out to Calgary I get interviewed regularly by the press and I can tell you not a single person ever raises that topic or even knows who I am. You call up Joe Ricketts and ask him whether he's ever heard of Red Ed. You mean the guy that fights the fires? Red Adair, is that who you're talking about? He would have no idea about me."* Ricketts, he says, simply saw Clark as a businessperson with "a business proposition."

It was, however, far from that simple. The first embers of the deal were talks in a Citigroup boardroom in 2003 between Ameritrade's CEO, Joe Moglia, and Ed Clark's head of development, David Livingston. TD was attracted to Ameritrade in part because Moglia had been able to acquire a competitor called Datek that had slipped away from TD Waterhouse. Ameritrade's ability to get Datek, Moglia says, gave them some credibility

---

* Former TD Chairman John Thompson mentioned Ed Clark's past in his speech honouring Clark as CEO of the Year on February 17, 2011. "The path to the CEO's corner office does not generally begin with a PhD thesis on Tanzania's economic policy."

in TD's eyes. Eventually Livingston set up a meeting between Moglia and Clark in a Chicago hotel, roughly halfway between Toronto and Omaha, the hometown of Ameritrade. It would, however, be akin to a light switch going on and off for two years. For Ricketts, selling meant letting go, never easy for an entrepreneur.

"The Ricketts became more uncomfortable as their control was being diluted," says Moglia. "There were times we pulled away from it 'cause the Ricketts didn't want to do it."[*]

At one point, when Ricketts and Ameritrade pulled back, TD began to have discussions with E*TRADE. A couple of years into his tenure as CEO, Ed Clark was trying to figure out what to do with TD Waterhouse in the United States. At one point, the bank got very close to doing a deal with E*TRADE, but Clark says it fell through because of issues of control. Charlie Baillie adds another opinion as to why it didn't happen. "We could never get comfortable with the principals at E*TRADE. I couldn't. And then I got Ed involved and he couldn't."

Bottom line—at the time, E*TRADE's people weren't TD's kind of people. Clark says there were fundamental and philosophical differences. According to Clark, E*TRADE's CEO, Mitch Caplan, thought a combined entity with TD should give him control of the credit side. TD begged to differ. E*TRADE ended up getting into all the kinds of instruments TD had exited, and paid the price during the financial crisis.[†]

When the discussions between TD and E*TRADE ended, Joe Moglia went back to TD. Ricketts was getting more accustomed to the idea of the Canadian bank as a seller and investor, but he wasn't fully convinced yet. E*TRADE still looked like a better proposition to him, in spite of its financial condition, because it would give him more say. Ricketts would have ended up with the

---

[*] Joe Ricketts declined an invitation to do an interview for this book. Ricketts announced his retirement from the board of TD Ameritrade on September 16, 2011. His son Todd would take his seat as a director of the company.

[†] In January 2012, Frank Petrilli, the former president of TD Waterhouse, became non-executive chairman of E*TRADE, raising the question of whether TD (now TD Ameritrade) might ultimately buy E*TRADE. Through a spokesperson in June 2012, Clark said that Petrilli's presence at E*TRADE "has no impact."

biggest stake in the combined company, not having to play second fiddle to TD Bank. It may have meant majority ownership, but a merger of Ameritrade and E*TRADE would also have resulted in a smaller pie, and financial hell a few years down the line because of E*TRADE's exposure to the subprime mortgage market.

Normally, David Livingston would do the bulk of the heavy negotiating. In this case, however, Clark himself had to spend time getting the entrepreneur comfortable with selling. The TD CEO stayed overnight at Ricketts' ranch, looking for common ground. Ricketts had a lot of pride of ownership, Livingston says.

Neither he nor Clark hides the fact that the talks were tough. Livingston is more to the point, laughingly describing Ricketts as "a piece of work." Aside from valuation, the big issues were the number of board seats TD would have, who would pick the CEO and what veto powers the bank would get.

"They were difficult negotiations. But most deals are," Clark said in June 2011. "You have to be willing not to do deals. I do not let my ego or emotions make business decisions. I don't yell, I don't pound the table. When you do deals, you just stay calm, you let the guy yell at you." Nonetheless, TD's CEO had to go the extra mile with Ricketts. For sure, Ricketts would be a stickler. Clark may claim to compartmentalize his emotions, but building a business is an emotional process. Giving it up is even more gut-wrenching.

Clark explains, "This was a very difficult stage in [Ricketts'] life. He built this company. It was a great company. That's a very emotional thing. You have to kind of establish a human bond with him," and at the same time remain independent. In the end, the bank made a deal with Ricketts "that made him a very, very wealthy man, forever."

For TD, buying 51 percent of Banknorth not long before was the offensive, strategic transaction that gave TD its entry into retail banking in the U.S. In contrast, a stake in a merged Waterhouse and Ameritrade was a defensive transaction, and a bit of financial engineering. TD wasn't going to be a seller of its online brokerage, but it wasn't stepping up to buy Schwab or Fidelity either. Then the question became, according to Livingston, how do you convince everybody that you deserve control if you're not taking more than half of the new company? He said the trick was persuading Ricketts and other investors that the deal was good for the new company. "There were big synergies, and so there's big profit uplift from doing that," he explains. The bank had to not only convince Ricketts and Co., it had to convince analysts and investors in the bank that this was a deft move.

Conference calls between companies and analysts in the United States are peculiar things. Frequently, they feature a lot of obsequious comments and questions. Analysts tell executives how great a deal they've just done, or congratulate them on their latest quarter. Rarely do these encounters get testy. The June 22, 2005, conference call following the announcement of the creation of TD Ameritrade was no exception. Even analysts on the Canadian side of the border were slobbering over Ed Clark, his CFO and the executives at Ameritrade. The CFO of Ameritrade, Randy MacDonald, jokingly called Ed Clark his new best friend—new boss, new best friend. In the deal, TD bank swapped its TD Waterhouse business, now deemed to be worth $3.1 billion ($2.69 billion USD), for the biggest share in a combination of Waterhouse and Ameritrade. It was a cagey move. As with Banknorth, Clark was moving like a jungle cat, taking just enough to direct the proceedings. Although TD would not have 51 percent, as it did with Banknorth, it had enough. It had five spots on a twelve-seat board and Clark himself would take one of the seats.

Nine years after Keith Gray first took TD on its biggest acquisition adventure ever and its first significant retail purchase in the United States, Clark had fashioned a combination with Ameritrade and a huge stake of the merged entity, making TD now a major player in online brokerage and asset gathering. Gray's $715 million purchase of Waterhouse in 1996 had, in just nine years, appreciated in value to over $3 billion. Waterhouse, because of the bonus of Knight/Trimark, was a freebie acquisition for the bank. Not only had the Waterhouse acquisition provided the firepower for Charlie Baillie to buy Canada Trust and bring Ed Clark onboard, TD would now be the biggest shareholder in TD Ameritrade. That's not counting the many millions Green Line and Waterhouse and now TD Ameritrade had made for the bank each quarter over the years. By 2012, TD's share in the company would be worth as much as $5 billion. So much for that "schlocky" little business. Arguably Keith Gray had made billions for TD.

Fred Tomczyk, however, credits Charlie Baillie with the Waterhouse transaction. "TD bet on discount brokerage way back when. Charlie just kept going. Everybody thought he was crazy at the time. He took a lot of heat back then." "It never would have happened without Charlie Baillie," Gray concurs.

Once again, the roots of TD's U.S. expansion could be found in the blood and sweat of entrepreneurs. On the retail side, it was the entrepreneurialism of Bill Ryan and Vernon Hill. In brokerage, Gray's Green Line had overtaken the entrepreneurial Waterhouse, and now Waterhouse was being combined with Ameritrade, the entrepreneurial grit of Joe Ricketts and his squad from Omaha.

Ameritrade in 2001 had only a $700 million market value and was often ignored in the press. The man who came to run it for Joe Ricketts and other investors that year was a New Yorker who'd cut his teeth at Merrill Lynch, which until it flopped into the arms of Bank of America in the calamity of 2008 had been the premier "Main Street" brokerage in the United States. Joe Moglia (who stepped down as CEO in 2008 but remains chairman) was a salesman, and like many in the financial world, also a sportsman—his game was football. Moglia, who has a lopsided grin that masks the inner toughness of a football fanatic, now coaches the Coastal Carolina Chanticleers of the Big South Conference. Make no mistake, he brought his rah-rah ways to Ameritrade and loves to compare what's necessary on the field to what's necessary in business. "Everything you do in football is about people. You've got to motivate. You've got to discipline. You've got to inspire. You've got to be good under stress," he preaches.

On the conference call when the deal between TD and Ameritrade was announced, Moglia was the lead speaker, peppering his remarks with sporting references. "I think most of you know that 75 percent of most mergers wind up failing. The single most significant reason why that happens is because companies fail on the integration. In the last three years, we have done seven integrations. We are seven and zero in the execution of those integrations, and we absolutely plan on continuing that undefeated streak."

Spoken like a true gridiron coach. Among the acquisitions he'd made while running Ameritrade: National Discount Brokers (NDB) and Datek, a firm Frank Petrilli had wanted to buy a few years earlier when he was running TD Waterhouse.

As much as Moglia talked about seven seamless integrations, the knitting together of Ameritrade and TD Waterhouse would not be easy. In the winter of 2011, almost six years after the deal was announced, when Fred Tomczyk was asked whether Ricketts and TD were aligned, he said candidly, "In the last 12 to 18 months, I would say that's true." A person familiar with what went on after the deal said, "Integration and governance were a nightmare at first."

Although Frank Petrilli and David Livingston are full of praise about the level of professionalism the Ameritrade CEO brought to the job, Moglia and Clark would not be in the same book club, even though they both happened to have worked for Merrill Lynch. Clark may not have been a controlling shareholder, but he was the closest thing to it, and Omaha heard Toronto's footsteps. Clark's old boss in Ottawa, Mickey Cohen, who had been on the TD board, was now one of his directors on the TD Ameritrade board. Cohen says that Clark did not micromanage the company from afar, but he allows that the situation had similarities to a private equity investment. "You don't own 25, 35 or 45 percent of the company and come to the board meeting to find out what's going on. You're dumb if you do," says Cohen.

Meanwhile, Moglia got deeply absorbed in preparing for the media interviews he would do on the day TD Ameritrade's quarterly earnings were released. It's not unusual for CEOs to prep for these sessions and for their communications staff to prepare a list of the most likely questions and coach the boss on how to spin the answers. However, it is unusual for CEOs to spend several days working this. Someone familiar with Moglia's process said his staff would flash cue cards to help him rehearse answers for his television appearances, even down to throwaway questions about sporting events. Moglia, ever the football coach, wanted to know the playbook cold so that on game day he would be ready to execute and catch whatever was thrown his way.

He is unapologetic about his level of preparation. "That was my job," he declares. His goal was to project a trustworthy image to investors, so they would say, "I kinda like that guy, I trust him."

Results are what matter and Moglia did deliver. Although Clark's man,

Tomczyk, took over as CEO, Moglia remains the chairman of TD Ameritrade, an indication of the bank's confidence in him.

Following the Ameritrade call, TD held its own conference call to discuss the impact on Toronto-Dominion Bank. Clark's key line was: "The new brand, TD Ameritrade, will be a powerhouse brand in the industry and will also increase the penetration of the TD brand in the United States." TD will be everywhere, is what he was saying. In a few years, when Clark would buy more banks and change the signs to TD, people wouldn't think the two letters meant touchdown. "It will carry the TD brand across America," he said of TD Ameritrade.

Clark explained that, from a financial point of view, rather than just take $50 million USD in earnings from TD Waterhouse USA, after tax TD could have a 40 percent interest in a newly combined entity that had earned $325 million in the past twelve months.

One analyst who did not engage in cuddly comments was Mario Mendonça of Genuity Capital, now Canaccord Genuity. He wondered if TD was simply becoming a holding company in the U.S. Clark responded by saying, "We would rather own less than 100 percent and have a skilled player with the capability of continuing to consolidate than own 100 percent and be stuck with an entity that may be strategically challenged three or four years from now. I put enormous emphasis on having a strong management team with great operational excellence, and I like to let people run their businesses. So I don't happen to find it particularly challenging to have strong, independent management teams. I think I'm perfectly capable of making my influence felt by having as good an argument, and if I don't have a good argument, then they probably shouldn't listen to me. . . . And so frankly again, as a foreigner operating in the United States, I like—I have all you guys on their back as well as me on their back."

Once the deal closed, Fred Tomczyk would be on the board of TD Ameritrade. Eventually he would be chief operating officer and is now CEO. According to him, the fact that both TD Ameritrade and TD Bank, America's Most Convenient Bank, both boast the TD shield means they do help each other, from a brand perspective. In 2012, he would spend $235 million on marketing, a significant chunk of his annual revenues of $2.6 billion, about double what the TD Bank spends in the U.S. pumping its name, which cannot hurt the bank's profile in the United States. "They are huge marketers by anybody's standards," Clark says.

Tomczyk says that TD is getting a bigger and bigger brand name in the U.S., and the more than 1,300 branches that it now boasts give Ameritrade more physical points of distribution. One of his core strategies is to build on Ameritrade's relationship with TD.

Truth be told, it really is more than a relationship. It is the next best thing to ownership, and among the executive set at TD there is a strong sense that the bank owns TD Ameritrade, rather than just being a 45 percent shareholder. Tomczyk says he thinks Clark would say it's his company.

Another indication of the tight relationship between the two companies is how Tomczyk interacts with TD Bank. The CEO of TD Ameritrade says he sits in on senior management meetings at the bank via video conferencing from his office in Jersey City, across the Hudson River from Manhattan. He recuses himself during certain discussions that he should not be hearing. When in Toronto (four times a year or more) he uses his old office on the fourth floor of the TD Tower, just a few doors down from Ed Clark's office. He assures me other executives also use the office. There is nothing on the desk except for Tomczyk's iPad.

But what does it matter if he has paperweights? He is swimming in cash, excess cash, he says, a good problem for a CEO to have. Tomczyk claims to achieve the economics of deposit banking without the capital cost or credit risks. He points to a credit rating upgrade during the crisis in 2009, when the company refinanced all of its debt and bought thinkorswim, the largest option and derivative online brokerage trader in the U.S., for $600 million. He claims that's where the growth is in trading, which is why in the same week Charles Schwab bought Options Express. Under Tomczyk, TD Ameritrade has also initiated shareholder-friendly moves. The company bought back 9 percent of its stock and started paying a quarterly dividend.* TD Bank gets 45 percent of that dividend.

---

* Stock buybacks are theoretically good for existing shareholders because the outstanding number of shares is reduced, meaning any earnings are distributed among fewer shares.

Will Tomczyk make other acquisitions? "Absolutely," he says.

The company has cash, debt capacity and could easily issue more shares, he says. He also adds that when interest rates finally begin to rise in the United States, TD Ameritrade will make a lot of money, given the cash it has sloshing around.

\* \* \* \*

Brokerage is not Ed Clark's first love like retail banking, but it's a good business and he likes it just the way it is. When he took over from Charlie Baillie, after Keith Gray left the bank, Clark sold off the brokerage operations in Australia, closed Hong Kong and shut down a joint venture in India with the sprawling Tata Group. Clark didn't like the volatility of the brokerage business. According to some, he has had a change of heart, and is eager to spread the gospel of discount brokerage to the two global economic juggernauts, India and China. Selling those operations outside of North America may be one of the moves Clark now regrets. "We're sorry we left India," Clark concedes. "Now Ed wants to get back into India. [But] the Tatas think we screwed them," one former TD executive says.

India and China aside, the United States is lots to handle. TD Ameritrade may be a separate publicly traded company based in the U.S., but it is for all intents and purposes supervised by TD Bank in Toronto. It is part of a grander scheme than simply discount brokerage or even asset gathering. It is another extension of the TD brand in America. Whether you see a TD Bank sign or a TD Ameritrade sign, it's only logical you'd make some connection, either consciously or subconsciously. And as the future unfolds, the two companies will do more and more business with each other, even if TD continues to cap its share of TD Ameritrade at 45 percent. Back in the days when Keith Gray was building Green Line, Robin Korthals and Dick Thomson were not just thinking about brokerage clients. Like Ed Clark, Bharat Masrani and Fred Tomczyk, they were just as interested in how many new banking clients with fat bank balances Green Line would bring to TD. In some ways, times haven't changed that much.

# 14

# TD UNIVERSITY

*Indoctrination Camp for Bankers*

The Westin Hotel at the corner of Fellowship and Highway 73 in Mount Laurel, New Jersey, could be a TD Bank dormitory. At breakfast, the room teems with people jockeying for the buffet, and most of them are wearing TD's signature green lapel pin, always on the left side, aligned with the heart. The hotel is just minutes from the bank's U.S. headquarters and the home of TDU, or TD University. Although there have been no reported toga parties at the Westin, there are thousands of students a year, all coming through to learn the TD way.

Across the street from Rodeway Inn and just down the road from Cadillac, Lexus and BMW dealerships, TDU is a 6,500-square-metre (69,414-sq. ft.) showpiece of modern architecture, completed just before Toronto-Dominion scooped up Commerce Bank in late 2007. TD not only bought a U.S. deposit machine, but also picked up this modern training centre, modelled on the "universities" of fast food titans like McDonald's. It's not a surprise. Vernon Hill, the ousted founder of Commerce Bank, who also owns Burger King franchises, has leased real estate to McDonald's.

On one side of TDU, there is a large red cube building that curves outward. The midsection looks like a greenhouse with a vaulted ceiling, and on the other side it morphs into suburban office space. It is part of a complex of nine build-ings housing 3,500 employees, which makes the bank a major employer in the state. In the parking lot, every car seems freshly washed. Prominently parked is a green panel van. Painted on the side of the van is the word "WOW," the bank's call letters in the United States. In the lobby, another buffet has been laid out, including two orange boxes of Wheaties to match the bouquets of orange gladioli decorating the table.

Climbing up through the glass atrium is a sweeping staircase. The centre hall is used not only for business and training, it has also been a wedding venue, hosting the nuptials of two TD employees who met while at TDU. The interior has a playroom feel—curved silver doors that resemble the hall of mirrors in a carnival funhouse, with some doors cut in non-rectangular geometric shapes sporting deep blue panels. All around, the feel is light, with bright colours and even beach umbrellas.

It won't make the Top 40, but a soundtrack has also been commissioned by TD and is piped into certain proceedings. TDU is where you learn the rules and secret ingredients of service that would make any self-respecting Canadian sneak a giggle. Listening in on any of the sessions by outsiders is verboten. The magic mash is closely guarded so no competitor can get an advantage. And competition can be stiff. On this day in May 2011, *The Wall Street Journal* carried a rehash of the story that Royal Bank of Canada was in the process of selling its U.S. retail banking division, which had been a money-losing ball and chain for RBC. (It would sell a month later.)

A black 7-series BMW pulls up in front of TDU. The bank's CEO in the United States, Bharat Masrani, gets out of the front passenger seat, his white shirt brilliant in the May sunshine. He takes his suit jacket out of the back seat and the car pulls away. Masrani is speaking this morning in the 400-seat theatre at TDU. Bankers from Maine to Florida, and some from Canada as well, are here. There are classrooms named *Passion, Culture, Innovation* and *Magic*. There are classes for new tellers, with simulated counters just like in a real bank, as well as a phony but realistic vault they can walk into as they would in a branch. Another room is set up to train people who work in call centres. (Note: TD says it does not outsource its call centres.) In one class-room, fifteen people listen to the teacher at the front until he sees visitors peering through the windows, at which point he leads a cheer, presumably without knowing who is out there. It wouldn't be surprising if he had been forewarned, such freaks for detail are the bunch at TDU.

As of the end of 2011, almost 18,000 first-timers at TD had received a six-hour session in "traditions"—indoctrination into the history of the bank, its brand, model and culture.

"They try to create a Disney-type atmosphere, that this is more than just a bank," says Fred Graziano, the head of retail banking for TD in the United States. "You get pinned! You get to drink the Kool-Aid for the first time." He refers to Jim Collins' business bestseller *Good to Great* as a book that's mentioned with frequency at TDU, along with his personal favourite, *212°: The Extra Degree.* "At the end of the day, that's all we have," Graziano says. "This is not a bank—it's a retail organization," comes the line again.

Throughout the U.S. system, there are fifty satellite TDUs, but nothing on such a grand scale as Mount Laurel, which also houses the human resources and the WOW departments. In 2011, the bank spent $79 million on training, almost $1,000 for every employee in Canada and the U.S. Shannon Peck, program manager for the WOW department, gives the tour. A short young woman with long black hair and smooth skin, she has the rap down pat. "Branding is everything," she says, rhyming off the slogans. "WOW is in the details. Banking is a utility, right? What separates us? Service. People want to be treated well."

The door handles, she shows, sport the TD shield. On Fridays, staffers are encouraged to wear their best green outfits. She cites an explicit definition of WOW: "Always exceeding customer expectations and creating surprise and delight." On the wall of a conference room upstairs, huge letters proclaim "Awesome Model + Passionate Execution = WOW." It's all a bit much, and the leaders in Toronto acknowledge some discomfort, but embrace the model because it seems to work.

"It's not me, but it's obviously successful," says Chairman Brian Levitt. "Once you decide something's not a moral question, success in business is giving customers what they want at a price they're willing to pay for it. And it definitely works."

He says to get a message out to 27,000 people—the number of employees the bank has in the United States—you have to "oversimplify and exaggerate," and that's what WOW does. Why are McDonald's or Shoppers Drug Mart so successful? "It's consistency, you know what to expect."

Fred Graziano says the bank's model of service has to be in the very DNA of the business. Every branch should look and feel the same, and his team is pretty "fanatical" about its sites. Besides, Ed Clark came from Canada Trust, a financial services company that invented plenty of its own rules and marketing hooks. Funnily enough, though, both program manager Shannon Peck and Rebecca Acevedo, a senior PR exec, refer to the bank as having just 27,000 employees, leaving out the 57,000 that work in Canada. This is clearly still an American bank, albeit with a Canadian parent, and both women are former Commerce employees.

In the lobby, in big letters, are the words "Get SMART." For anyone raised on mindless 1960s TV shows, this leads to a double-take. The exhortation has nothing to do, though, with the hilarious spy comedy starring Don Adams as the bumbling, shoe-phone toting Maxwell Smart, Agent 86, battling his archrival Siegfried at KAOS. Get SMART here is more saccharine than comedic. *S* stands for "Say yes." *M* means "Make each customer feel special." *A* is for "Always keeping promises." *R* stands for Recover, as in "To err is human, to recover is divine." *T* is for "Thinking like our customers." And there's a footnote to *S*. If you can't say yes to a customer, you bump the file up to a manager or supervisor to find another way to "WOW" that person.

If you're really into it, you might join the Alpha WOW Omega Program, a frat club of sorts for the eager beavers of WOW, volunteer employees who drive around in the lime green WOW van making surprise visits to branches to celebrate outstanding workers. Are these the "whack jobs" Vernon Hill wanted to hire? Peck compares the program to "Ed McMahon's Publishing Clearinghouse" of TD Bank. WOW the customer, and prizes ye shall get. One of the power WOWers is the Penny Arcade coin counter. You dump your coins into the mouth of Penny—a freckle-faced little girl with pigtails—and she automatically counts it and spits out a statement. Once the change is poured into the machine, the screen starts to look like a slot in Vegas, with similar sounds. You can also guess how much you've fed into the beast, and if you're within $1.99, you get a prize, like a TD tape measure. There's also Mr. TD, a greenish mascot character who looks a bit like an older, plumper Gumby.

"He's our culture. He's the idea of TD," Peck says, not quite making clear what a chubby Gumby has to do with banking.

There's some anxiety in TD's Canadian retail operations that the "whack job" approach in the States, and the WOW, will make its way north into the more uptight Canadian atmosphere. "You're fucking kidding, right? I'm not doing that stuff," says a former Canadian TD executive. "I think what Ed has done is a great job creating the culture. You all wear your little green pins. The question is, how real is it? This is bullshit. At the end of the day, it's trying to make the most money."

\* \* \* \*

Bharat Masrani's office in Cherry Hill, New Jersey, is on the second floor of TD's U.S. headquarters. He is the bank's number one man in the United States and one of the select few talked about as possible successors to Clark. He's a lifer at the bank, starting out as a lending trainee in 1987, working his way up to the bank's chief risk officer. It's a mystery to Vernon Hill why you would put someone who's a former risk officer in charge of what he thinks should be an entrepreneurial organization. That said, Hill doesn't know Ed Clark, and although TD stays away from risky financial products, it has risked a gigantic amount of capital in the United States. TD Bank, America's Most Convenient Bank, accounts for nearly a third of TD's 85,000 employees and a little under a quarter of its annual earnings.[†]

To be or not to be? To be Canadian, or to hide it? Although the bank would squirm at this question, it is surely obscuring some of its true identity to "pass" for American. Most of the major Canadian banks have resorted to alphabet soup names as they've embarked on international expansion. Royal

---

\* Bank of Montreal now has automated coin-counting machines in Canadian branches, although they don't have names like "Penny Arcade." In the spring of 2012, Ed Clark said TD might bring the machines to branches in Canada.

† In the 2011 fiscal year, TD reported net income of $5.889 billion ($6.251 billion adjusted). $1.256 billion in earnings came from its American personal and commercial bank. It had 25,387 full-time equivalent staff south of the border with 1,281 branches. By the end of September 2012, it had 1,304.

Bank of Canada is RBC. Bank of Montreal is BMO. Canadian Imperial Bank of Commerce is CIBC. One could argue that it would be a competitive advantage to operate a Canadian-run bank in the United States in the post–financial crisis world. U.S. banks screwed up. Canadian banks didn't. Why not fly the flag unabashedly south of the border? But Americans don't want this fact shoved in their faces.

Bharat Masrani's office has glass walls. One allows him to see into the office of his number two, Fred Graziano, a holdover executive from Commerce. Another allows him look down, like a count watching over his minions, on a massive branch of the bank. It could be slightly unsettling to be a teller and look up and see Bharat staring down at you.

In the fierce U.S. retail and banking markets, TD has to nurture its American business model and continue to showcase and prove its niche in the sector. "We don't make cars and screwdrivers. We're in the people business. When we say 'TD Bank, America's Most Convenient Bank,' it's not a tagline. It's who we are as a company. That's what we do for a living," says Masrani.

Unlike RBC, TD has recognized that it is operating in a different culture and accepts that fact. While getting the opportunity to buy Commerce Bank was a lucky break, getting the training centre as part of the deal turned out to be lucky too. As odd as it might be in Canada, where the TD way of doing things has been absorbed over 150 years of development, TDU is the means by which the U.S. division maintains distinctiveness and integrates acquisitions. All employees of companies TD has bought since Commerce have had to go through their indoctrination at TDU. It's also where Canadian employees come to learn about how to "bank" the United States, and perhaps return to Canada with new approaches. You come to TDU to be indoctrinated into the TD way of life, and if you want to succeed in the fraternity of "TD Bank, America's Most Convenient Bank," you ask for more.

# 15

# ED'S PERSONAL SHOPPERS

*The TD Acquisition Team*

Some guys know baseball. They can recite batting averages, earned run averages for pitchers, and tell you which hitter is most likely to smack a double on a third pitch when there's a wind from the south. Riaz Ahmed knows banks like those guys know baseball. A slender man of medium height with black hair streaked with grey, he is dressed predominantly in black, with no sign of TD green. Ahmed is Ed Clark's chief personal shopper. He and his team pick and choose the banks and other institutions that TD should or should not buy in TD's footprint, the strip along the eastern seaboard from Maine to Florida.

"I troll the U.S. market. I keep in touch with bankers," Ahmed says.

By his own modest estimation, he knows the vitals on some fifty banks, the ones with at least $10 billion in assets. He knows their balance sheets, their income statements, their management teams, their cultures, whether they are capital constrained, whether they have liquidity problems, whether they paid back government bailout money. Ahmed and his team of half a dozen scan, study and chart them, and then wait for the right moment to pounce.

"I know them pretty well," he says, dripping with understatement.

It may be false modesty, but Ed Clark wants to make it clear that the CEO doesn't do the acquisition, at least at TD. He characterizes his role as the sponsor, the guy who will write the cheque. He credits Ahmed's corporate development team with evaluating the possible targets and probably turning down ten times as many as the bank actually makes a move on. He explains:

"You ask Goldman Sachs or Morgan Stanley or JPMorgan or whatever, they would say we have one of the best corporate development groups, clearly, in the world. They celebrate when they turn a deal down. It's the same celebration in their group as when they do a deal, and they're very disciplined about saying that. We had one where they worked for months and months and months. We bid, we didn't get it. I said, 'Okay, champagne time.' What terrifies me is hubris. I mean assets [loans], acquisitions and egos—those are the three things that bring down banks. I mean, imagine, you know, buying something over the weekend. What kind of ego do you have to have about your judgment that would let you do that?"

Clark is full of disgust for those companies that do acquisitions because the boss gets an idea and says, "I want to make the big bold move here," calling it a formula for failure. He may very well be right. Big corporations are extraordinarily complex. A sensible consumer who's buying a car or computer might shop around more and do more due diligence than a macho CEO who wants to be perceived as a man of action. Even Vernon Hill is on the same page as Clark on this one.

This viewpoint harkens back to the first conversation I ever had with Clark, back in 2003. At the time, he said the hardest thing to do was nothing.[77]

TD may finalize a deal over a weekend, but pulling the trigger on a purchase takes the corporate development team months of planning and research—maybe not as long as Keith Gray took getting to know Larry Waterhouse, but months.

Riaz Ahmed is much more deliberative than Gray. Although Gray quietly processes his ideas and strategies over time, he is at heart an entrepreneur. Ahmed approaches acquisitions differently, more like a scientist. He is also as modest as he is soft-spoken. When asked to compare himself to Bill Ryan of Banknorth—famous for driving three hours to simply have a coffee with a banker he wanted to get to know who one day might be a seller—Ahmed thought about their differences. "If I could ever be as good as he was. He was a master at that. He approached it from a relationship perspective. I approach it from a technical perspective."

"Super smart guy," Angus Rigby, a former TD executive, says of Ahmed. "Ed relies on him a lot on the acquisitions."

Among the executives at TD Bank, Riaz Ahmed is one of those who have probably known Ed Clark the longest. A chartered accountant by training, he was twenty-five in 1988 when he went to work for Clark at the shattered organization known as Financial Trustco, a clean-up job if there ever was one. Ahmed was one of four men, including Clark, who came in and restructured it.

"Just going through that experience with him at Financial Trustco for three years restructuring, doing a lot of deals, negotiating your way out of difficult contracts—it was a fantastic experience for me in terms of learning. You just can't find a richer environment to learn stuff," Ahmed says, calling his time with Clark "a tremendous exercise in growing up and maturing as a deal maker."

In 1991, after the foursome put away the mop, everyone scattered. Clark went to Canada Trust as COO. Ahmed went to work for Citibank, which not surprisingly was also sinking at the time, a victim of a commercial real estate collapse. Citibank (which later became known as Citigroup and was bailed out during the 2008 financial crisis) had to be rescued then as well—by Saudi Prince Al-Waleed bin Talal, the same investor who threw a life preserver to Four Seasons Hotels in the early 1990s.

Ahmed spent the next five years at Citibank, getting a taste of U.S. banking culture, before landing at TD Bank in 1996. Clark was by then CEO of Canada Trust. The two stayed in touch during their separation. Ahmed would go see or have lunch with Clark for career advice. They would be reunited when TD bought Canada Trust and Clark became CEO of the bank.

"A transformation of TD started with Canada Trust," says Ahmed. "That is the defining moment of how we got where we are, which includes the U.S. strategy." Had TD not bought Canada Trust, he says, it might not have understood Commerce Bank, which they all call the "Canada Trust of the U.S."

Commerce would, he says, have the same transformative effect on Banknorth as Canada Trust had on TD—the zany culture, Sunday hours, lapel pin. "We saw value in that. Any other bank operating in the New York market probably wouldn't have understood," he explains.

Although Ahmed and Clark had worked together at Financial Trustco, Ahmed actually went to work for TD before Clark. In 2003, they started talking about Ahmed working with David Livingston, who was then heading development for TD. Ahmed joined the department in October 2004, not long after TD had announced the Banknorth acquisition, and he worked on closing that deal. The first year was about "making sure that we were building decent scale in the United States so that if we were going to build a presence in the United States then it had to be a presence that could survive." Scale, he says, builds capability, and gets the bank to a safe spot.

"If we didn't do anything more, we'd be all right," he says, in reference to TD's initial 51 percent stake in Banknorth. It had almost $30 billion in assets, but it could be grown. Hudson United and Interchange added more than $10 billion, bringing the total to over $40 billion. Commerce then added $48 billion to bring the assets to about $90 billion. With other acquisitions and organic growth, the bank has a scalable platform in America. At the end of July 2012, TD had $208 billion in assets in the U.S. By that measure alone, it is a big bank in the United States. "We wouldn't feel compelled to do anything else from here," Ahmed says, shutting down any questions about further acquisitions.

The only banks ahead of TD now in the U.S. are major ones—Bank of America, JPMorgan Chase, Citigroup, Wells Fargo—and super regionals like US Bancorp. Being the number nine bank in the U.S. (the sixth biggest in North America when the Canadian division is included), but in a very specific geographic region, gives TD concentration, so it seems even bigger. And the Manhattan presence gives it the media attention it wouldn't get if it were focused on Arizona. Ahmed also knows the history of the bank, that back in the 80s, when Canada had independent brokers and the banks all started buying them, TD did not.

"TD decided at the time to focus on online brokerage, which at the time was called discount brokerage," he recounts, speaking about Gray's legacy. That belief in online and discount brokerage emboldened the bank, he says, to acquire Waterhouse in the U.S.

Ahmed says "if you just follow the cash," from the IPO of Waterhouse, to buying it back and then the stock swap to get the biggest share of Ameritrade, "effectively that investment has been for free for TD." Ironically, the Waterhouse brand came north and became the wealth management brand in

Canada, whereas it has disappeared in the U.S., where it started.[*] In the U.S., where TD is not well known as it is in Canada, TD Bank and TD Ameritrade give TD two marketing "shields."

When asked, "Have you made progress in making TD a household name in the U.S.?" he replies, "We're on the journey." Excluding the Waterhouse purchase, the bank has been in retail in the U.S. only since 2005. Regis and Kelly have helped, and being a triple A–rated bank hasn't hurt. Also, adds Ahmed, "many people came to us and said, 'We don't want to [do business] with a TARP bank.'"[†]

David Livingston left in 2006 and the former CFO Dan Marinangeli supervised the development department briefly. Ahmed jokes that Clark put Marinangeli there to make sure that he, Ahmed, was growing up. Soon though, Clark's young protégé was in charge of development. It was crucial timing. In August of 2007, Goldman Sachs called and said Commerce Bank was up for sale. Ahmed's intimate knowledge of those fifty U.S. banks was about to pay off. Ahmed was now the personal shopper, whose job it was to squeeze the fruit. Commerce felt like good fruit.

"We were aware of it. We knew of its strengths. The fact that it came up surprised us because we didn't think it was up for sale. We jumped on that right away. Goldman said to us this would need to be a quick transaction," Ahmed explains.

In an unusual move, TD took most of the SET, the senior executive team (Bharat Masrani, Tim Hockey, Riaz Ahmed, chief risk officer Mark Chauvin and Ed Clark), down to see the "property"—the eureka! moment for the group. The TD brass quickly recognized the similarities to Canada Trust. It also made an impact on Commerce's team when they saw the whole front line from TD come for a visit. "We think you're the only guys who will understand us," Ahmed recalls a top Commerce executive saying.

---

[*] Robin Korthals thinks TD managers made a mistake letting the Green Line name disappear in Canada. "I thought it was idiocy," he says. The Canadian discount brokerage still has 50 percent market share.

[†] TARP stands for the Troubled Asset Relief Program, which was enacted during the financial crisis to allow the U.S. government to take stakes in at-risk banks.

Time, though, was crucial. Bill Ryan, the boss of Banknorth, who knew Commerce and Vernon Hill, jokingly said to Ahmed, "Don't let Ed screw this up." After staying up all night finalizing details, TD announced the deal on October 2, 2007. "That was one of the longest days of my life. I literally went home, had a shower, changed my suit and came back in. I didn't even go to sleep," Ahmed recalls.

"The valuation exercise [was] pretty typical," he says. Looking at profitability, his team attempted to restate earnings with TD as owner, adding new branches, assessing the branch maturity rate, always with the question "Could we realize that growth or not?" As with any financial modelling, there are always lots of assumptions, and models are only as good as those assumptions. "You never get one and say, 'Well that was easy.' They're not," Ahmed declares.

In analyzing which banks to buy, Ahmed is the subject matter expert. Then there are the valuation experts. Mark Chauvin does the risk analysis. Ed Clark calls each of these areas of responsibility "neckties," the implication being that you could hang from your tie if you're wrong. Ahmed has the corporate development necktie, and asks the big question: Do we hear anything in this transaction that makes us choke? "We've walked away lots of times. We might get the feeling we're not hearing transparency."

Ahmed says you can sit around a table for three or four hours and know whether you're getting the straight goods or not. If you feel like you have to ask the right question in order to get the right answer, "that doesn't go over well with us."

One extremely big question is the quality of the loan book at the target bank. Enter another crucial member of Ahmed's team—Al Jette, TD's executive VP of treasury and balance sheet management, an executive with deep ties to Ed Clark going back not only to Canada Trust days but to Clark's tenure at Financial Trustco.

"Al is a genius," says David Livingston. "Relatively quiet, very smart, a very analytical guy who is an aggressive mountain biker." Jette, Livingston says, always created worry at the bank that he'd do something fatally hare-brained on his bicycle. Jette is like a maestro when it comes to interpreting balance sheets, understanding assets and liabilities and whether they are properly matched. Mismatches mean trouble. If you borrow short and lend long, it could result in disaster. When things go well, you can make lots of money under that scenario. But when things go badly, you can lose a lot.

"Al's view is you don't want either one," Livingston says. If earnings come from a mismatch, TD does not consider them to be core earnings. Livingston says that Al is a major force inside TD when it comes to taking risks and how to factor that into the deal price. He says Jette, along with Clark, and Ahmed, who now occupies Livingston's job at the bank, "understand this the best. The three of them together would be an analytical force."

\* \* \* \*

TD hasn't been the only one interested in buying banks in the United States. There are those who pick away at left-for-dead community banks, putting them in rehab until they have enough assets to achieve efficiencies. Billionaire investor Wilbur Ross is one of those. Now in his mid-seventies, Ross is one of the most respected financiers in the United States. Of modest height, with a balding head that suits a man of his vintage, Ross occupies an elegant office high above the Avenue of the Americas in Manhattan. The walls are festooned with avant-garde photographic art, something of a surprise given that Ross himself comes across as a straight-up, meat-and-potatoes guy. As in offices of most corporate champions, there is the requisite wall of fame, here a series of photos of Ross with world leaders (Clinton, Blair, Mulroney), royalty (Prince Charles) and other business titans (the Mittals of India, to whom Ross sold revived steel mills).

Ross made his name with the legendary Rothschild family as a turnaround man and is known in some circles as a vulture. "Vulture" is street lingo for a savvy investor who buys distressed assets on the cheap and makes them worthwhile (read: saleable) again. Ross was doing exactly that with graveside banks in the United States, post–financial crisis.

During his pursuit, he has bumped up against Ed Clark's group under Riaz Ahmed. TD was the underbidder of a bank that Ross bought in Florida.* Ross

---

* Ross beat out TD for BankUnited. In the summer of 2011, with BankUnited trading publicly, Ross told CNBC his investment in the bank had tripled in value in a year and a half.

was also buying up little banks in New Jersey. Once again, he was in TD territory. There's good reason why the two keep meeting. Ross says New Jersey has the highest per capita income of any state in the union and is the most rapidly growing. That's good, for retail banking and commercial lending. Florida is a good property too. With no state income tax and no inheritance tax, it's a magnet for those in high-tax jurisdictions elsewhere in the U.S. The demographic math is there as well, given that the state is bulging with affluent retirees.

Ross says the consolidation of the U.S. banking system will be a multiyear process. There are 7,300 banks, and only eighty of them have assets of $10 billion or more. "People don't realize, Canadians especially don't realize, how fragmented the [American] banking system is. New Jersey alone has 110 banks—110 separate independent banks—all below $2 billion [assets] in size," Ross adds. He says there are 700-odd banks on the FDIC (the U.S. Federal Deposit Insurance Corporation) watch list and his best guess is that 500 of them will fail.*

He thinks the ideal size for a regional bank is something approaching $10 billion. That means it's big enough to have all the sophisticated products and sophisticated systems, but not so big that it loses contact with its customers.

Of course, this raises questions about just how big TD is. Is it too big? With $806 billion in total assets, and within that, just over $200 billion in the U.S., it's a Goliath. "I'm not sure that after a certain point you don't have a reverse scale that sets in," Ross says.

He talks about how a broad geography with lots of branches requires additional layers of management. In other words, it makes no sense for a New Jersey bank to have branches in Colorado. You'd need someone there to oversee things, whereas with a few banks with a few hundred million in assets in New Jersey, once you slam them together there are all kinds of economies of scale. Ross is of the belief that he can create a series of separate banks that are each around $10 billion or so in assets. "We're already there in Florida, we're at about $11 billion."

---

* According to the FDIC, there were just three bank failures in the U.S. in 2007. There were 25 in 2008, 140 in 2009, 157 in 2010 and 92 in 2011. As of August 3, 2012, there were 40 more. That's 437 since the start of 2007.

As for TD's big move into the U.S. with Commerce Bank, "They paid a very aggressive price, so clearly they were taking a very long point of view and I think given the strength of their capital position and given the strength of their basic balance sheet, rather than investing in bad loans I think I'd rather pay a little aggressive price for a decent bank in a decent territory," is how he describes TD's strategy. He says he thinks that it will probably take ten years to show signs of working.[78]

It took between fifteen and twenty years for Canadian banks to become active in the United States after Bank of Montreal's purchase of Harris in Illinois in 1984. Matthew Barrett, the former chairman and CEO of BMO, who then followed up as chairman and chief executive at Barclays in the U.K., said in the fall of 2009 that Canadian banks faced headwinds for a number of years whenever they looked at buying anything in the United States. Barrett explains, "Historically, Canadian banks were at a disadvantage acquiring in the U.S. [because] you had a sort of medium currency, the Canadian dollar, PE [price to earnings] ratios were much higher in the United States, so it was prohibitively expensive and dilutive for many, many years. Now, if you could find the target, particularly if you can convince the FDIC—who are doing it every day, by the way—to ring-fence any toxic assets inside it, it may be a once in a lifetime opportunity. And it's my guess, I don't know, but it's my guess that the Canadian banks are throwing a line over that as we speak."[79] He was right at the time about both TD and BMO. Each would do more deals in 2010.

During the crisis, the first U.S. banks to fail were in the West, and TD started to take notice. It then developed a close relationship with the FDIC, putting what Ahmed described as a tremendous amount of effort into this in 2009.

The FDIC was established in 1933 to deal with the thousands of banks that failed in the late 1920s and early 1930s. The agency identifies failing banks and conducts a ninety-day process to find a qualified buyer that includes valuing the bank's assets and marketing the wobbly institution to healthy purchasers that then make bids for it. The whole idea is to protect customers' deposits and to seamlessly shutter the bank on a Friday afternoon and open it on Monday morning with a new owner.

As for the FDIC process of buying dying banks, "We had to learn it. We didn't know what really happens when banks go under," Ahmed says. As a result of the learning curve, Ahmed says TD "missed a couple of transactions along the way." But by 2010, the bank was ready and bought three institutions in Florida. Prior to the deal, TD had just nine branches in the Sunshine State that had come courtesy of the Commerce acquisition. Long term, the bank had plans for Florida but expected the buying process or the build-out to take years. The financial crisis and bank failures sped everything up. In April 2010, TD bought the carcasses of three banks in the state (Riverside National Bank of Florida and two smaller ones) with the assistance of the FDIC, which suddenly gave the bank sixty-nine more branches there.

\* \* \* \*

Colleen Johnston comments on the prolific amount of modern art adorning the halls and rooms of the fourth floor at TD's Toronto headquarters. She says she doesn't care for a lot of it. We pass a large, purplish painting. "Not my taste," she says.

Sitting in a corner of her office is a pair of black high heels ready to go if she needs them. After a hectic week that included a visit to the U.K., she is wearing flatter shoes. There are photos of her two daughters, one of her with actor Christopher Plummer, and a painting on the wall by an artist who had a stroke. This resonates deeply. Her brother, a young man, suffered a stroke a few years earlier. There is also a framed five-dollar bill issued by the Bank of Toronto, from a time when Canadian banks issued currency.

As for opportunities in the United States, she says that in the fall of 2008 acquisition targets were plentiful. With every weekend bringing the likelihood of a major bank failure, there was a steady handful of possibilities, large and small. TD was tempted, but continued to debate internally whether to play offence or defence.

"You don't want to catch a falling knife here. You'd rather have the knife bounce off the floor and maybe lose a bit of value but have better visibility," Johnston says, quoting Ed Clark's philosophy.

In 2009, however, as the financial world continued to writhe in pain, TD got in line to make a run for BankUnited in Florida. The Canadian bank didn't win that auction. Wilbur Ross did.

"We, I think, may have bid sixty-seven cents on the dollar plus the FDIC guarantee," Johnston recalls. "What it turned out to be was a learning process for us." TD was not experienced in looking at troubled or distressed assets, but it was definitely disappointed to lose that.

The other internal debate was whether to stay in footprint or stray out of it. Some banks coming up for sale not only had branches in Florida, where TD wanted to build its presence, they also had them in Las Vegas, Arizona and California, areas hit extremely hard by the collapse in housing prices. While not ruling out a move outside of its footprint, Johnston indicated the decision was to stay inside it.

TD was most likely to do a deal with a guarantee from the FDIC and, like it or not, the FDIC deals were going to be in the Sun Belt, where most of the scorching had occurred. Much of Florida had also experienced a crash in real estate values, but at least TD had a couple of dozen branches there as a start. In some cases, TD had already been speaking with small, distressed banks to try to arrange a private deal.

"It wasn't as if we got a covert call from someone saying, 'Hey, you might want to come in and take a look here.' You have to be prepared to go in quickly. The bank is being seized." The FDIC process is a disciplined one that has to stand up to public scrutiny, Johnston explains. "It's not as if Sheila Bair phones up Ed [Bair being the head of the FDIC at the time]. I think there's sometimes this sort of folklore that someone gets a call saying, 'Hey, will you buy this bank now?'"

The FDIC-assisted purchases of the three Florida banks—Riverside, AmericanFirst Bank and First Federal Bank of North Florida—were assigned the codenames "Romeo" and "the Juliets." "Romeo" was for Riverside. The smaller of the three were "the Juliets." Essentially, the FDIC would absorb 50 percent of any loan losses up to certain thresholds and up to 80 percent in excess of them. This vastly limited the risk to TD and in exchange, the FDIC got a credible bank to keep the branches of those crippled banks open. There would be no material earnings impact on TD or impact on its capital. As Ed Clark puts it, the deal was such that it was cheaper than building new branches.

Just weeks later, on May 17, 2010, TD announced yet another acquisition of a distressed bank in the United States. This time it was South Financial Group (SFG), giving TD another 176 branches in the southeastern U.S., mostly in the Carolinas, but also another sixty-six in "deposit-rich" Florida. To get these new "stores," TD was paying $61 million in cash or TD stock. Although it differed from "Romeo and the Juliets" because there was no guarantee from the FDIC, TD was still dealing with the U.S. government. SFG had received TARP money from the Treasury Department during the dark days of the crisis. As part of this deal, TD would pay Treasury $130.6 million to buy preferred stock purchased by the U.S. government under TARP.

Here was a Canadian bank taking another troubled bank off the hands of U.S. taxpayers. This one gave TD another $9.8 billion in deposits and $8 billion in loans. Given that the bank was also getting another 176 branches, Bruce Campbell, a conservative Canadian money manager who was once a bank analyst at RBC, said TD was essentially getting each branch for a little over $1 million a piece, adding that you couldn't build them for that. "It's almost like you're getting the deposits for free," he said.[80]

This time Morgan Stanley contacted TD about South Financial Group. The deal was code-named "Hunt" by TD, not using the convention of having the first letter of the code match the first letter of the target. At first blush, Colleen Johnston says, the bank would not have been interested, even though Clark says TD had been watching South Financial for a long time. "We as an organization didn't know much about the Carolinas or real estate lending in the Carolinas," he says.

Again, though, South Financial Group was a company that had lost its founder and leader in the fall of 2008. The new CEO was an executive by the name of Lynn Harton. Riaz Ahmed and others from TD went to Greenville to meet Harton and his team. "It became apparent to us that they had just run out of time. This was a class management team and we wanted to have them on our team," Ahmed recalls.

\* \* \* \*

When the larger financial world talked about emerging markets, it used to mean China, India and Brazil; more recently countries like Turkey, Indonesia and Vietnam are included. When TD talks about emerging markets, it means New York City, Boston and Florida, with maybe a little bit of the Carolinas and Washington, DC, thrown in for good measure. While it brags about a Maine to Florida footprint, the foot is missing a toe. That toe is Georgia. It is not by design that TD has no branches there—it hasn't been avoiding it—but an acquisition has not yet presented itself.

"It would be on my target list, obviously," Graziano says. Masrani, who claims to speak with Ahmed often, says having Georgia in TD's swath doesn't matter to him. Sun Belt demographics are tempting to follow, he says, but can be misleading. Masrani is clearly more cautious in what he says than Graziano. The fact, however, that Graziano sounds ready to add Georgia to the fold makes observers think that's the case. Snowbirds driving down I-95 to Miami from Maine in the winter suddenly see TD drop off the map in Georgia, leaving them with no place to roll their coins for free.

"We want to be there because that would certainly fill out the entire east coast," Graziano says. "Atlanta, it's definitely a market that fits us. It really needs to be in our footprint."

Graziano sees the consolidation trend in the United States continuing apace. There were 15,000 U.S. banks in the 1990s; there are 7,300 now, and he sees that number being cut in half again by 2014–15. TD, via Ahmed's team, will assess anything and everything of the right size and shape that might be available in its footprint.

Fred Graziano is a lean, tanned, middle-aged man of medium height with short grey hair. Like many a banker, he wears a blue-striped shirt. His conservative tie has diagonal slashes, one of which is the magic colour, green. He wears TD cufflinks with the same logo that appears on the now-famous lapel pin. His office is separated from his boss's lair by a glass wall. He can see who's in with Bharat Masrani, Masrani can see who's in with him. The most noteworthy object in his office is a large map of the eastern seaboard of the United States. It sits on a stand and in one glance you can see the swath TD now cuts from Maine to Florida, with that one exception of Georgia.

As for how big TD could get in the U.S. market, Graziano unabashedly uses the word "unlimited," citing the bank's "unique model," again going much further than Masrani. He says it's not about brand awareness, a concept many companies embrace. He cites BP, which as a result of the spill in the Gulf of Mexico has a lot of brand awareness, just the wrong kind. He prefers to talk about "brand consideration," meaning people will think about giving TD a shot.

Although the bank boasts about its Maine to Florida footprint, there are really three areas of intense interest—metro New York, Boston and Florida, the bank's emerging markets. Graziano refers to them as "primary markets." That means that 70 percent of all new stores the bank builds will go into those zones. Graziano says he would not be tempted to plunk a new bank in upstate New York, where he'll get $70 million USD in deposits, versus a new bank in metro New York where he'll garner $300 million.* The average in the system is about $89 million.

"You can't replicate that anywhere in the world," he says. "There's nowhere that I can think of in the world that's greater than metro New York." The Philadelphia area, where TD's U.S. headquarters sits, about half an hour from downtown, is a mature market, according to Graziano.

"Florida is a minimum 400-store market for us," he says. Metro Boston could handle sixty-seven new locations. Metro New York could grow from 250 to 400. In New York City, Ed Clark envisions another sixty branches, each costing somewhere between $4 and $5 million apiece to build, higher than elsewhere. All told, Graziano says, TD could easily add another 1,000 locations in the United States. "A thousand stores, that was without doing any analysis around it, but easily a thousand." He says he wishes he had unlimited capital. "Metro New York is endless."

At the current rate of building thirty-five to fifty new stores a year, that could take twenty to thirty years. Another 1,000 stores implies more

---

* The TD branch at Two Wall Street was the first in the bank's system to hit $1 billion in deposits.

acquisitions, more targets among those fifty or so banks with assets of $10 billion or more, the kind that Riaz Ahmed follows closely.

"I would be surprised if ten years from now we haven't done any [more] acquisitions," Clark says, adding that the U.S. growth strategy is not dependent on acquiring.

John Thompson, the former chairman, speaks highly of South Carolina, where there are lots of car manufacturers, in addition to Boeing. It also has the same "right to work" anti-union laws as Texas, another state that he mentions, even though it is outside TD's current footprint.

"So, would I go into California now? No, right? Midwest? No, I don't think so. Some parts are good, but you want to be in Detroit? I don't think so. Could you be in Texas? Yes, sure."

Thompson says that after Banknorth, Commerce, the smaller acquisitions in the southeast and then Chrysler Financial in late 2010, the bank is in a phase of "absorbing what we've got." He says it's best to slow down, get it all humming and then think about next steps. "The one thing about TD is that we don't make acquisitions that aren't on strategy," he says firmly. "So the way we do this is we create the strategy first without knowing exactly where we're going in terms of that bank or this bank or that area or whatever. And you get strategy right, and then you start to look at how you're going to execute the strategy second. But we're not an organization where the next investment banker that walks in through the door and says, 'Hey, I've got this one to sell,' and we say 'Oh, boy, maybe we'd like that one.' That's not how we work here."

Ed Clark says, "I don't wake up every morning and say, 'Jesus, if I don't get another acquisition done, I'm toast.' That's not how we feel. But I think they'll just naturally come our way."†

Thompson, however, is struck by the strength of Riaz Ahmed's team and the level of analysis and scrutiny it lays as the groundwork for any acquisitions. "Their ability to look at a demographic area and find out what the parameters are—How much money's there, what's the characteristics of customers? How

---

† At TD's Investor Day on April 17, 2012, Clark said the bank is "on hold" when it comes to more acquisitions in the U.S., and if it were to do one, it would be small.

concentrated are they? What's the balance between retail commercial, what does the real estate look like?—you know, all those things, he's very good at that."

Ahmed's job is really to help Ed Clark assess the big picture. But as Clark's chief buyer, he laughs at the question of whether he ever has buyer's remorse. He allows that not all of the bank's acquisitions have done as well as hoped. "Some meet their business cases, some don't," he says. The biggest issue for Ahmed is "tail risk," those risks that are low probability but can cut you off at the knees. "We don't do those deals," he says, like a wily batter who's learned how to pass on a crummy pitch.

Notwithstanding crises and bad lending practices, the major Canadian banks are, at their core, cash machines, pumping out profits year after year if management doesn't get distracted and lets them operate. The biggest risk is doing something stupid like making a bad acquisition that turns a strong institution into a weak one. The essential challenge facing Canadian bank CEOs is what to do with all the cash that builds up. They can increase dividends, buy back stock to increase the value of the shares left outstanding, or spend it buying businesses. The latter is the riskiest, but there is often pressure from analysts, investors and the media to act. It's as if there's a constant voice in the head of the bank CEO saying, "You're being paid all this money, don't just sit there, do something." There is also competitive pressure. If the bank across the street is embarking on something bold, what should the response be? That's why doing nothing, as Clark once said, could be the hardest thing. But you have to be *ready* to do something. Once or twice in a career, opportunities like Canada Trust or Commerce Bank do come along, particularly in what Ed Clark calls "disruptive" markets, the kind that have existed since the onset of the financial crisis. Assets he never thought would be available are suddenly on sale.

# AND CAR LOANS TOO

*Buying Chrysler Financial*

CEOs don't usually find out their company has failed while watching live national television. Tom Gilman is the exception. On April 30, 2009, the CEO of Chrysler Financial found himself standing in front of a TV monitor in Reagan National Airport in Washington, DC. Gilman, a three-and-a-half-decade veteran of the auto lending business and his CFO, Lee Wilson, had been shuttling back and forth from Detroit to Washington, trying to keep their company alive during the searing recession that followed the financial crisis. Barack Obama was now on the screen saying he was not going to provide any assistance to Chrysler Financial and that the company was not viable. Gilman was stunned.

"You're the CEO of a company that the President of the United States has just declared not viable," Gilman recalled in an internal TD speech on June 10, 2011. "At this moment, you have 4,000 employees watching this press conference live at all your business operations—what do you do tomorrow?"

Gilman said he had been told by the government to liquidate the company that had been providing auto financing for more than forty years. He then told the TD group what he had said to his employees the next day: "You know what? The government isn't always right."

Gilman, it turns out, *was* right. Both Chrysler and General Motors had filed for bankruptcy and would require a financial intravenous from the U.S., Canadian and Ontario governments, but somehow, Chrysler Financial stumbled through. The rescue would, however, take radical measures. Gilman had to slice his staff in half, and managed to pay off $1.5 billion in TARP money his company had received from the U.S. Treasury in January 2009. Chrysler Financial stopped originating new auto loans but continued to run off what it had and paid off other debts. It would, however, require a new owner.

The proprietor of Chrysler Financial back then was Cerberus, a revered private equity company that had made a mistake by buying the automaker Chrysler. Cerberus had been so brimming with confidence in itself as a turnaround specialist that it was convinced it could revive the Detroit legend. While the private equity house is named for the mythological dog that guards the gates of hell, it seems even the sentries of Hades don't have a perfect record. Chrysler and Chrysler Financial were dogs of another sort, and Cerberus wanted clear of them.

Chrysler's CEO during that period was Bob Nardelli, the former CEO of Home Depot. Nardelli had drawn criticism from shareholders and corporate governance experts for taking a $210 million severance package from the home renovation retailer. At best, his goodbye package was seen as an insult to Home Depot shareholders. At worst, it was seen as morally wrong. Nardelli was a tough guy, for sure, but his pointed style was not enough to make Americans buy Chryslers.

Cerberus was, however, superbly connected. Its nominal chairmen were former U.S. vice-president Dan Quayle and former U.S. Treasury secretary John Snow. Snow seemed annoyed at any questions vaguely implying criticism of private equity, the secretive and often unimaginably lucrative corner of the financial markets. Private equity firms focus on companies viewed as inefficient, take them private and give them a management transplant. Frequently, workers are fired, costs shaken out and the company is taken public again, often at great profit. Secretary Snow is also the former CEO of the huge U.S. railroad CSX. With a steely face, his teeth gritted as he stares down an impudent reporter, he says that Cerberus manages money for school teachers' pensions, like that of his dead mother.[81] It's tough to respond when someone conjures the ghost of his late mother.

TD was introduced to Chrysler Financial by none other than Goldman Sachs.

Goldman was working for Cerberus, but TD had also been using Goldman to great effect to conduct acquisition surveillance in the United States. According to Riaz Ahmed, Goldman told TD, "Chrysler Financial would love to have some funding and you're in search of assets so you should go meet them."

Assets meant loans, and TD was indeed in search of them. With Commerce in the U.S., it had a deposit machine, but those deposits had piled up and weren't being lent or put to work. If TD owned a major auto-lending unit, it could provide a natural loan destination for all those deposits. Ahmed sent Barbara Hooper and some other members of his crack corporate development team down to meet with Chrysler Financial. When they returned, they "batted it around" for a few weeks.

"I said to Barbara, we should buy this thing. Why don't we just talk to them about buying them?" Ahmed recalls. He says Hooper then phoned to float the notion and the seller was receptive. Ahmed describes the ensuing process, using an unlikely term for a capitalist enterprise. "We started socializing the idea," meaning they discussed it around the shop, talking to Ed Clark and other members of the senior executive team. They warmed up to it.

"There is an element of courting each other," CFO Colleen Johnston says. "We only want to do this deal if management [the target company] wants to do the deal—that makes it infinitely easier."

Contrast that approach with BHP Billiton's clumsy hostile bid for Potash Corporation of Saskatchewan in 2010. Here was the world's largest mining company flying in from a foreign country on the other side of the globe, making a lowball bid for a world-class asset without developing a relationship or boning up on local Saskatchewan politics, which ultimately foiled any chance for the deal to succeed. In the case of Chrysler Financial, TD held a lunch at headquarters to start to get to know the people from the company, to build trust. Not quite the Keith Gray or Bill Ryan method. More like speed dating, but dating nonetheless. "You're really trying to gauge compatibility," Johnston says.

Negotiations for the deal, code-named "Colt," were more than the usual slog. In this case, even though Cerberus hadn't been able to make a go of Chrysler and Chrysler Financial, TD was on heightened alert. It knew it was dealing with a group that had a reputation for being sharks.

"I think with someone like Cerberus, they're a very sharp organization," Johnston says, barely suppressing a smile. "You just have to make sure you're going through and understanding every, every single aspect of the deal. I think that was probably a tougher deal to negotiate. They were tough." And TD was tough, she adds.

"There wasn't going to be a lot of money left on the table," says Tim Hockey, the executive in Toronto now responsible for North American auto lending. "They were interesting, but frankly, we probably feared more than we actually experienced."

The stamp of approval came from TD's chief risk officer, Mark Chauvin, whom Johnston describes as "steely-eyed." When Chauvin says he's comfortable, everyone around the table breathes a sigh of relief. The deal did raise questions, though, about how active TD had become as an acquirer in the United States. "We're not deal junkies," Ed Clark felt compelled to say on the Chrysler Financial conference call, after the deal was announced just four days before Christmas 2010.

Maybe not, but this would be the third significant deal for TD in the same year. In the spring it had done the FDIC deal for three banks in Florida, then a month later it had taken out South Financial Group in the Carolinas. It had just closed the huge Commerce deal in the spring of 2008, and it had been prominently mentioned in the hunt for BankUnited, which it lost to Wilbur Ross. Investors worried that TD's name was associated with rumours about every major deal. Was it looking too aggressive with the U.S. economy still fragile?

Given the fact, however, that TD was a healthy financial institution, its name would logically surface as a possible buyer of almost anything and everything mentioned for sale. The news about the bank's interest in the auto lender had leaked two weeks before when Bloomberg News fired out blaring headlines. Again, like Commerce, it was another example of a company coming up for sale that TD could never have envisioned being available. Only in times of financial distress did opportunities like this present themselves.

As Ed Clark explains, "We certainly can't take any credit for it, because we went into the United States in a disruptive period. We're being able to do things in the United States that I never would have dreamed. Who would have thought that we'd own Chrysler Financial, right? I mean, it never had occurred to us."[82]

The rationale for the purchase was curious. TD was looking for a place to put money to work. The bank was generating so much money in deposits in the United States—it had $80 billion USD in excess deposits in its investment portfolio—and it needed to find a home for them. This was the situation Canada Trust had faced in the 80s and 90s. TD was sitting with an eastern seaboard presence, but Chrysler Financial would give the bank "national asset gathering" in the United States. Clark says that 90 percent of Americans need a loan or a lease to buy a car and the natural people to provide the financing are not the auto manufacturers, which generally don't have the money. "People with money are the natural people and that's what we are."

At the time of the Chrysler Financial announcement, TD had U.S. deposits of $130 billion. If it owned Chrysler Financial, it could lend out a chunk of that money to auto buyers. After mortgages and credit cards, the third biggest area of consumer lending is cars. In spite of a stubborn 10 percent unemployment rate and annual auto sales in the U.S. sitting at 11.5 million units, well below the peak years of 16 to 17 million units, Clark made the case that people needed their cars to get to work. Furthermore, investors should not worry about people who were bad credit risks. Chrysler Financial would be focused on so-called prime and near-prime customers, people who made their payments and had solid credit histories.*

For each of its major deals, the TD communications branch has been masterful at composing its message. In the case of Chrysler Financial, the bank has repeatedly trotted out the argument that in the U.S. people are more likely to walk away from their houses than their cars. And if you default on your mortgage, it might take thirty months for you to be evicted. But if you default on your car loan, it takes thirty days for the car to be repossessed.

The bank acquired Chrysler Financial for $6.3 billion USD, although TD

---

* At an investor conference on April 17, 2012, the bank was still ruling out getting involved in subprime auto loans in the U.S., but only in the short term.

would claim it was really costing the bank only about $1 billion. In the days prior to announcing the deal, Colleen Johnston was asked at a Goldman Sachs conference whether TD would be a buyer. She replied that the bank wasn't looking at anything significant. That comment resulted in the market thinking there would not be a deal. First, there had been the news report citing three sources, then the CFO had apparently thrown cold water on the report. Then on December 21, 2010, the Bloomberg report was proven to be true.

How exactly was $6.3 billion not "significant"? The way TD explained it was as follows. It was buying $5.9 billion of assets (auto loans) in the Chrysler Financial portfolio that were active but, for the most part, running off and would not exist in a few years. The bank was then adding $400 million for what's known as goodwill—i.e., how much over market value it paid for intangibles like the name and brand. For accounting purposes, this number has to be recorded and it is deducted from the bank's core regulatory capital. In addition, TD would be setting aside $500 million to maintain the bank's capital standards because it was taking on assets (loans) that carried some risk. It's a bit of contortionist math, but that's the way it was explained. It's not a $6.3 billion purchase, the bank argued, it's actually $900 million of invested capital (the $400 million for goodwill plus the $500 million for the capital cushion). That $900 million was not deemed "significant," given that the bank had approximately $620 billion in assets at the time. Technically, Johnston was right. It was not significant in the strictest sense, but Chrysler Financial was a big name and the bank was playing it up as a potentially powerful new unit that could help foster lending and produce earnings in the U.S.

The big issue would be dealer relationships. At the time of the purchase, Chrysler Financial had more than 2,000 dealers in its network. The stated target was to get to more than 5,000, "a very achievable goal given a national universe of 18,500 franchised dealers in the U.S.," according to Tim Hockey, who spoke on the conference call to analysts and investors.

The bank was very bullish on the call, saying it could ramp up to $1 billion USD in loan originations per month by 2013. It was promising shareholders a 20 percent return on invested capital within three to four years and

$100 million in earnings in 2012. Again, as it had with Banknorth, Commerce and South Financial Group, TD would keep existing management. The CEO of Chrysler Financial, Tom Gilman, would continue to run that business out of Detroit, under the supervision of Hockey in Toronto. On March 1, 2012, during the bank's first-quarter conference call, Ed Clark said revenue at the division was "still challenged."

\* \* \* \*

The sixteenth floor of the TD Tower feels very different from the fourth floor, Ed Clark's habitat. You hear voices. Even the decor is friendlier than on the fourth, less in the mode of the Museum of Modern Art. The sixteenth has a vaguely suburban feel. It's the headquarters for TD Canada Trust, the retail division of TD in Canada, the very turbine of the bank's profit machine. This is Tim Hockey's part of the bank.

Hockey is another one of the contenders for Ed Clark's job when the CEO leaves his post. Hockey is a lifer at the bank. He started as a part-time teller in 1983 at Canada Trust in Ottawa, where he studied public administration at Carleton University. This is no Harvard boy, although in 1997 he obtained his MBA at the University of Western Ontario. He moved rapidly through the ranks, through the loans trainee program, and ultimately became district vice-president within ten years before moving into a regions office, where he worked in, among other things, information technology, mutual funds and credit cards. He jokes that he's had twenty-six jobs in twenty-eight years. As with Ed Clark, whose natural path would have been to enter academia, Hockey was advised by his father to leave the bank and do something else. "That's the only piece of advice from him I've never taken," Hockey says.

Good thing. Hockey was one of the strongest early proponents of American expansion during the Clark era, now makes millions of dollars a year and is in line for the top job. Even though many point to the fact that Hockey's résumé doesn't have the breadth of Bharat Masrani's, he is Ed's protégé, according to a former executive. Some have described Clark and Hockey's relationship as almost like father and son.

Hockey is as driven as one needs to be to be a top bank executive. Like most who make it to the upper ranks, he has energy to spare. Saying he doesn't require much sleep, he's up at 4:30 a.m. and rides his bike the thirty kilometres from Port Credit to downtown Toronto. He then shows up at the gym, where he works with a personal trainer for half an hour, getting to his desk by 6:15, where he stays until 6 p.m. At that point, he rides his bike the thirty kilometres back home, timed to fifty-two minutes door to door.

As Vernon Hill says, at TD they measure everything, and Hockey is proud of that, at least about himself. Written on the front of a fat white binder that had been prepared for the Q2 2011 conference call is the statement "26 down, 58 to go." Hockey is tracking the quarters until his scheduled retirement age of sixty-three. It's not because he doesn't enjoy the job. It's how he looks at the world. Six years earlier, he participated in his first conference call for the bank, a "rite of passage" because analysts and media are listening and quoting. Afterward, his wife asked him how it went. "One down, eighty-three to go," he said. His wife didn't understand. He explained that he was forty-two, and if he stayed at the bank another twenty-one years until the bank's customary retirement age, which is what he intended to do, that would be eighty-four conference calls in total. "You can't do anything in a quarter. It's a blink of an eye. But you can change the world in eighty-four quarters," Hockey preaches.

More interested in bicycles than automobiles (he bought a vacation home in Greenville, South Carolina, because the cycling is good), Tim Hockey talks enthusiastically about car loans, saying it was fascinating to watch how auto loans performed during the crisis. It was that old communications team cue card again—people kept paying their car loans, whereas they would walk away from their homes. TD Auto Finance, as it's now called, is running ahead of forecasts, with Hockey telling investors in April 2012 that 8,000 dealers were signed up, originating $800 million in loans in the prior month.[83] In September, he told a Barclays investors conference that TD would soon be one of the top three auto lenders in North America. "We hugged Tom [Gilman] and we 'pinned' him," Hockey says, when the bank closed the deal.

The hardest part of any of these purchases is the integration, and it's getting harder for TD, even though the bank has now done many. Colleen

Johnston says that the bigger you get in the United States these days, the more the regulatory spotlight shines on you. "Once you move out of your home market, it gets tougher. Growth in Canada is safer."

With Chrysler Financial, however, it wasn't like integrating another branch banking operation. It could be run as a separate business and that made it easier for TD. Johnston says Gilman and Hockey became quite compatible working together, even though "they're like chalk and cheese, in a way." Gilman, she says, is no-nonsense, not using any more words than he needs. "Not to be too schmaltzy, but when you look at these kind of deals, the people are a really important facet," she says. Folks from other companies can have different styles, but have to have the same values.

TD executives, however, don't use a deal as an excuse to party. Upon sealing the Chrysler Financial transaction, about ten people simply went up to the fifty-fourth floor to the well-reviewed restaurant Canoe for a drink. Johnston says she ordered something without alcohol that night. Although she will have the odd drink the night before she has to make a presentation, she won't have anything alcoholic the evening prior to an earnings report or a deal announcement.

"It's not our culture to be crazy celebrative," Hockey confirms. Hubris and "counting one's chickens" are out, he says. It couldn't have been written more clearly in the Ed Clark rulebook.

That rulebook, however, will soon have a new author. Whoever the board decides should take Clark's place, that new CEO will either follow the Clark way or write a fresh chapter, just as Thomson did after Lambert, Baillie after Thomson, and Clark after Baillie. As *New York Times* columnist Russell Baker said after being asked whether he'd like to be the successor to Alistair Cooke as the next host of *Masterpiece Theatre,* "My reply was I'd like to be the man who succeeds the man who succeeds Alistair Cooke."[84] Ed Clark, the unlikely bank CEO, may yet be the toughest act to follow at TD Bank.

# THE ERA OF ED

*The Legacy*

On February 17, 2011, a jazz quintet played "Satin Doll" as the glittering crowd mingled among the dinosaur skeletons at the Royal Ontario Museum. On the tables, towering candelabras sprouted flowers, not candles. On the menu was fennel and pear salad with Ontario smoked trout and honey citrus vinaigrette, sprinkled with lemon dust and finished with a pear chip. For the main course, guests had a choice of beef tenderloin in a red wine reduction or seared halibut with smoked bacon in a preserved lemon and clam broth paired with winter vegetables and *pommes fondant.* For dessert, chocolate *crème brûlée* with house-made raisins, port compote and hazelnut brittle.

This was the twenty-first annual ceremony for Canada's Outstanding CEO of the Year, a black-tie affair. Among those in attendance to honour Ed Clark: Sonja Bata, the elegant octogenarian wife of the late Tomas Bata of the Bata shoe empire; Ed Clark's predecessor, Charlie Baillie, who wore a tuxedo jacket with large green checks on the traditional black; Purdy Crawford, former chairman and CEO of Imasco; Brian Levitt, the new chairman of TD and also a former CEO of Imasco, wearing a patterned cummerbund; John Thompson, the former chairman of TD and his wife, Melinda; Judith Cohen (wife of Mickey Cohen, former deputy minister of energy from Clark's days in Ottawa); Roger Greenberg of the real estate company Minto Group, a client of the bank since the merger in 1955; Bill Downe, CEO of Bank of Montreal, who two months before had announced his own $4.1 billion acquisition in the U.S.; Paul Godfrey, CEO of Postmedia Network; and Hal Kvisle, former CEO of TransCanada and the previous year's honouree.

The room was also stacked with TD executives, including Bharat Masrani, Tim Hockey and Colleen Johnston. Former premier of New Brunswick and ambassador to the U.S. and now TD's deputy chairman, Frank McKenna, was working the room. The former president of TD Waterhouse, Frank Petrilli, was in from New York. Fred Tomczyk, CEO of TD Ameritrade, was there, as was Roger Phillips, former CEO of Ipsco and former TD board member; Clark's longtime executive assistant, Janis Dixon; as well as head of human resources at the bank, Teri Currie, who is largely unknown to the public but a highly regarded TD executive.

Clark, dressed in a black tux sporting that ever-present green TD pin on the lapel, claimed to be uncomfortable receiving awards, but seemed genuinely moved. Choking up when he mentioned her in his speech, he paid tribute to Fran, his wife of forty-two years, a retired psychologist, mother of four and now a grandmother, calling her his "competitive advantage." He also said the award he was receiving half belonged to his departing chairman, John Thompson, who had been with him every step of the way. The video tribute included words from TD execs; Clark's four children; the former governor of the Bank of Canada, David Dodge; as well as the current governor, Mark Carney.

Fran Clark is a friendly, calm woman who knows how to carry on an easy conversation. Two of the Clarks' children were in attendance—Hugh, who was studying at Harvard and would soon be off to Mumbai for his work, and Carrie, who is a psychologist like her mother. They too seem to have an effortless ability to be sociable. In my pre-dinner conversation with Carrie, Ed jumped in to say that running the bank was just as much about psychological behaviour as numbers.

In his speech, Clark graciously mentioned the leaders before him—Allen Lambert, who built the first skyscraper in Toronto, a landmark that put TD on the financial district map; Dick Thomson, who led from the top for an astonishingly long and profitable stretch, managing the bank adroitly for its shareholders; and Charlie Baillie, who had a vision to take the bank into new frontiers like Waterhouse and Canada Trust.

Canada is a country in pursuit of what's known in the business world as national champions. Nortel Networks was, for a brief shimmering moment, a Canadian trophy company, shining on the global stage. In 2000, before it began its painful slide into oblivion, Nortel comprised 35 percent of the entire value of the Toronto Stock Exchange. It was mentioned in the same breath as Cisco Systems. Research in Motion vaulted a Canadian product into the hands of heads of state, government officials, captains of industry, and worker bees all over the planet. RIM, however, strains to keep up and by May of 2012 was for sale as Apple and Android continued to dominate the smartphone market, where RIM once ruled. In tablets, Apple has been a clear winner with the iPad.

It's not just in technology that Canada has struggled to maintain world-beating status. In mining, Canada lost control of a large chunk of the base metals industry in 2006 when Brazil's Vale took over Inco while Xstrata of Switzerland gobbled up Falconbridge, Inco's neighbour in nickel-rich Sudbury, Ontario. It was only in late 2010 that the federal government stepped in and nixed BHP Billiton's plan to purloin Potash Corporation of Saskatchewan, the humongous fertilizer resource thought to be so precious that it was not deemed in the national interest for a company from another country to buy it. The list goes on, with Molson, the famed beer company, Four Seasons Hotels, Hudson's Bay Company, Fairmont Hotels, CP Ships, Dofasco and Stelco, all dined on by foreigners. In 2011 and 2012, Ed Clark would be an instrumental behind-the-scenes player, trying to maintain Canadian financial sector control of the TMX Group, operator of Canada's largest stock exchange, by successfully scuttling a bid by the LSE Group in London.*

The major Canadian banks, of course, have a legal shield, a law that protects them from takeover. No single entity can own more than 20 percent of the voting shares of any one of them. They therefore have a moat—a protected oligopoly—that can help them attain championship status. The Big Five achieved global renown during the financial crisis, singled out by the World Economic Forum as the soundest in the world, not one of them requiring a capital injection by taxpayers. While TD has most certainly

---

* In July 2012, the Maple Group, a consortium of four banks (including TD), as well as other financial institutions and pension funds, obtained the final regulatory approvals to take over TMX Group.

moved up versus its competitors, the other large Canadian banks are very profitable and have handsomely rewarded shareholders. In fact, among the Big Five, Bank of Nova Scotia has had the best return over the past twenty years. On August 28, 2012, the *Globe and Mail* reported that Scotiabank topped the list with a 15.5 percent compounded annual growth rate. Royal Bank and TD were tied at 14.8 percent. CIBC was fourth best with 12.9 percent and BMO fifth at 12.6, still highly respectable. Arguably, they are already national champs, and TD, as a challenger to Royal Bank as biggest, clearly has quality written all over it.

But to be a truly iconic national company, does a firm have to make it elsewhere too? General Electric is known the world over, as is Procter and Gamble or Boeing or Apple. Manulife Financial has sought championship status, but was perhaps too aggressive in trying to win it. The company did not protect some of the guarantees it made on certain products it sold in its John Hancock division in the U.S. and elsewhere—principally variable annuities, designed to provide periodic pension-like payments to holders over time. In order to reserve against these products or liabilities, charges to earnings had to be taken if the company did not adequately hedge, or insure, against a decline in market value. As a result, it had not protected itself against the guarantees made to the holders of these products. In a great irony, here was an insurance company that decided not to buy insurance to protect against market risk associated with these liabilities. When the financial crisis hit, Manulife's vulnerability was laid bare and its earnings were hurt as it took charges to strengthen reserves associated with its guarantees. Shareholders were hit hard and the stock has still not recovered to pre-crisis levels. While its 2004 purchase of John Hancock in the United States was for many years thought to be an inspired acquisition, the largest by any Canadian company until then, lifting it to championship status, that success has been largely overshadowed by Manulife's market woes.

The state of affairs that has plagued Manulife since late 2008 has not only tormented shareholders but is also a profound blow to the pride of former CEO Dominic D'Alessandro, who took the company public and led the building of it for a decade and a half before retiring in 2009. It all looked great until it didn't. Donald Guloien, D'Alessandro's successor in the top job, has spent much of his tenure as CEO dealing with the fallout.

So what of TD, then? Will the $19 billion USD it has spent in the United States turn out to be a good investment? Or will it produce pedestrian returns, or worse, unanticipated troubles for the bank? Will TD get tangled in a country that lost its triple-A credit rating in the summer of 2011 and may be stuck with a stagnant Japanesque economy, suffering from deep fiscal problems and a political system so paralyzed by extremes that it can't come up with a long-term credible plan? Would Ed Clark have been better off if he'd behaved like Dick Thomson, returning that $19 billion to shareholders in the form of dividends and share buybacks? If TD's service is so superior to that of other banks, should he have redirected some of that money to marketing in Canada to try to steal more market share from the rest? Protected by an oligopoly, should he have focused on safer, Canadian-based expansion, perhaps in western Canada, where the resource industry has blossomed in lockstep with China's growth and demand?* Did he avoid that because of his own complicated personal history with Alberta? Or will his plan work, with TD continuing to grow, specifically in the U.S., and morph into the biggest and best Canadian bank ever, playing a leading role on the global banking stage?

"The U.S. will really start to thrive, probably after Ed has retired. This isn't about Ed," Colleen Johnston says, mouthing Clark's own line. "We are stewards of this organization and we have to leave the organization stronger than how we inherited it." Frank Petrilli says, "Watch out, B of A. Watch out, JPMorgan Chase. They [TD] are going to be one of the top three, in my humble opinion. They don't get distracted by nonsense."

* * * *

It's May 26, 2011, the day of the bank's release of its second-quarter earnings report. Ed Clark is sitting in front of a camera at the Toronto Stock Exchange

---

* As of the end of the third quarter of 2012, TD's return on equity exceeded 44 percent for its key personal and commercial banking division in Canada.

for an eight-minute interview on CNBC with Maria Bartiromo. She gives him an easy ride. Although Bartiromo can be a formidable journalist and interviewer, she isn't quite as pointed during this segment, ignoring the story of the quarter with TD. Its main retail business was experiencing margin pressure and it did not meet the consensus earnings estimate, an average compiled from a poll of analysts. Twice during the interview, Bartiromo tells Clark he's made a good point. After he explains why TD and a group of other banks and pension funds have gone hostile in their bid for the TMX Group, Bartiromo says he's given a great analysis. Clark has just gotten exactly what he wanted—eight minutes of free advertising in the United States. Ed Clark wins again. He's clearly delighted to go on Bartiromo's show each quarter, even though more than 80 percent of the bank's profit is generated in Canada and the Canadian stock market, for all intents and purposes, sets the price of TD's shares. It's no coincidence that Clark does not appear quarterly on television in Canada. He leaves that to his CFO, Colleen Johnston. Canadians, it seems, don't mind if he spends time tilling other fields.

Still, those American fields are not quite producing a primo crop yield. When it comes to the question of return on equity, both Fred Graziano and Bharat Masrani get antsy, if not a touch defensive. In the spring of 2011, the two top executives in the United States are under the gun, with TD earning just 7.4 percent on all the billions the bank has invested in the U.S. operations. By the end of the third quarter of 2012, the number has slipped to 6.4 percent (8.1 percent when adjusted for unusual or one-time items), still not beating the bank's cost of equity. Sounding counterintuitive, Graziano says that "what keeps it down is the growth. If you wanted to get double digits, stop doing acquisitions, stop opening new stores and we'd get there real quick."

"When we started off and we bought Canada Trust, the same discussions were ongoing. *How does this make sense? When are you ever going to get your returns up?* Well, ten years later, no one's asking that question. So my expectation is that we will repeat that," Masrani says.

Bob Falese, CEO of Commerce Bank before TD bought it, also says he is not worried. "Eventually the United States will come back to a level of growth that will reward TD," he says.

He continues to invest in Toronto-Dominion. Larry Waterhouse hasn't sold a share either. Nor have others no longer associated with the bank, even early critics of Clark who now allow, in the words of one, that he has done a fantastic job.

In truth, TD in the U.S. has to move beyond being obese with deposits. It has to lend all that money, as it hopes to via Chrysler Financial. Its American employees have to learn how to sell other products beyond deposit accounts, and Clark says it takes a massive amount of training for them to become familiar with complex offerings. A top TD executive from Toronto, Brian Haier, who used to run human resources and then the branch network in Canada, moved to New Jersey in June 2011 to make sure that happened. Tellers have to learn to *sell, sell, sell*—not a necessity back when Commerce Bank was happy to take people's deposits and give out dog biscuits.

As well, the cost of complying with new financial regulations developed in the wake of the financial crisis means smaller banks will have a hard time staying small.* Wilbur Ross, the U.S. billionaire bank buyer, says that the 7,300 banks in the United States will shortly end up being 5,000 banks.[85] Ed Clark says that also means its American competitors, the "super regionals" like PNC and U.S. Bancorp, could accumulate more scale and be fiercer competitors. TD's market share grab will start to slow down, he says, even as the bank fills in gaps in its footprint down the eastern seaboard and intensifies its presence in the deposit-rich cities like New York, Boston and Miami.†

"These are countries. These are certainly provinces in Canada," he says, expressing amazement that the metro New York, northern New Jersey and Long Island area alone have deposits roughly equivalent to all of Canada's.

Since the merger of the Bank of Toronto and the Dominion Bank in 1955, when combined assets were a relatively piddling $1.3 billion; to the years of entrepreneurship of Keith Gray under the reluctant Dick Thomson; to the

---

* In 2011, TD hired Edward Silverman, the former staff director of the U.S. Senate Banking Committee, as its head of government relations in the United States. The chairman of the committee at the time was Christopher Dodd, co-author of the Dodd-Frank Wall Street Reform and Consumer Protection Act.

† Among the top ten metro areas in the U.S. for available deposits, TD has branches in five—New York, Philadelphia, Miami, Boston and Washington. Total deposits in those five areas are $1.6 trillion, with just over $1 trillion of that in metro New York alone.

global aspirations of Charlie Baillie; to the exploits of Ed Clark, who has told his executives the U.S. expansion will be his legacy, TD is undoubtedly a continental colossus, the sixth-largest bank in North America. Its assets as of the end of the second quarter of 2012 totaled $806 billion.

"No one sees us as scale-challenged," Clark says.

With just over 1,300 branches, a former executive says, "They're past the failure point in the U.S. They're not going to fail. The question is, How successful are you going to be?"

\* \* \* \*

It's the first Friday of June, 2011, the day of the release of the monthly non-farm payroll report, the most-watched gauge of job creation in the United States. The markets are expecting 165,000 new positions to have been created in May. They get a measly 54,000.* This is after a week of other lousy data points. The housing market is experiencing a double dip in price drops. The manufacturing sector is slowing, the consumer is less confident. The next month's job data are equally pathetic and the members of the American political class are clawing at one another over whether to raise the country's debt ceiling to avert a default. The U.S. is not Greece, Ireland or Portugal, but the country is facing its own fiscal choke point if Republicans and Democrats can't agree on how to approach the federal debt. The mighty U.S. economy is spooling downward again. The Federal Reserve has been throwing cheap money at the economy for almost four years, but the turbine just can't seem to keep spinning without all that extra lubrication. By August it's worse. S&P takes away America's triple-A credit rating for the first time in history, stock markets are spooked and people are wondering if this, plus the wobbly euro zone, could mean 2008 all over again.

---

* On September 7, 2012, the non-farm payroll report showed only 96,000 new jobs were created in August 2012, showing the economy is still sluggish. The U.S. economy requires several months in a row (if not years) of 200,000-plus job growth to make a meaningful dent in the unemployment rate and indicate a solid recovery.

* * * *

In October 2011, in what was once the trading floor of the Toronto Stock Exchange, Ed Clark is on stage with fellow CEO Larry Fink, who heads up the world's largest money management firm, BlackRock, with $3.6 trillion USD under its roof. Beneath the Art Deco murals of the historic exchange, the two are being interviewed in front of a select crowd from Toronto's financial district.

Clark talks about when the U.S. debt crisis peaked in early August, after the downgrade by Standard & Poor's. He says it was "like someone pulled the power switch on loan demand." Suddenly there wasn't any. He said customers in the U.S. had decided they might not have a country anymore, believing it was going to default. Demand soon came back, but this was the economy on which he had placed TD's chips, where the politics and realities over the next twenty years are unlikely to get friendlier as boomers head into retirement and healthcare dependency. Then a surprising statement tumbles out of his mouth in front of a financial sector audience and an American CEO who is paid more than $15 million a year: "Globalization doesn't make everyone else better off. [It's] in the process of destroying the middle class." Despite having taken on America with brio, he deeply understands the forces that could tear that society apart.

A few weeks later, on a blustery and wet October night in 2011, Ed Clark is getting yet another award, in a year during which he has been drenched with them. This time it's from Canada's pre-eminent business school, the Ivey School of Business at the University of Western Ontario. Tim Hockey, an Ivey alumnus, introduces him. At the podium that evening at Toronto's Four Seasons Hotel, Clark gives one of the most important speeches he's ever given. As his tenure at the top of the bank turns the corner into his last years on the job, he is speaking out on socio-economic issues, showing his bent for being part of the public policy debate. He is talking about demographic forces, the uneven benefits of globalization, the pressure on the middle class and the hard political choices he sees in the future. Ed Clark still wants to change the world. Maybe there is still a bit of the hippie in his closet. One can't help but think he's conjuring up his own history and evolution as a guidepost to the future.

*Income gaps have widened. The middle class has shrunk. And the working class struggles, while the highest income earners have become better off. Without fully understanding the forces at play, people get it. They recognize the prize has just got smaller—and their instinct is to protect their share. The Tea Party in the United States is an obvious example. Don't focus on their particular solutions. Focus on what drives this movement. This also happens to be a message being delivered by those in the "Occupy" movement. . . . Their message is the same—they don't like how the world is turning out. . . . We need leaders who can make the complicated simple—without demonizing. . . . We must help our politicians be the leaders we need, leaders who understand the issues, who choose the pragmatic over the dogmatic.*

Make the complicated simple. Pragmatism over dogmatism. Clark is—perhaps unconsciously—describing his own skills. One former executive, upon reading the speech, remarked, "I think it is an application for his next job. Not sure where he is going—academia, international finance, i.e., World Bank or Canadian politics. Maybe even Bank of Canada. Not sure, but he will not be playing golf every day."

Whether that's true or not, Clark is clearly talking about leaders who are like him, and he may very well be right that his sort is the sort that's needed. Making complicated things simple and choosing the pragmatic has worked in spades for Ed Clark. He's a businessperson who innately understands politics. Through Frank McKenna, he gets private time with the likes of Bill Clinton and Tony Blair. He recently began attending meetings of the elite global group Bilderberg, rubbing shoulders with the prime ministers of France and Italy.

Clark may get many accolades, but his peers in Canada are hardly slouches. Scotiabank's Rick Waugh is respected globally as vice-chairman of the Institute of International Finance, a worldwide industry association. During his tenure as CEO, Waugh has been almost as acquisitive as Clark, spending billions buying banks in Asia and Latin America, not to mention businesses in Canada. Royal Bank's Gord Nixon, who has also been CEO of the Year, has run the bank for almost twelve years, an amazingly long stretch given the recent financial mayhem. BMO's Bill Downe has enlivened what had been the sleepiest of the big five, making a major acquisition in the United States. And CIBC's Gerald McCaughey has stabilized what had been the clumsiest of the group.

But given Clark's outsized investment in the U.S. market, does he sleep nights? Clark's made the call, he knows the problems, but he's sticking to his script. He argues that in spite of the comatose housing market and frightfully high unemployment during and since the Great Recession, "we've been able to grow through that." What about planning for something bigger and more calamitous, though? "We can't outrun a world collapse. You can't run a business on the basis of that either," he says.

In fact, amidst the August 2011 rubble, Clark and TD were buying again from those desperate to sell. In this case, it was the monster-sized Bank of America, still in pain from the U.S. housing collapse, looking to unload assets. Around the same time, Bank of America would sell a chunk of its interest in a Chinese bank and Warren Buffett would step in and invest in the moribund bank as he did with Goldman Sachs and General Electric during the 2008 crisis. Working secretly on the deal for months under the code name "Alpha,"[86] TD stepped up and bought the company's Canadian MasterCard portfolio, run by MBNA. The cash consideration was $7.5 billion to cover the amount of outstanding credit card receivables, but the total amount the bank was really investing was about $1 billion, not a huge amount for this blossoming bank. In September 2011, Ed Clark told an annual banking conference there were still huge opportunities for TD in the U.S, not the least of which would be pumping up its presence in New York City.

Back in 2005 the *Globe and Mail*'s Sinclair Stewart wrote, "Ed Clark is congenitally unable to sell."[87] That may have been the case then, but it is not the case now. He's frequently in sales mode, and sometimes by underselling, he is conducting the most persuasive sales job of all. "Okay," you say to yourself, "he's not snowing me." Most of the superficial views of Clark can be turned on their head. He is not a capitalist or a socialist or an ideologue. He is a realist, a pragmatist and a businessperson. That's all. When the assignment was to write a thesis about Tanzanian socialism, he did it. When the assignment was to draft the National Energy Program, he did it. When the assignment was to mop up Gerry Pencer's mess at Financial Trustco, he did it. And when the assignment was to take TD Bank to the next level, he did it.

"He's your ultimate rational man," says money manager Michael Decter, who's observed Clark since taking an introductory economics course from him at Harvard in the early 1970s.

Clark's frequent proclamation that he is a "people person" also catches some who know him by surprise. It's the rare intellectual who can also be comfortable having a beer with Joe Six Pack. His characterization of himself is also at odds with his own admission to Sinclair Stewart in 2005 (or this reporter for that matter) that he doesn't like small talk or the social circuit. Frank McKenna was brought in partly to schmooze with big clients because that's not what Ed likes to do. One former diplomat says everyone likes McKenna, and he plays well in western Canada, a big help to Clark. "A touch stiff" is another description applied to Clark, but staffers also paint him as being able to be very "on" and social when he needs to be, and as having an uncanny ability to shut off that side of his personality. Many effective people have that ability. They are multitalented and gregarious when called for, introverted and focused when they need to be.

On charitable giving, Clark says, "I don't want to get into the details, but I give away a very substantial amount of my net worth. But I always say that's a totally selfish act. I mean, let's not pretend that it's anything but that, because the charge that you get when you buy a piece of land for Habitat for Humanity, build sixteen houses on it, feed sixteen families and give them houses, I mean what could be better? So for me it's enabled me to do things that I never thought I could do in my life."[88]

He told Sinclair Stewart that he is shocked at how little rich people give away. "I mean, what toy could I possibly acquire that would give you the same sense of satisfaction as when you take thirty women who literally have been fucked around by men, and transition their lives so that they and their children's lives aren't on welfare?"[89]

He may give away a lot of his net worth to charity (in Q2 2008 he announced he would exercise 10,000 stock options a week, giving 40 percent of the pretax profit to charity), partly out of feeling guilty about how much money he's earned in his life, but he's proud to defend his pay based on shareholder returns.* He also likes to defend his record, loving nothing more than laughing in the face of his critics, rhyming off a list of his moves since 2005.

"I got out of structured products and everyone said, *Stupid.* I go into the United States. *Stupid.* I stay out of subprime lending and therefore my lending volumes grow less quickly than the U.S. players—*You're stupid.*" On whether he ever gulped hard, he refers to his wife, Fran. "She can count the number of days in my last twenty years of my career that I came home stressed out.† But if you say, do I wear this job every day? Yes," he concedes.

On the question of whether he will be more conservative in his last years as boss, he answers, "The truth is, I don't know. Legacy is a bad word. I think it causes CEOs to do wrong things. So you don't have to worry that I'm going to do something to establish my legacy. I equally think it's not right to stop and say, if there's an opportunity . . . to say I'm going to deny doing it. If you feel that way and you're nervous about it, then get out of the seat and give it to someone else."

Which raises the succession question at TD. There are two strong candidates (Bharat Masrani and Tim Hockey) with perhaps a third, the outlier of the group, Mike Pedersen, the head of wealth management.‡ Who might the successor be?

"All of them," Clark says, brushing off his public relations person, who is shaking his head, signalling him to avoid taking the bait and not give any sort

---

* Clark's total direct compensation for 2011 was $11.275 million vs. $11.275 million in 2010. Under the plan, he would have been eligible for a 6 percent increase. However, due to the economic outlook, the compensation committee recommended and the board approved leaving his compensation the same as the year before. Clark voluntarily deferred his cash bonus ($1.96 million) into deferred share units, making all his "incentive compensation" equity based to "maximize alignment to long-term shareholder value." According to TD's proxy circular of February 2012, the value of Clark's share ownership in the bank was $85,838,453. Upon retirement, his annual pension for the rest of his lifetime will be $2.4885 million. When he dies, his surviving spouse will receive the full annual amount for the rest of her life.

† This is slightly at odds with Clark's earlier comment about not having developed the skill to sleep through the night, in particular during the financial crisis.

‡ Aside from Pedersen, there may be other outliers: Colleen Johnston and Fred Tomczyk, CEO of TD Ameritrade. Complicating the choice between Masrani and Hockey is age. Masrani was born in May of 1956, Hockey in May of 1963. The longer Clark stays on as boss, the more it reduces Masrani's chances and improves Hockey's.

of answer to this highly sensitive question. "I think every one of those you named. Other people would hire them as their CEO to run a large organization. The bank would follow any one of the three."

Colleen Johnston gets sentimental (but not overly so) about Clark, about his values and decision making, but also knows that there is a reality at any institution like a big bank, and TD is no different. "You know, when I talk to investors, clearly Ed is an iconic CEO. And from where we sit, it's hard to imagine a world without Ed, for sure. But the way investors look at it is, investors deal with companies all the time, and they realize that CEOs at some point will retire and that is a fact of life. So what they look at is the process around this, and what they worry about is, will the successor come from within or outside the company? Do I know who those successors could be and what do you think that'll do to the strategy? Because investors invest in a strategy."

Others disagree. A former high-ranking TD executive who says Clark is "nothing but impressive" calls him a "one-man show" and pointedly raises the question about whether there will be a vacuum when he goes. "The guy's still making all the decisions in the bank and many of the minor ones for that matter. How much are you concerned when he's not there? Not one of those guys makes a decision without checking with Ed. You get a lot of *Ed said, Ed said*. And when that person's not there anymore, what happens?"

There may be few quite like Ed Clark, though. As John Thompson pointed out at the dinner honouring Clark in February 2011, "How many other great CEOs have also been named the top civil servant of the year?" But what is the risk that it all goes to his head? One of his biggest fears for the bank, Clark says, is hubris, in spite of being criticized as a know-it-all and smartest kid in the class when he first arrived at TD.

"If you think of what blew up financial institutions, it's this image of the super strong leader: *I know what to do, stop questioning me, we're going to go and conquer the world.* And that's really, really dangerous in a financial institution. It's also dangerous for you as a human being because you lose what is actually important to you."[90]

Says a global banking expert: "There are no geniuses in banking. If someone were really a rocket scientist, he wouldn't be in banking. There's always the possibility he will blow up." But who tells Ed Clark he's wrong? A former TD executive says not many people do, calling the atmosphere at the bank "quite sycophantic under Ed," something Clark disputes vigorously.

He recounts this anecdote. "The other day I was saying to a fellow who was working on a project, 'You know, I think I've got to get in here and do this.' And he said, 'Would you just shut up? Take a Valium. Let me deal with this, you're just going to mess this up.' And this is someone in the middle level ranks of TD. And everyone laughed and said, 'Okay, back in your box, Ed.'"

"I'm going to end up at eighty-five wearing diapers," Clark says, "and the only thing that's going to matter to me is whether my kids or grandkids want to see me. Matt Barrett [former BMO and Barclays CEO] had a great expression. You went from *Who's Who* to *Who's that?* Now if you don't keep reminding yourself that the day I walk out of there it's going to be *Who was he?* you don't get the real world."[91]

* * * *

How odd life can be. Thirty years before, he couldn't have set foot in this town. But on the evening of November 24, 2011, Ed Clark is sitting at one of the tables of honour under the dining room chandeliers of the elegant Fairmont Palliser Hotel in Calgary. It's just a few blocks from the Petroleum Club, the place where oilmen passed around "Red Ed's" doctoral thesis on Tanzanian socialism all those years ago. In between the Petroleum Club and the Palliser Hotel is the TD Canada Trust Tower, right in the centre of town. Clark arrived after the pre-dinner cocktail party, thereby avoiding small talk with the hordes, but if he feels even a scintilla of discomfort in this Alberta ballroom, he doesn't show it. He is a man of immense and easy self-confidence. At one point, he stands up to accept a bear hug from Dick Haskayne, a legendary member of the Calgary energy and resources community, a mentor to several of the major CEOs in the sector, and a man who would have been in his prime when Clark's National Energy Program hit Alberta's oil patch like a dagger.

Whether you buy into the cult of Clark or not, it's hard to deny he's at the top of his game. He's in Calgary to hand over the mantle of Canada's

Outstanding CEO of the Year to the next recipient—an oilman, no less—Pat Daniel of the pipeline company Enbridge, which supplies two million barrels of oil a day to the United States. While Clark has been making friends in the U.S., Daniel has been the one making nice after one of his lines leaked 20,082 barrels in Michigan in 2010. His handling of the crisis—spending two months there, listening to locals and managing the situation on the ground, after the world watched BP mishandle its calamity in the Gulf of Mexico— won Daniel the award.* As they like to say at TD University, "To err is human, to recover is divine."

\* \* \* \*

For a self-proclaimed people person, albeit one with a punishing schedule, Clark has a strong dose of ice water in his veins—or what Keith Gray calls "shit in his blood." However, perhaps the core of Clark's modus operandi for the bank is, as he says, winning the hearts, minds and souls of the employees. On that score, he seems to have done it to the max, even at the upper reaches of the bank. Tim Hockey thinks back to when he first met Clark. "I remember in 1991 when I was a branch manager he walked into my branch. That was a pretty big day in my life." The branch was in Orleans, Ontario. Hockey was twenty-eight years old. He's been reporting directly to Clark since 2005, and has long been a devotee. In the late 1990s, before TD bought Canada Trust, Hockey and his wife lost their two-year-old daughter to a very rare disorder. After the little girl's death, he received a handwritten note from Ed Clark consisting of just four words: "Whatever you need, Ed." Hockey has tears in his eyes when he says, "You'll cut your right arm off to work for a guy like that. The best leader I've ever seen."

---

* In July 2012, the U.S. National Transportation Safety Board publicly criticized the way Enbridge had handled the spill.

# EPILOGUE

*Keith Gray's Moment*

After forty-three years working for TD Bank, Keith Gray was enjoying his retirement. In the eighteen months following his departure from the company, he and his wife, Wendy, had climbed Mt. Kilimanjaro, they'd run the New York Marathon, and he'd volunteered to spend six weeks in Kyrgyzstan to advise local authorities on banking and stock exchanges. The couple had sold their home in tony Lawrence Park in Toronto and bought a gorgeous "cottage" on ritzy Lake Muskoka. The summer home has a large stone hearth and features post-and-beam construction. On the wharf, there is a boathouse with an apartment above it for guests. Below is the berth for his and hers motorboats that are hydraulically lifted out of the water after use. A Mercedes E550 sits in front, parked next to a Lexus SUV.

In August of 2000, on a beautiful night in the district where Ontario's well-to-do "summer," Keith and Wendy were picked up by a boat to be taken to another cottage for a dinner party. The social scene in Muskoka requires stamina. After a lovely evening, which included fine wines, they returned to their home around midnight. Wendy checked for phone messages. There was one for Keith from Steve McDonald, the CEO of TD Waterhouse. Wendy told Keith that McDonald wanted him to call back. It didn't matter what time it was.

TD Waterhouse was listed on the New York Stock Exchange and the Toronto Stock Exchange and had a market capitalization, or market value, of about $10 billion at the time, representing approximately half of the market value of TD Bank.

Gray had no idea why McDonald was calling but he phoned him back at around 12:30 a.m., getting him out of bed. "In his usual gruff manner he said he wanted me to be in New York for a press conference on Monday morning," Gray recalls. When he asked why, McDonald told him that the chief operating officer of Waterhouse, Frank Petrilli, had resigned to go run E*TRADE and that Gray was the new COO.

Gray told him to wait just a minute, that he would have to think it over. But McDonald shot back, "You'll be here in New York, though?" Gray told him he was enjoying his retirement and wasn't sure he wanted to go back full-time, particularly to New York City. He asked McDonald how much he would be paid. "We'll work that out," McDonald said, telling Gray that the job would be temporary until they could find a new COO, and that he should speak to the human resources department. Gray said he wouldn't commit until he had the details worked out and told McDonald he'd call the bank's HR people in the morning. That was the end of the phone call.

It was now one in the morning and Gray sat down on the deck with Wendy and another bottle of wine to discuss what had happened. Gray said two words: "Payback time." Wendy was in full agreement. "It's not *if*. It's *how much,*" she said. Gray decided he wanted what Frank Petrilli had been making, which was $200,000 a month. For three months' work, he wanted $600,000 and the bank agreed to it.

In the end, Petrilli surprised everyone by asking Baillie if he could return to TD after just a week at E*TRADE. He said the culture was akin to life on Mars compared with what he was used to at Waterhouse; he realized he'd made a mistake, and apologized. Baillie agreed to have him back. With Petrilli gone for only a few days, McDonald tried to wiggle out of paying Gray the agreed-upon $600,000, but ultimately he got the money. Compared with many of today's executive packages, it's not an outlandish sum. For Keith Gray though, whose salary when he left the bank at the end of 1997 was $260,000 a year, a pittance compared to CEOs, this was a major amount and he felt he'd earned it, given how much money the bank had made from the discount brokerage business he'd built. Compensation is a scorecard, says Ed Clark.[92]

Sitting in the sixty-fourth floor of Scotia Plaza in what was once the office of cable baron Ted Rogers, Steve McDonald is now a top executive at Bank of Nova Scotia, co-chairman and co-CEO of its investment bank. From his window, he looks down on the TD Tower, his old haunt. He doesn't dispute Gray's story about the phone call and the money. "He was arguably the founding father of discount brokerage" at TD, McDonald admits. Gray was never paid anything like the other top dogs at the bank, yet "he was writing these massive cheques to these people [for acquisitions]. It had to get to him. He'd been unrecognized. In the end, I did write him a cheque. Not for the one week. I was paying him in some small way for what he'd achieved for the bank," McDonald says.

In all likelihood, there would be no place for a Keith Gray inside Ed Clark's bank. TD has grown by orders of magnitude since Gray's time. As a result, there is more process and procedure to maintain control of an enormous organization. To have a free-range entrepreneur like Gray running around wouldn't work in today's TD. As the former CFO of Commerce Bank, Douglas Paul, says, "The hardest thing about becoming a big bank is not becoming a big bank."[93] The bigger you get, the bigger the risk you become sclerotic and bureaucratic.

If you can criticize anything about TD, it's that it has become a bit self-righteous. Its executives have no hesitation telling you how great they are at what they do, while at the same time decrying hubris as the germ that brings banks down. There is a lot of TD theology that can get wearisome. But it's hard to argue with the results. TD Bank is a flourishing institution, continuing to evolve to new levels of success. As of the third quarter of 2012, it's on track to earn approximately $6.5 billion in profit for the year. That's $18 million a day, every day of the year.*

Why has TD succeeded so far? While being mindful of risk, it has a history of embracing entrepreneurialism. Allen Lambert brought the bank into the modern age by bringing in world-renowned architect Mies van der Rohe to erect Toronto's first financial skyscraper, which puffed up the chest of TDers who laboured in the smallest of the Big Five, giving them a reason to be proud.

---

* The 2012 year-end results will be announced after this book has gone to press. For 2011, *Report on Business* magazine ranked TD the most profitable company in Canada.

Dick Thomson followed with an astonishing multi-decade profitable tenure as boss, carrying the bank to the upper echelons of corporate lending, bringing TD to the top of the heap globally when it came to providing financing for the cable and telecom industries. He and Robin Korthals also tolerated a loose cannon like Keith Gray, allowing him to build a business within the bank.

Beyond its own tolerance of entrepreneurialism inside the institution, TD bought the fruits of others' dreams and efforts. It purchased the achievement of Larry Waterhouse, who constructed a business from nothing. Charlie Baillie then bought the sassy Canada Trust, which had become renowned for its free-wheeling, underdog retail banking tactics that so appealed to Canadians. TD then welcomed the big-brained but controversial Ed Clark, Mr. Retail himself, who went on to carry that torch into the United States. He bought Banknorth, assembled by an old-school schmooze artist named Bill Ryan. In short order, TD combined its Waterhouse division in the U.S. with the online brokerage of another entrepreneur, Joe Ricketts, and finally, the *pièce de resistance,* buying what Vernon Hill and his "whack jobs" at Commerce had built, allowing TD to puncture the Manhattan, New Jersey, Philly and Florida markets much faster than it ever imagined.

The current TD Bank is a heady brew fermented by the imaginations and perspiration of a relatively small group of people, people who broke the mould of banking and financial services in Canada and elsewhere. In ten or twenty years, investors will know whether TD's U.S. invasion was the best use of the bank's capital. The next leader, Clark's successor, will embody an as yet unknown theme. Beyond that, given the bank's growing presence in the U.S., Teri Currie, the head of HR at TD, says that the next generation of leaders will require significant on-the-ground experience in the United States to qualify for the top job.

As for Keith Gray, he wasn't one of the anointed ones. His picture won't be among the past CEOs in the hall of fame on the fifty-fourth floor, but he made it a long way for a boy who could have spent his life in a foundry. In a scrapbook in the study of his Toronto condominium, where he keeps souvenirs such as original trading tickets from the early days of Green Line, there is a page torn from the 1998 annual report of TD Bank. Gray proudly points to the list of the people in the upper left-hand corner, the senior executives at the bank. Right under the chairman, president and CEO and vice-chairmen are the executive vice-presidents. Among them is W. Keith Gray. By the time his name appeared in that coveted position, he was sixty-three, the mandatory retirement age at the bank. He'd made it to the top tier just in time.

In 1980–82, Gray was manager of the main branch of TD, the plum branch job in the country. A blue-chip lawyer who did business there, a client of Gray's, suggested it was time he moved up in the world and joined the exclusive Rosedale Golf Club and that he, the lawyer, would be happy to sponsor him. Gray wrote to his division office, which sent the letter on to the corporate division. A phone call came back saying he should not pursue the application further, because "it's Dick's golf course."

In 1994, when Gray had become president of the Royal Canadian Golf Association, he was in Dick Thomson's office and put the CEO on the spot, saying he would like to join Rosedale. Gray recalls, "He said, 'Sure. I can't sponsor you, but I can second it.'" While it may have sounded to Gray like a social snub, Thomson was simply obeying the rules of the club. He could not sponsor an employee—a common rule at prestigious clubs—but he could (and did) second his nomination. "I was always in favour of other TD people coming into Rosedale," Thomson says.

Years later, after he'd retired from the bank, Gray ran into his former boss at the Rosedale Golf Club. Thomson, in an instance of generosity toward Gray, said that he'd noticed that other former bank executives were improperly taking credit for making the acquisitions that built the brokerage business. Thomson seemed in a mood to set the record straight.

"That was you," Thomson told him.

For Gray, hearing this simple sentence from Thomson was the trophy he'd long been seeking. When asked what he thinks was his greatest accomplishment, Gray laughs and summons all the conviction of someone who knows he could have landed somewhere very different, making a labourer's wage.

"I survived," he says. "I survived."

TD in its various incarnations goes back to 1855, almost 160 years. It was only when Keith Gray finally caught Larry Waterhouse that the bank entered the retail market in the U.S., albeit in discount brokerage, with only a sideline in banking. Since then, Ed Clark has poured $19 billion USD more into rapidly establishing a branch network and business that exceeds the number of branches it has in Canada. But will his strategy work out the way he wants?

On Thursday, March 29, 2012, TD shareholders gathered at the Glenn Gould Studio at the CBC Broadcast Centre in downtown Toronto. It was the 156th annual meeting of the bank, but the first time it had been held in Canada's biggest city in fifteen years. And there was a twist. Ed Clark would not be there, at least in person. He would appear virtually, via satellite from New York City, accompanied by Colleen Johnston and members of the board of directors. By law, the formal meeting had to be held on Canadian soil—and it was, overseen by Chairman Brian Levitt. But just as he appears on CNBC regularly (he had done so the night before), Clark was in New York to make a point. TD is taking Manhattan away from the other banks. The message was one he'd sent before, that TD would move from number five in New York City to number three by 2015, adding another fifty branches where it already had eighty-nine.

He and the TD board also sent another message. Clark would be CEO for longer than expected. His contract had already been extended beyond the standard retirement age at TD. In October of 2012, he would be turning sixty-five, and his extension was set to take him to at least April 2013, through the next annual meeting. It had been left open-ended. But on this day, no successor was named. What shareholders heard from Brian Levitt was that Ed "plans to be around for a while yet." Clark added that he was in the "final years" of his CEO tenure. "I am in no hurry to leave," he said, adding that he loved his job.

That may very well be true. His bank has a platinum credit rating, it recorded another year of record profits and he is continually showered with awards. The first time I met him, during the early years of his reign, he threw his arms up in the air and said, "It's a great job." There may be other reasons he's not leaving so soon. High among them is the possibility that his successor is not ready. If it's Tim Hockey, there may be the sense among board members that he needs more time to broaden his résumé, at least to the breadth of Bharat Masrani's, which includes having been chief risk officer, considered a crucial qualification in today's banking world. It could be that Clark hasn't yet

found something that would give him as much of a kick or intellectual challenge as running TD. He is, after all, a thoroughbred who needs to run. The
other possibility is that he wants to stick around to make sure his invasion of
the U.S. really pays off for the bank, reaching double-digit returns before he
vacates his post. He dismisses this, but perhaps he has his father in mind, a
man who suffered a heart attack not long after he retired. One person who
knows him well says that Clark "still has a young mind. He's the smartest guy
I've ever worked with. He's a proud guy. He doesn't want to leave [the bank]
in the midst of a financial crisis."

One former bank executive, however, thinks Clark is being selfish, that it's
time for him to give someone else a chance. "Ego is an amazing thing. History is
full of leaders who stayed in charge too long. Ed could be one of them," he says.

Or not. Clark has railed publicly against the hubris of bankers. For him
to be driven by ego would leave him wide open to criticism should anything
go awry. Given his record, Clark could go on to further successes, make more
acquisitions, drive more improvements in the bank and contribute more to
public policy and the community. His record has shown that it's been unwise
to bet against him. Like Keith Gray, he too has survived, and thrived.

# ACKNOWLEDGEMENTS

It should be said that two people don't create an institution. But to tell the story of a large organization, a writer has to make choices. Keith Gray and Ed Clark were my principal choices, the main actors that take you, the reader, through the dramatic journey of TD Bank. Of course there are countless "supporting characters." I use quotation marks because they are not players in a theatrical production. They are the people involved or qualified observers and I spoke with many of them.

Some notes about the making of this book and the people who helped. Unless otherwise noted, any quotations are from interviews I conducted. The process formally began in January 2010 over a burger and a beer at a pub on College Street in Toronto with Keith Gray, with whom I've had the pleasure of sharing numerous lunches or dinners since the late 90s. Somewhere along the way I lost count of the hours of conversation we had about the bank over meals in various Toronto pubs, and in Muskoka, Sarasota or in the car to Wyoming, not to mention the many emails and phone conversations over the same period. I'd like to thank Keith and his wife, Wendy Leaney, for their friendship, patience and unlimited co-operation. Thanks also to Keith's sister Lois Marley and her husband, Paul, who still live near the family farm. What Keith's parents bought in 1940 for $1,000 recently sold for $1.15 million.

By the summer of 2010, my agent, Michael Levine, had enthusiastically agreed to try to find a publisher for the project (Michael, I have to say, was available at all hours). I thank him for his unflagging spirit and encouragement, and I am also grateful to his assistant, Maxine Quigley, and to Carolyn Forde and all the good folks at Westwood Creative Artists.

Once the official search for a publisher was on, I approached the bank. I'd like to thank Ed Clark for taking my call during the last week of July 2010. His longtime former assistant, Janis Dixon, arranged a meeting with him without any of his handlers. That's when I told him my idea, while confessing I had never written a book. He was immediately enthusiastic, saying he was a fan of books about Canadian business history. He wondered how long it might take me to write it. At the time, I said three years, not knowing how long it would take to find a publisher. (It took until December 2010, when Jim Gifford of HarperCollins Canada signed on.) I suspect Ed was thinking about his own retirement timeline, which remained something of a mystery throughout the writing of the book.

The nub of my discussion with Ed was a request for interviews with him and with many members of his team. I said to him in no uncertain terms that I would not be writing an "authorized" book and he said he would not want that kind of book anyway. Although he was supportive, Clark said he would have to speak with his chairman, John Thompson. Ultimately, the bank gave me meaningful but limited access to Ed and other executives. There were many names on my wish list for which the bank did not provide interviews or access. In all, I was granted upwards of 25 hours of interviews from TD, including four hours with Ed; two hours with Colleen Johnston; two hours each with U.S.-based executives Bharat Masrani and Fred Graziano; an hour each with John Thompson, Brian Levitt and Tim Hockey; an hour with Teri Currie and an hour with Riaz Ahmed. I also got a tour of TD University in Mount Laurel, New Jersey, in addition to a pit stop at a preselected branch in the area. One retired executive, John Davies, requested we do the interview at TD headquarters with a bank public relations person present.

Thanks to all listed for your time and comments. At all of the above interviews, a member of the bank's communications department was present. In spite of their trying to contain me, I thank them for their help: Neil Parmenter, Mo Nakhooda, Wojtek Dabrowski, Rebecca Acevedo, Susan

Donlan, Simon Townsend, Maria Leung, Stephen Knight and Elizabeth Lewis. I'd also like to give a shout-out to Dianne Salt, the longtime head of communications at TD, who was just leaving her post when I began, and to Anne Spruin, the bank's archivist.

In all, I conducted more than 100 interviews, resulting in well over 200 hours of conversation. That does not include the countless number of interviews I have done on television over the years with TD executives or about the bank (at BNN and elsewhere before that) or off-camera conversations with sources I had prior to beginning this project.

Many people spoke with me for this book, including retired and former executives of the bank who spoke freely and without the presence of TD minders. Many spoke on the record. Among them are former CEOs Dick Thomson and Charlie Baillie and former president Robin Korthals. All three were generous with their time and helpful. Special thanks to Charlie's and Dick's executive assistants, Janice DaCosta and Josephine Munroe—also to Rita Venantius in Colleen Johnston's office and Carol Simpson, executive assistant to John Thompson and Brian Levitt. In the U.S., Larry Waterhouse, Frank Petrilli and Richard Neiman shared their recollections freely.

Thanks as well to Fred Tomzcyk, Bill Ryan, Peter Verrill, Joe Moglia, Bob Kelly, Vernon Hill, Bob Falese, Peter Maurice, Purdy Crawford, Mickey Cohen, David Livingston, Steve McDonald, Stephen Jarislowsky, Keith Howlett, Bud McMorran, Bill Brock, Jim Peterson, Scott Clark, Kevin Doyle, Heather Conway, Lawrence Bloomberg, Tom MacMillan and Frank McKenna.

I cannot possibly thank everyone, so if I have missed you, I apologize. I thank all those who spoke to me on the condition of anonymity, and whose names do not appear. They know who they are. When dealing with direct quotes, at times I have tidied up what people have said, removing *um*s and *ah*s and *gotta*s, while trying to remain faithful to the essential, core message.

Two former prime ministers graciously took my calls and gave of their time. Thanks to the patient Rt. Hon. Paul Martin, who found himself on the other end of a disconnected Skype line during our interview. Cradling my laptop, I frantically ran up and down the stairs of our house, trying to re-establish an Internet connection with the former leader of the country. The Rt. Hon. Brian

Mulroney was also patient when our dog began barking in the background, something that no doubt came through loud and clear on Skype.

Additionally, Anastasia Hare did library and article searches for me that saved me a lot of time. Sommelier Anne Martin helped instruct me in the differences (and similarities) between Château Le Pin and Château Petrus. Jeremy Gutsche and Amber Mac gave me helpful advice, particularly about social media.

With my commitment to be on the air Monday through Friday at BNN, I wrote this book in my spare time or during chunks of time I could get away from my program, which gave rise to mixed emotions. I've always treated my show like the family store, and shopkeepers don't like to be away for too long. My thanks to my loyal and talented core team at BNN's *Headline* (Roula Meditskos, Zena Olijnyk, Kristine Owram, Jillian Glickman and Lois Lee) for minding the shop in my absence, and to Paul Waldie, Kim Parlee and Jacquie McNish for sitting in for me.

BNN, under Jack Fleischmann and Lesley Harmer, was very supportive, as was the network's marketing chief, Jeremy Roach. It didn't hurt that the network for the first time was a sponsor of Canada's Outstanding CEO of the Year Award in February 2011. By total coincidence, the honouree was none other than Ed Clark. I had been master of ceremonies the year before—when BNN was not a sponsor—and was asked to be so again, and as it turned out, Ed appeared on my program the day he received the award. Outside of interviews specifically for this book, I have interviewed him and Colleen Johnston numerous times on television, as well as Charlie Baillie, Tim Hockey and other bank executives.

I would be remiss if I did not mention someone who inspired me greatly from the beginning of my career. The late Brian Nolan was one of my professors at Carleton University's School of Journalism in Ottawa. Although not given to hero worship, I always marvelled at Brian. He had a singularly triumphant career as a television journalist and documentary filmmaker. He was in Dallas in November 1963 and was an eyewitness to the shooting of Lee Harvey Oswald. While at Carleton, he wrote books, and that made me think, "Gee, I'd like to do that someday." Brian died in 2006 of lung cancer. After I graduated from Carleton, we continued to correspond until just weeks before his death. He was, and continues to be, an inspiration.

Around the time of Brian's death, I had the luck to become a Knight-Bagehot Fellow at Columbia University in New York, a joyous learning experience. Without a doubt, my year there made me think more deeply about my work and allowed me to be inspired by those friends I met as a Fellow. I might not have written this book without having taken that time to intensify my focus and knowledge. In addition, three friends with expertise in business, banking and financial markets generously took the time to review the manuscript. My thanks to Tony Griffiths, Malcolm Knight and Bruce Campbell for their suggestions and support.

A writer is lost without an editor. I want to thank Jim Gifford of HarperCollins Canada for his quiet yet firm guidance and wisdom. He was at once encouraging and critical, two things an editor needs to be to nudge an author to the finish line. Jim saved me from my worst tendencies. Our coffee meetings at the Royal Conservatory café were both productive and fun, and he made countless suggestions that improved this book beyond measure.

Other people at HarperCollins I would like to thank are Noelle Zitzer, Anne Holloway, Allegra Robinson, Liz McKeen and Kelly Hope. They have done their very best to root out errors in the text, and any that remain are mine and mine alone. Thanks also to Cory Beatty, Rob Firing, Iris Tupholme, Shannon Parsons and Norma Cody. I am also grateful to Alison Woodbury for her legal advice.

Most important, I would be nowhere in life without my family. My parents deserve particular mention. My mother, Roselle, is a brilliant woman (one of two women to be admitted to Dalhousie Law School in 1947). Well into her eighties, she is still a university student, even though she has many degrees already. She reads constantly, and her lifelong curiosity and pursuit of learning have been a beacon. She also provided some of my favourite foods from her repertoire while I was closeted away writing the book. Thanks, Mom. My father, Saul, passed away on March 15, 2005. Ironically, I was supposed to interview Ed Clark at that time because it coincided with the closing of the bank's purchase of Banknorth. Obviously, I missed that interview. My dad, like my mom, was a best friend. He supported me unconditionally—as he did my two sisters and brother—through all of his days, and I am immensely grateful for his love, wisdom and sense of humour. Deep down, I think he had wanted me to be a medical doctor like himself, but at the last minute, even though I was accepted by Queens for biochemistry (pre-med they called it), I chickened out and went to Carleton for journalism. Ultimately, he wanted me to pursue what I wanted and took pride in what I chose to do for a living. I wish he could have read this book.

I'd also like to thank my sisters, Marcia and Susan, for their encouragement and for showing the way. The former is a librarian and has read more books than anyone I know. The latter did her PhD at night and is an example of the discipline necessary to write a book. My brother, Morris, is a fine photographer who has taken many a picture for me when I've asked, including the one on the Westwood website and my Twitter feed. I must also thank our dog, Daisy, a very low-maintenance schnoodle who kept me company and provided the distraction of walks to break up the many long hours in front of the laptop.

This book is dedicated to my spouse, Lynne Heller, who encouraged me to write it from the get-go, and gave me the necessary pep talks during the many times when I hesitated. She is truly a loving and generous partner who knows more about living life and embracing opportunities than anyone I know. She is also an excellent editor and computer support department. She knows me and she knows what's authentic. She also knows people, and has read the complete works of William Shakespeare, which I have not. Thank you, Lynne, for your love, encouragement and laughter.

# TIMELINE

*Note: Dollar figures are expressed in*
*Canadian currency unless otherwise stated.*

Toronto Dominion Bank purchases Waterhouse Investor Services on **April 10, 1996**, closed **October 15, 1996**, for $38 USD per share, totalling $715 million CDN.

Initial public offering of TD Waterhouse Group Inc. occurs on or about **June 28, 1999**, at $24 per share, 11.2% of the company sold to the public (12.4% with over-allotment). It raised $1.122 billion.

TD Bank Financial Group purchases CT Financial Services Inc. (operating under the name Canada Trust), announced **August 3, 1999**, closed **February 1, 2000**, for $7.998 billion.

TD Bank Financial Group acquires TD Waterhouse shares that it did not own (privatization), on **November 26, 2001**, at $9 per share, for total consideration of approximately $605 million.

TD Bank Financial Group purchases 51% of Banknorth of Portland, Maine, announced **August 26, 2004**, closed **March 1, 2005**, for $5.1 billion—$3.112 billion in cash, $1.988 billion in stock.

TD Bank Financial Group sells TD Waterhouse USA to Ameritrade Holding Corporation, announced **June 22, 2005**, closed **January 24, 2006**, for 32% stake in combined company (stake valued at $3.1 billion). By **October 31, 2006**, TD had increased stake in TD Ameritrade to 39.8% by purchasing $1.052 billion in shares through open market purchases. As of **July 31, 2010**, TD Bank owned 45.95% of TD Ameritrade. The bank periodically adjusts its share ownership to maintain stake at 45%.

TD Banknorth purchases Hudson United, announced **July 12, 2005**, closed **January 31, 2006**, for $2.2 billion stock—$1.073 billion in cash, the balance in stock.

TD Banknorth purchases Interchange, announced **April 13, 2006**, closed **January 1, 2007**, for a total cash consideration of $545 million.

TD Bank Financial Group purchases remaining shares of Banknorth, announced **November 20, 2006**, closed **April 20, 2007**, for $3.7 billion.

TD Bank Financial Group buys Commerce Bancorp, Inc., of Cherry Hill, New Jersey, announced **October 2, 2007**, closed **March 31, 2008**, for $8.5 billion.

TD Bank Group acquires the assets and certain liabilities of three Florida banks—Riverside National Bank of Florida, AmericanFirst Bank and First Federal Bank of North Florida—in an FDIC-assisted transaction on **April 16, 2010**. The FDIC would assume 50% of loan losses up to a certain threshold at each bank, then 80% of loan losses beyond stated thresholds.

TD Bank Group buys South Financial Group of Greenville, South Carolina, announced **May 17, 2010**, closed **September 30, 2010**, for $64 million in cash or stock, plus $134 million to repay U.S. Treasury's Troubled Asset Relief Program (TARP).

TD Bank Group buys Chrysler Financial, announced **December 21, 2010,** closed **April 1, 2011,** for cash consideration of $6.39 billion. Of that, the bank said it was investing capital of approximately $900 million—$400 million set aside for goodwill, $500 million added to capital.

TD Bank Group buys MBNA MasterCard portfolio from Bank of America for total cash consideration of $7.5 billion (approximately $1 billion in invested capital), announced **August 15, 2011,** closed **December 1, 2011.**

TD Bank Group buys Target Corporation's existing U.S. Visa and private label credit card portfolio, with a gross outstanding balance of $5.9 billion USD, announced **October 23, 2012.** Price was not disclosed. In a separate announcement, Target said it would report a pre-tax gain of between $350 million USD and $450 million USD in connection with the sale.

# ENDNOTES

## INTRODUCTION
1. Pencer, *The Ride of My Life,* p. 92.

## CHAPTER 1
2. *Mansbridge One on One,* CBC Television, December 11, 2010.
3. Greenwood, "Green Lantern."
4. Stewart, "Cult of Ed Clark."
5. Donald Reilly, cartoon, *New Yorker,* date unknown.
6. Larry Stevenson, interview, *Headline with Howard Green,* Business News Network, August 30, 2011.

## CHAPTER 2
7. Gladwell, *Outliers,* pp. 133–34.

## CHAPTER 4
8. Schwab, *How to Be Your Own Stockbroker,* pp. 16–19.
9. Ibid., pp. 21–23.
10. Ibid., p. 24.
11. Ibid., pp. 24–25.
12. Ibid., p. 89.
13. Ibid., p. 60.
14. Srikantiah, "The Toronto-Dominion Bank," p. 2.

15. Ibid.

16. Schwab, p. 60.

17. Ryans and Henderson, "The Toronto-Dominion Bank: Green Line Investor Services 1996," p. 4.

18. Ryans, "The Toronto-Dominion Bank: Green Line Investor Services, p. 5.

19. Jobs, *I, Steve.*

20. Kador, Charles Schwab, p. 160.

21. Order, in the Superior Court of Hong Kong High Court.

22. Kador, p. 168.

23. Ryans, p. 6.

24. Toronto-Dominion Bank Investor Services Division, internal memo, February 10, 1997.

## CHAPTER 5

25. Ryans, "The Toronto-Dominion Bank: Green Line Investor Services 1996," Exhibit 6.

26. Ibid., p. 20.

## CHAPTER 6

27. Ed Clark, interview, *Headline with Howard Green,* Business News Network, February 17, 2011.

28. Garcia Márquez, *Love in the Time of Cholera,* p. 117.

29. McQueen, "'Red Ed' Clark."

30. Foster, *The Sorcerer's Apprentices,* pp. 52, 74–75.

31. Clark, *Socialist Development,* pp. xii, xiv.

32. Ibid., p. xv.

33. Ibid., pp. xv, 4.

34. Ibid., p. 237.

35. Ibid., pp. 258–59.

36. McQueen.

37. Stewart, "Cult of Ed Clark."

38. Ed Clark, interview, *Headline with Howard Green,* Business News Network, February 17, 2011.
39. Howlett, "Clark to Join Trust Company."
40. Stewart.
41. Ibid.
42. McQueen.
43. Howlett, "It's Fun to Play on a Winning Team."
44. McQueen.

**CHAPTER 7**
45. Paul Martin, interview with author.
46. Willis, "The Courtship of CIBC and TD."
47. Ibid.
48. McCarthy, "Martin Shrugs Off."
49. Willis and Waldie, "Deal Hatched over Eggnog."
50. Toronto-Dominion Bank 2000 Annual Report, p. 67.
51. Smith, *The Trust-Builders,* pp. vii-viii.
52. Ibid., p. 170.
53. Ibid., pp. 171–72.
54. Ibid., p. 171.
55. Ibid., p. 209.
56. Ibid., pp. 209–10.
57. Ibid., p. 181.
58. Halberstam, *The Fifties,* pp. 173–79.
59. Macklem, "TD Bank Aims at U.S. Market."

**CHAPTER 8**
60. Bill Downe, interview, *Headline with Howard Green,* Business News Network, January 11, 2012.
61. Smith, *The Trust-Builders,* p. 190.

## CHAPTER 10

62. Nomura Fixed Income Research, "CDOs in Plain English."

63. Buffett, Letter to Shareholders, February 2008, p. 3.

64. Chant, "The ABCP Crisis in Canada," pp. 4, 19.

65. Knight, "Surmounting the Financial Crisis."

## CHAPTER 11

66. Tully, "Vernon Hill."

67. Frei and Hajim, "Commerce Bank."

68. Commerce Bancorp, Inc., Form 10-K, p. 15.

69. Ibid., p. 49.

70. "OCC Enters into Cease and Desist Order."

71. Ed Clark, interview, *The Business News with Howard Green*, Business News Network, October 2, 2007.

72. Ibid.

73. Ed Clark, interview, *The Business News with Howard Green*, Business News Network, March 31, 2008.

## CHAPTER 12

74. Reucassel, "If Everyone Likes TD Shares."

75. Colleen Johnston, interview, *Headline with Howard Green*, Business News Network, May 24, 2012.

## CHAPTER 13

76. Neuman, "But by No Means Least."

## CHAPTER 15

77. Unrecorded conversation with author in Clark's office, autumn 2003.

78. Wilbur Ross, interview, *Headline with Howard Green*, Business News Network, August 27, 2010.

79. Matthew Barrett, interview, *Headline with Howard Green*, Business News Network, November 5, 2009.

80. Bruce Campbell, interview, *Market Call*, Business News Network, May 17, 2010.

**CHAPTER 16**

81. John Snow, interview, *Headline with Howard Green*, Business News Network, December 10, 2008.
82. Ed Clark, interview, *Headline with Howard Green*, Business News Network, February 17, 2011.
83. TD Bank Group, 2012 All Investor Day, April 17, 2012, transcript, p. 7.
84. Kolbert, "A New 'Good Evening.'"

**CHAPTER 17**

85. Wilbur Ross, interview, *Headline with Howard Green*, Business News Network, August, 2011.
86. Tim Hockey, interview, *Headline with Howard Green*, Business News Network, August 15, 2011.
87. Stewart, "Cult of Ed Clark."
88. Ed Clark, interview, *Headline with Howard Green*, Business News Network, February 17, 2011.
89. Stewart.
90. Ed Clark, interview.
91. Ibid.

**EPILOGUE**

92. Ed Clark, interview, *Headline with Howard Green*, Business News Network, February 17, 2010.
93. Frei and Hajim, "Commerce Bank."

# BIBLIOGRAPHY

## BOOKS

Clark, W. Edmund. *Socialist Development and Public Investment in Tanzania, 1964–73.* Toronto/Buffalo: University of Toronto Press, 1978.

English, John. *The Life of Pierre Elliott Trudeau.* Toronto: Alfred A. Knopf Canada, 2006.

Foster, Peter. *The Sorcerer's Apprentices: Canada's Superbureaucrats and the Energy Mess.* Toronto: Collins, 1982.

García Márquez, Gabriel. *Love in the Time of Cholera.* New York: Alfred A. Knopf, 1988.

Gladwell, Malcolm. *Outliers: The Story of Success.* New York: Little, Brown and Co., 2008.

Greenberg, Alan C. *The Rise and Fall of Bear Stearns.* New York: Simon & Schuster, 2010.

Halberstam, David. *The Fifties.* New York: Villard Books, 1993.

Jobs, Steve. *I, Steve: Steve Jobs, in His Own Words.* Chicago: Agate, 2011.

Kador, John. *Charles Schwab: How One Company Beat Wall Street and Reinvented the Brokerage Industry.* Hoboken, NJ: John Wiley & Sons, 2002.

Kuralt, Charles. *A Life on the Road.* New York: Putnam, 1990.

McQueen, Rod. *Manulife: How Dominic D'Alessandro Built a Global Giant and Fought to Save It.* Toronto: Viking Canada, 2009.

Pencer, Gerry. *The Ride of My Life: A Memoir.* Toronto: Key Porter Books, 1999.

Pound, Richard W. *Stikeman Elliot: The First Fifty Years.* Montreal/Kingston: McGill-Queen's University Press, 2002.

Schull, Joseph. *100 Years of Banking in Canada: A History of the Toronto-Dominion Bank.* Vancouver: Copp Clark, 1958.

Schwab, Charles. *How to Be Your Own Stockbroker.* New York: Macmillan, 1984.

Smith, Philip. *The Trust-Builders: The Remarkable Rise of Canada Trust.* Toronto: Macmillan of Canada, 1989.


## ARTICLES

Alexander, Doug, and Sean B. Pasternak. "Canadians Dominate World's Strongest Banks." Bloomberg, May 2, 2012.

Argitis, Theophilos. "Canada's Bank World's Soundest for Fourth Year." Bloomberg, September 7, 2011.

Austen, Ian. "Toronto-Dominion's Chief Continues a Run at the Border." *New York Times,* June 21, 2011.

———. "U.S. Entices Big Banks in Canada." *New York Times,* December 27, 2010.

Blumenthal, Jeff. "Former Commerce Bank Chairman Hill Cleared in Investigation." *Philadelphia Business Journal,* November 19, 2008.

"Canada Trust Buys Citibank Canada Retail Branches." Canadian Press, May 13, 1999.

"Canada Trust CFO Steps Down, Clash of Egos Rumoured as Gunn Moves On." *Globe and Mail,* April 15, 1994.

"Canada Trust Parent Plans U.S. Move." *Kitchener-Waterloo Record* (from Canadian Press), February 10, 1993.

"Canada Trust Takeover Approved." *Cambridge Reporter,* February 1, 2000.

Canfield, Clarke. "Banknorth Rises from the Ashes Suddenly." Associated Press, January 4, 2004.

Craig, Susanne. "Canada Trust Rules Out Sale." *Globe and Mail,* April 21, 1998.

———. "TD's Baillie Is Talk of the Street." *Globe and Mail*, September 20, 1999.

Dash, Eric. "Chief Steps Down, and Commerce Bank Agrees to End Business Deals with His Family." *New York Times,* June 30, 2007.

Daw, James. "CT Financial Scores Profit on Bank; Sale Shedding U.S. Unit Brings Gain of $320 Million." *Toronto Star,* August 23, 1996.

DeCloet, Derek. "What's Big, Green and User-Friendly?" *Canadian Business,* August 27, 1999.

———. "When Slow Growth Is Not an Option, Make a Full-Speed Assault." *Globe and Mail,* July 16, 2005.

DiStefano, Joseph N. "Shirley Hill Ordered to Pay TD Bank $1.6M: Report." *PhillyDeals,* February 11, 2010 (based on *Courier-Post* report by Eileen Smith).

———. "Vernon Hill Is Back: PA Commerce Bank + 1st Republic = Metro Bank." *PhillyDeals,* November 10, 2008.

Feder, Barnaby J. "Leslie Quick Jr., A Pioneer in Discount Stock Brokerage, Dies at 75." *New York Times,* March 9, 2001.

Foster, Peter. "The Reform of a Bureaucrat." *National Post,* August 7, 1999.

Freeland, Chrystia. "Ed Clark on CEOs and Risk Taking." *Financial Times* video, ft.com. "View From the Top." November 1, 2007.

Gladwell, Malcolm. "The Sure Thing: How Entrepreneurs Really Succeed." *New Yorker,* January 18, 2010.

*Globe and Mail.* "CT Chief Has Surgery." June 24, 1995.

*Globe and Mail.* "CT Financial Sells S&L." August 23, 1996.

Goff, Sharlene, and Patrick Jenkins. "Hill Steps Aside to Enable Metro Approval." *Financial Times* website, ft.com, January 22, 2010.

Graham, Natalie. "My First Million: Vernon Hill of Metro Bank." *Financial Times,* October 29, 2010.

Greenwood, John. "A Fine Balance: Canada's Outstanding CEO of the Year." *Financial Post,* January 15, 2011.

———. "Green Lantern, Canada's Outstanding CEO of the Year." *Financial Post Magazine,* February 2011.

Greenwood, John. "TD Steals a March from Competitors: Nabbed CT Financial: Despite Death of Mergers, the Bank Got Bigger—Fast." *National Post,* December 4, 1999.

Griffiths, Katherine. "Barbarian at the Gates Puts Faith in Good Service." *Times of London,* May 9, 2011.

———. "The Battle Cry for a Banking Revolution—Have a Nice Day." *Times of London,* May 9, 2011.

Haliechuk, Rick. "Canada Trust Boss Ranks with Bankers: Salary and Bonus Top $824,000." *Toronto Star,* March 2, 1994.

———. "Canada Trust Targets 20% Jump in Profit." *Toronto Star,* March 29, 1995.

Howlett, Karen. "Canada Trust Hops Borders." *Globe and Mail,* October 1, 1993.

———. "Clark to Join Trust Company." *Globe and Mail,* August 8, 1991.

———. "It's Fun to Play on a Winning Team: When Edmund Clark Needed Advice, He Turned to Peter Maurice." *Globe and Mail,* August 10, 1991.

———. "TD Appoints Clark to No. 2 Job." *Globe and Mail,* July 7, 2000.

———. "TD Reaps Rewards for Buying CT Financial." *Globe and Mail,* May 24, 2000.

Knight, Malcolm D. "Surmounting the Financial Crisis: Contrasts between Canadian and American Banks." *American Review of Canadian Studies,* 2:3, 311–20. First Thomas O. Enders Memorial Lecture, Johns Hopkins University, May 3, 2012.

Kolbert, Elizabeth. "A New 'Good Evening' for Masterpiece Theater." *New York Times,* February 24, 1993.

Kruger, Daniel. "Best Managed Companies in America." *Forbes,* January 12, 2004.

Langan, F.F. "Orillian Rose from Lowly Bank Clerk to President of Toronto-Dominion: Orillia Native Ben Boyle Dead at 92." *Orillia Packet and Times,* date unknown.

Loomis, Carol. "The Remarkable Departure of Vernon Hill." *Fortune,* July 2, 2007.

Macklem, Katherine. "TD Bank Aims at U.S. Market: Plans to Capitalize on Strength of TD Waterhouse." *National Post,* November 18, 1999.

Mahood, Casey, Andrew Willis and Ann Gibbon. "TD Buys Canada Trust, Expects Martin's Approval." *Globe and Mail,* August 4, 1999.

McCarthy, Shawn. "Martin Shrugs Off TD Chief's Remark." *Globe and Mail,* May 30, 1998.

McClearn, Matthew. "Jean Coutu." *Canadian Business,* June 16, 2008.

McKenna, Barrie. "Big Banks Don't Scare Canada Trust's New Boss." *Globe and Mail,* March 30, 1994.

McQueen, Rod. "'Red Ed' Clark Takes On Toughest Task Yet." *Financial Post,* July 17, 1993.

Neuman, William. "But by No Means Least." *New York Times,* April 9, 2006.

Newman, Richard. "Commerce's Founder Sued by TD Bank; Was to Use Logos in Presentation." *Bergen County Record,* November 20, 2008.

Noble, Kimberley, Jennifer Hunter, Danylo Hawaleshka and John Geddes. "Going Green." *Maclean's,* August 16, 1999.

———. "It Will Be the End of an Era If Ottawa Approves TD Bank's Purchase of Canada Trust." *Maclean's,* August 16, 1999.

Norris, Floyd. "At Schwab, Unkept Promise to Investors." *New York Times,* January 14, 2011.

Partridge, John. "Canada Trust Ditches Johnny Cash." *Globe and Mail,* September 9, 1993.

———. "Canada Trust Makes Treasury Changes." *Globe and Mail,* August 31, 1994.

———. "CT Financial 'on Track' for Profit Rise." *Globe and Mail,* March 29, 1995.

———. "Move Aims to End CT Financial Talk." *Globe and Mail,* July 22, 1997.

———. "Ottawa Nixed CIBC, Canada Trust Deal." *Globe and Mail,* July 19, 1997.

Pasternak, Sean B., and Matt Walcoff. "TD Bank Wins Highest Valuation Since 2007 after U.S Expansion." Bloomberg, August 3, 2011.

Perkins, Tara. "Rolling the Dice on a U.S. Recovery: Some Say TD Paid Too Much for a U.S. Bank During the Start of the Subprime Crisis. But If There Is a Turnaround It Will Be Worth It." *Globe and Mail,* March 6, 2010.

Peters, Jeremy W., and Eric Dash. "A Banker's Last Day at the Office, in a Bank He Built Aggressively." *New York Times,* July 31, 2007.

Pooley, Erin. "The Medicine Man." *Canadian Business,* May 21, 2007.

Robertson, Grant. "TD, RBC Battle for Top Bank Honours." *Globe and Mail,* September 2, 2011.

Sidel, Robin, and Caroline Van Hasselt. "RBC Puts U.S Bank on Block." *Wall Street Journal,* May 11, 2011.

Sorkin, Andrew Ross. "Commerce Founder Gets Back into Banking." *NYT Dealbook,* June 10, 2008.

Steiner, Robert. "DOA in the U.S.A." *National Post Business,* October 1999.

Stewart, Sinclair. "Cult of Ed Clark." *Globe and Mail,* June 24, 2005.

Strauss, Marina. "Tim Hortons Retreats in Battle for U.S. Market." *Globe and Mail,* November 12, 2010.

"Top 200 CEOs." *Financial Post,* November 1, 1994.

Toulin, Alan. "Turbulence Follows Former 'Trudeaucrat': Profile of Edmund Clark." *National Post,* August 9, 1999.

Tully, Shawn. "Vernon Hill Is the Best Damn Banker Alive (Just Ask Him)." *Fortune,* September 15, 2010.

Willis, Andrew. "The Courtship of CIBC and TD." *Globe and Mail,* April 18, 1998.

———. "Project Kaiser Took Shape in a Thick Cloud of Smoke." *Globe and Mail,* August 4, 1999.

Willis, Andrew, and Paul Waldie. "Deal Hatched over Eggnog." *Globe and Mail,* January 24, 1998.

Willis, Andrew, and Richard Blackwell. "Vice-Chairman Kelly Departs TD Bank." *Globe and Mail,* July 8, 2000.

Wirebach, John. "Canadian Tire Closes U.S. Subsidiary Auto Source." *Automotive Marketing,* February 1995.

"The World According to Rob." *Toronto Life,* February 2011.

## OTHER SOURCES

Affidavit of Tom D. Seip, in the Supreme Court of Hong Kong High Court, between Charles Schwab & Co, Inc., Plaintiff, and Wang Teh Huei, 1st Defendant; Shui Hing Investment Co. Ltd., 2nd Defendant; Yick Fung Estates Ltd., 3rd Defendant, October 21, 1987.

BMO annual reports.

Board of Governors of the Federal Reserve System. Large Commercial Banks data.

Buffett, Warren E., Chairman, Berkshire Hathaway Inc., Letter to Shareholders, February 2008.

Canadian Bankers Association. *Banks in Canada.*

Chant, John. "The ABCP Crisis in Canada: The Implications for the Regulation of Financial Markets." Research Study Prepared for the Expert Panel on Securities Regulation, 2008.

CIBC annual reports.

Commerce Bancorp, Inc. Form 10-K, Securities and Exchange Commission, fiscal year ended December 31, 2007.

Federal Deposit Insurance Corporation (failed bank list).

Forbes, Steve. Speech to Knight-Bagehot annual dinner, New York City, autumn 2009.

Frei, Frances X., and Corey Hajim. "Commerce Bank." Harvard Business School Case Study, October 3, 2006.

Global Discount Brokerage. Board of Directors presentation, September 18, 1997, Green Line, Toronto-Dominion Bank.

Nomura Fixed Income Research. "CDOs in Plain English: A Summer Intern's Letter Home." September 13, 2004.

"OCC Enters into Cease and Desist Order with Vernon W. Hill, II." Office of the Comptroller of the Currency, November 17, 2008, NR 2008–135.

Order, in the Superior Court of Hong Kong High Court, in the matter of an intended action between Charles Schwab & Co, Inc., Plaintiff, and Wang Teh Huei, 1st Defendant; Shui Hing Investment Co., Ltd, 2nd Defendant; Yick Fung Estates Ltd., 3rd Defendant, October 22, 1987.

Personal papers of W. Keith Gray.

RBC quarterly and annual reports.

RBC Capital Markets Conference. Bloomberg, January 11, 2011.

Reucassel, John, CFA. "If Everyone Likes TD Shares, Why Do They Trade at an Average Multiple?" BMO Capital Markets Report, April 12, 2012.

Ryans, Professor Adrian. "The Toronto-Dominion Bank: Green Line Investor Services 1996." Richard Ivey School of Business Case Study. University of Western Ontario 9A97A010.

Ryans, Professor Adrian, and James Henderson, Research Assistant. "The Toronto-Dominion Bank: Green Line Investor Services," Richard Ivey School of Business Case Study. University of Western Ontario 9-88-A016.

Scotiabank quarterly and annual reports.

Smith, Brad. "Collins Amendment May Have Teeth after All." Stonecap Securities. April 15, 2011.

Speech by Ed Clark, President & CEO, TD Bank Financial Group, on occasion of being honoured as Canada's Outstanding CEO of the Year for 2010. Delivered February 17, 2011, at the Royal Ontario Museum.

Speech by John Thompson, Former Chairman, TD Bank Financial Group, on occasion of Ed Clark honoured as Canada's Outstanding CEO of the Year. Delivered February 17, 2011, at the Royal Ontario Museum.

Srikantiah, Ashwini, under the direction of Professor Joe Martin. "The Toronto-Dominion Bank and Canada's Little Bang of 1987." Rotman School of Management Case Study. University of Toronto. February 8, 2012.

Statement of W. Keith Gray, June 17, 1983, to G. Heintzman, Q.C., of McCarthy & McCarthy, for OSC hearing into establishment of Green Line.

TD Bank and TD Ameritrade annual reports.

TD Bank regulatory filings, quarterly earnings reports and prospectuses.

TD Waterhouse Group, Inc. Common Stock Prospectus, June 23, 1999.

Toronto-Dominion Bank Investor Services Division, Internal Memo, February 10, 1997.

Video tribute to Ed Clark on the occasion of being honoured as Canada's Outstanding CEO of the Year, February 17, 2011.

# INDEX